The
Cornucopia
of Substance

The
Cornucopia
of Substance

Kenneth G. Mills

Sun-Scape Publications
Toronto • Stamford

© 2004 by Kenneth G. Mills
All rights reserved, especially the right of reproduction in whole or in part in any form without written permission except in the case of brief quotations utilized in critical articles and reviews.

Unfoldment is a trademark of Kenneth G. Mills.

Canadian Cataloguing in Publication Data

Mills, Kenneth G., 1923–
    The cornucopia of substance / Kenneth G. Mills

Includes index.
ISBN 0-919842-60-7

    1. Spiritual life.   2. Self-realization.   I. Title.

BF637.S4M553 2004   158'.1   C2004-903404-9

Sun-Scape Publications
A Division of Sun-Scape Enterprises Limited
tel.: 800-437-1454
e-mail: info@sun-scape.com
Web site: www.sun-scape.com

P.O. Box 793, Station "F"
Toronto, Ontario M4Y 2N7, Canada
tel. 905-951-3155, fax 905-951-9712

65 High Ridge Road, Suite 103
Stamford, Connecticut 06905, USA
tel. 800-437-1454

Credits
Original painting incorporated into cover design: *Vortex* by Kenneth G. Mills
(acrylic on canvas)
Design: Margaret MacQueen

Printed in Canada

Contents

About the Author vii
Foreword x
Acknowledgments xii
Editors' Notes xiii

I	The Fragrance of Grace	1
II	Sound Investment	25
III	Overview	39
IV	Resist Ordinariness	55
V	The Freedom of Love	67
VI	The Code of Your Unreality	83
VII	How to Reconstruct Your World	101
VIII	Re-minding	129
IX	Penetrating the Seeming	145
X	The Presence of Truth	171
XI	The Cherry	189
XII	The Palpability of the Invisible	211
XIII	The Continuing Evidence of the Unknown	227
XIV	The Pure Tone	241
XV	The Sublimity of a Free Spirit	257
XVI	The High Way of the Ultimate	271
XVII	A Meeting	283
XVIII	Perfection	289
XIX	Thought-probe into Time	301
XX	The I-thought	319
XXI	The Resolution of Chromaticism	337
XXII	The Precipice of Possibilities	349
XXIII	In the Floodlight of Meaning	363
XXIV	Where Words Are Not	373

Index 387

About the Author

The spontaneous lectures of Kenneth Mills have reached thousands of people from a wide spectrum of traditions and cultures. Flowing from a singular Standpoint, these lectures offer the receptive listener (and reader) a daring new view and comprehensive practicality. In describing his speaking, Dr. Mills has said: "The *Unfoldment*™ is really a projection from another dimension or plane of consciousness, causing those prepared to hear to awaken to the Higher/Greater possibilities of living beyond the limits of three dimensions and translating what seems to be the ordinary into another level of consideration."

The life of Kenneth Mills unfolds through a deep interest in music, the arts, and education, as well as in health, architecture, fashion, landscaping, and interior design. The boundless energy, innovation, and love that characterize his multi-faceted creative expression have come forth from his unswerving fidelity to his original vow, a vow that he made within himself that he would speak of his realizations if asked about them directly. These insights have since become a continued vocalization dedicated to sharing limitless possibilities with those who question the apparent state of affairs in their lives and in the world.

Trained for twenty-five years as a concert pianist, Kenneth Mills followed an intuitive prompting to decline the offer of a world concert tour. The major turning point in his life came in 1967 when he received an identical message from two people. Within a few weeks, an acquaintance whom he had known only slightly and a Buddhist monk whose lecture series he had just attended each told him: "You must learn to speak the Word again!"

Not entirely understanding the scope of this unusual message, Dr. Mills decided, "Since I of myself can do nothing, I will move with the statement from Psalms — 'May the words of my mouth and the meditations of my heart be acceptable in the Light of the One Altogether Lovely.' I will speak if I am asked and otherwise I will appear to speak like everyone else." Very soon thereafter, people began seeking him out to ask about their deepest questions and concerns; ultimately, the questioning became so frequent and the numbers so many that he turned to public lecturing to accommodate this. Since he began speaking publicly in 1968, he has given many thousands of hours of spontaneous *Unfoldments*.

The special genius of this man finds expression in unique and diverse forms. From Carnegie Hall to the great choral festivals of Europe, Kenneth Mills has appeared in concert, on radio, and on television with his internationally acclaimed choral ensemble, The Star-Scape Singers. He founded this ensemble in 1976 and has won the hearts of audiences around the world, serving as a powerful force for world harmony and unity. From China, Russia, Estonia, Lithuania, Latvia, Yugoslavia, Poland, Czechoslovakia, and across Western Europe, the invitations have come to Dr. Mills and The Star-Scape Singers for performances and broadcasts. Accolades have been received from many countries. With the principal composer, Christopher Dedrick, and others, Dr. Mills created over 150 original choral works. In 1992 he was awarded a MedArt USA Special Recognition Award "for the outstanding healing power of his art."

The lyrics for many of the works in The Star-Scape Singers' repertoire are taken from the poetry of Kenneth Mills. His poems are spontaneously created and given during lectures, or manifest themselves in his day-to-day activities. Over 3,000 of these spontaneous poems have been transcribed, and some of them appear in several published volumes. In response to the spirit of these poems, New York dramatist Dr. Barry Brodie formed the Earth-Stage Actors and a "Theatre of Philosophy" in 1987, dedicated to performing dramatic settings of Dr. Mills' poetry and prose.

Over the past several years, Dr. Mills' extensive musical training has also found expression in his own keyboard compositions and the release of four compact discs. This music reveals the Soul of one who defies the limitations of what would seem to be mere electronic keyboards and allows heart-feeling to come forth; this is well described by composer John Lissauer: "His ideas flow uninterrupted from his soul to his fingers to our very fortunate ears." In these extemporaneous compositions, Dr. Mills captures the essence of not only individual instruments but an entire orchestra of sound, interweaving extraordinary themes and melodies that echo long after the listening has ended.

About the Author

Majestic ToneScape, Dr. Mills' most recent release, was recorded at Manta Sound in Toronto with sixty-five of Canada's finest musicians joining forces under the baton of conductor Mark Skazinetsky (associate concertmaster of the Toronto Symphony Orchestra).

Art can be found in many forms, and Kenneth Mills' artistry with a paintbrush perhaps expands one's definition of "music," for just as music can have colour, his art exudes harmony, rhythm, and surprise, elevating the viewer and allowing thought to be suspended so that wonder is experienced. As he has said, "Life is music, and music is life." There are countless expressions of it!

Kenneth Mills' achievements have received wide recognition. PRIME Mentors of Canada selected him to be the 1997 Honorary PRIME Mentor "for being an exemplary mentor to many appreciative and devoted protégés and for serving as a role model par excellence whom society could look up to for inspiration and guidance." In addition, Dr. Mills received an Honorary Doctorate of Humanities from Wolfe's University of King's College, Cambridge, and a Senate of Canada Award of Excellence for outstanding achievement in Humanities, Education, Philosophy, and Arts.

Currently, Kenneth Mills offers lectures, workshops, and seminars and speaks with performing artists, public representatives, award-winning composers, and international figures. His meetings with members of the professional disciplines (such as teachers, designers, doctors, dramatists, musicians, dancers, singers, writers, and businesspeople) open the door to transformed insights into these fields, offering a freedom from the old views and a host of radical new ideas.

Foreword

Imagine you've come upon a chest, a very strange chest that appears to have no keyhole, no hinges, in fact, not even a seam. In total befuddlement you exclaim, "What is this?" Suddenly, the chest opens, as if your question was the key to its lock.

Eagerly you look inside expecting something of great substance: jewels, precious metals, perhaps even some arcane text that will reveal the great mysteries of the universe. Instead, you see a very odd assortment of objects that resemble tools of some kind. You then wonder at the value of what you have found.

But rather than close the chest and walk away, you decide to pick-up one of these alien instruments. Immediately, in the moment of activity, it reveals its use and you begin to discover the practicality of this substance you have found. The more you use it the more purposes it reveals. You find, as you return to the chest, each implement you grasp, in its utilization, reveals its value. What's more, as you continue to draw from this treasure trove, it dawns on you that there is an infinite supply!

Such is the book you have opened! Some question or even simple curiosity has prompted you to open it. In it you find words. But, as you know, words are of value only if they bear meaning, if they are lived.

These words in this book bear meaning because they were originally uttered as spontaneous *Unfoldment*™ from a man, Kenneth G. Mills, who is one with the Word, the divine Logos. These words came into sound because sincere seekers, such as you and I, asked. The humility of question coupled with the willingness to accept answer coaxed these words from a life dedicated to Principle, Love, Spirit, Truth — use any word you wish that points to the Ineffable, the Word-less.

So, dear reader, you have not so much opened a book as you have entered a life, the life of Kenneth G. Mills, whose words are given spontaneously, that is, they emanate directly from experience bypassing thought. Keep in mind that these words are not about ideas, they are the very sound fabric of this man's incarnation. As Dr. Mills himself says, "A word full of meaning is like a life full of love."

I am sure that you, as I, cherish books and the printed word; but having heard these words as they were originally transmitted into sound spontaneously, I liken these pages to postcards bidding us to set out and visit the regions of reality from which they are sent.

I shan't hold forth on the vast difference between the spoken word and the printed word, but would simply ask you to consider: Where do words come from and where do they go? I will, however, appeal to your sincerity of heart and your earnestness of quest to leave these words not on the page, but make them yield their meaning to you. Read them aloud, memorize them, sing them, wrestle with them, even (dare I suggest it!) try to prove them wrong. In any event your effort will not go unfulfilled, for you will find in no time your garden replete with abundance and you blessed with a cornucopia of substance!

Barry T. Brodie, Ph.D.
May 2004

Acknowledgments

Special thanks to those who helped to bring these Lectures into book form:

Design and production: Margaret MacQueen, Ellen Mann

Editing: David Kennet, Angela Wingfield, Barry Brodie, Scarlette Leach

Indexing: David Kennet, Kathy Taylor, Donna Carruthers, Lucille Joseph, Bill Wingfield

Proofreading: Kathy Taylor, Donna Carruthers, Bruce Philp

Transcribing: Kathy Taylor, Linda Petrunka, Rose Harrison, Gwynne MacHattie, Dorothy Mazeau, Blair Randle, Susan Shortt, Dorothea Overend, Barry Brodie

Editors' Notes

Kenneth Mills uses the words "you," "me," "I," and "I AM" in a very specific sense. The "you" and the "me," especially when emphasized, refer to the imaginary entities that we have created in our minds and claimed to be the identity of both ourselves and others. The "you" and the "me" represent the state of thought that believes itself to be embodied physically and thus part and parcel of a material world. It is our conceptual identity; it is a limited, corporeal self-image that we have been educated to construct on the premise of duality and materiality. In short, it is the human personality that parades one way one minute and another way the next.

The "I AM" is the infinite, the eternal, and the unchanging. The I or the I AM is our true Identity. The I AM is what we really are. It is beyond any thought that can be identified with the finite. It is not a conceptual identity, for it cannot be conceived, yet it is the Light to all conception. The I AM is synonymous with other terms appearing in the text: Consciousness, the Source, the Self, Christ, Truth, Life, Love, the Light, That which IS. Yet, we cannot think in terms of being That personally, because this would impose a limit on the I AM, which is limitless.

The use of "We," when capitalized, is explained by Dr. Mills:

> "We" always points to the all-inclusive nature used by royalty and is always considered a grace, for it is a divine all-inclusiveness, thus capitalized and set apart in the Lectures, pointing to the impersonal Nature and its all-encompassing activity.

Love!

Never, never, never permit a thought to come in that causes you to doubt Love! Never! As soon as you do, you have had it. Never let your work seduce you so that you devote all of your time to work and thus you forget "Love!"

– Kenneth G. Mills

The Fragrance of Grace

Chapter I

You should play with being a mortal, and fool everyone! Who would ever guess that right where the mortal is found enjoying himself or herself, the Divine is waiting to be seized by recognition?!

The Fragrance of Grace

Themes: Being ~ Presence ~ Conscious-awareness ~ Soul ~ Identity ~ Language of Spirit ~ healing ~ mind

This is the morning of April 19, 2003, and we are gathered together to celebrate the rebirth of a season of newness and wonder and to escape from the suggestion of a period of repression and dismay. We are moved into the sunshine, you might say, of *Grace* and into that place where man may worship in what is said to be holiness, as he ceases to dwell in the realm where he is ruled by the conflicts which arise from an involvement with the emotional nature of being "this" instead of That.

We are gathered together in an act that conforms to the promises of the past, in which people were together from all nations of the world, in a gathering place where the ones attuned to the ineffable wonder of Actuality find themselves congregated on behalf of those who would find this place of power within the sanctuary of the Heart and within the living rhapsody of having found. It is in this recognition that we know, without doubt, that the peregrinations of the mortal are all due to the unruly mind of dissatisfaction.

It is necessary for all of us who gather together in the name of the vanguard of the race to know, without doubt, that the recovery of the spirit of Allness and the rekindling of the ember of Promise are once again fanned in the remembrance pattern of those who were called out from the passage of time and found once again assembled in bodies and in this dimension, to carry forth the wonders and the possibilities that are indelibly written upon the Scroll of the Soul and just waiting for the Sound which will invest that one with a pure heart, to read without doubt the promptings of the quickening spirit as it is freed from the grave consequences of a false belief-system and regains, in its struggle to be free, the wonders of emancipation as the mind is once again brought under the jurisdiction of the divine impulse to set the captive free and be found, as the Soul once again flees to the assistance of those in doubt and raises once again its feeling so that the emotions may be quelled and the feeling of the totality of Being be a grace bestowed upon us as effortlessly as the sun shines upon this planet, upon which we endeavour to enact the drama bequeathed unto us from the Saints and the Sages of the Ages.

With these few words we are now ensconced in that place where we find ourselves approved, for we have gathered together on behalf of those who have not yet found the gathering place of those who would find a new spirit, a contrite heart, and a Soul embellished with the fire of emancipation.

We have always known the quixotic nature of the mind. We have constantly been impregnated with beliefs; we have been constantly developing the system which would support the beliefs; and we have been constant in attempting to live with this assortment of beliefs. But it is not even palatable, because it is not dipped in any succulent fare; it is only dripping with the disillusionment that comes with the attempt to bring incompatibles together. One of the greatest attempts we make is to make the mind to be more holy. Unfortunately it doesn't know anything about being holy and it doesn't know anything about being the mind! It's a belief that you have one. You also appear to have a grace, and that is the ability to think.

The ability to think is just nothing but the evidence of consecutive thoughts that seem to make sense when you live in the sensorial, corporeal situation! The sensorial data is always conditioned by the structure of the thought-patterns which you have found acceptable to live in with ease. You don't *want* to find those patterns of thought which will conflict with your comfortable state and your emaciated, spiritual state.

Now, a spiritual state, you say, is something that the mind dreams-up as the opposite of the material state. A spiritual state is usually nothing but a material state deemed to be intangible and, therefore, capable of being worshipped, but bearing very few fruits; usually they are the fruits of conflict. When the mind is present, one of the foremost demands is to find that it is controlled. **You would not have a mind in your dream sequence if it were not for the fact that it is capable of being trained. Just as a horse is capable of being trained in dressage, so is your mind capable of dancing with the cosmic waltz!**

You must understand that a mind given to speculation is a mind that ceases to understand the magnitude of the Conscious-awareness that is a bestowal of Grace. The Consciousness bears with it the corresponding identity we have called awareness, which allows us to appear as we seem to be. It is **Love,** as you know, that makes it appear that we *can* appear this way and be satisfied.

We never can be satisfied in fragmentation. It is the fragmentation which diminishes the development of the great thesis of Being Actual. You can't fit the incompatible with the facts of Being. You can't adjust the cut of the pieces of your jigsaw puzzle, as you wish to grab them and put them in place, when they don't really fit. You can't have a jigsaw puzzle done with ease unless you have some idea of the picture that is going to evolve as the pieces are rightly joined together. Neither can you have, in this life experience, the fullness of the picture if you cease to find the Centre around which all the pieces are fitly joined.

Your picture must not necessarily be one that is of this world; if it is, you will try to describe it in the realm of perspective, dimension, and masses. But in the realm of That which IS, you will find that it is the all-encompassing force of knowingness that allows us to treat our experience, on this platform of drama and experience, with the wonder or the magic of being in a state that appears transformational in the tonality of the words that are heard, and transcendent in your state of flying with them.

You must move from the coop of the mind to the state of Wonder beyond the top of the mountain. Never be satisfied with the top of the mountain; it is still a limit. Always fly beyond it and see if the mountain welcomes you with a volcanic eruption, and you dive into it and find the Dove carrying you aloft and depositing you once again in the foothills of time in order to bear the Message of simplicity and humility to those who would find the remnants of the edifice erected to the One altogether lovely, and waiting to be, once again, sounded through the avenue of tonality unto the vehicle of reception where the sound investment is a tonal investment.

In the vestment of Sound, may you come to see, as never before, that the purpose of your life is to witness involuntarily what it is to live in another state of awareness and yet allow yourself to appear to be "just human." Who will ever realize that in our "just human" state, the Divine resides as the Love that empowers and inflames the heart and enlivens our spirit of newness and emancipation in the wonders that are possible when men and women cease to find their example in the dust and again gain the reservoir of the unlimited Well of all goodness, and in so doing, find the unlimited Source as the evidence of a continuing supply of all that is needed to give unto those who come into their presence the feeling of gathering together from all the nations of the world on behalf of those who are waiting to find the gathering place that point of Power that enables one and all to rejoice in the Invisible and bear the fragrance of Grace.

Some of you have asked what it is to be the guardian of the race. I have always called you "the vanguard," and the guardian comes with it. There are so many people to-day who are fretful and weary, and yet know not that they are weary, because they are open to the suggestions of propaganda. This is where *your* presence is so important, because fear has come upon us. This is certainly the evidence of propaganda, because "the greatest thing we have to fear is fear itself." (Franklin D. Roosevelt) *Fear only arises when you feel the point of separation,* and this point of separation is always considered within the framework of the mind. It is this point of separation that usually impels most of us to seek, because we know within ourselves that there must be a point of unification otherwise we would not be impelled to be dissatisfied with the repression of expression!

We are impelled to move into that state where we know that it is not mind over matter but Mind instead of matter, and this is the matter: that very few people ever consider the mind to be other than what they think is contained in the cranium. That isn't the mind; that is the brain. It is amazing how some people love to eat it! [laughter] So, it can't be a terribly important consideration. The mind must be and have an origin in something that isn't so porridge-like; it must be a condition that we have made-up as a result of a belief-system, because we have been taught from childhood when we think: "Now, use your mind!" "Put two and two together correctly." "Yes, five." Then, you're told, "That is wrong. Pay attention, focus, get your mind on this." And what do you do? Get your mind on this. What does that mean? It means that you are contained in the scherzo of suggestion!

You must perceive that the mind is a suggestion that *it* possesses *you*, because you *think* you possess *it*. It is the thoughts that cause you to be bound to what-isn't. What happens? Most people are living mummies because they have an embalmed mind that has been strung down to you through the straws of suggestion! You are not this mind. If Mind is not what we *think* it is, then Mind must be everything that isn't thought. It is this very fact that allows us to perceive that **Mind has a corresponding identity as energy, and the energy uninterrupted is known as a ray; interrupted, it is encapsulated as a thought!**

This Mind that *must be* is evidenced as a thought, or the energy encapsulated. This is where tonality comes in, because a thought having a corresponding identity is a tonal experience. This tonal experience is thus two places removed from the origin. This is why, in the vocalization that can happen with a movement from mind to the mindless, we are able to offer to your attention that which that force termed "the mind" seeks after: releasement from the thought-pattern of limitation — and that is done through language! It is this language that is paramount for transcending the *veil* of mortality: the language of Spirit.

We have been told, "You must learn to speak the language of Spirit."

> The "language of Spirit" is such a command.
> When it was said to me, I thought and I thought
>   and I thought
> And I couldn't think anything spiritual, other than
>   what I'd been taught.
> It was only in the moment that my tongue was
>   loosed,
> On Hollywood Avenue at sunset one night,
> That it happened, and I knew at that moment
> That something had released me but I knew not
>   what
> Until I had to speak without thinking.
> This morning is the result of that.

If I had to *think* what I was going to say, I would be saying what I had been thinking, but the structure which you hear is as new to you as it is to me. So, the words are fitly joined together, and I'm sure they are a puzzle to your mind as to how it happens because to the mind they are always a puzzle. You need not know what you are going to say, for when the heart is right, it has a mode of expression that opens the attention to the possibilities of manumission, and man escapes from the fugacious realm of thoughts, for they are always — what? — fleeting. That is not the arena of the Light!

The Light is the constant presence of Power that allows, in the act of being Actual, alteration. Where does the alteration take place? Primarily through the mind, because the sound of Words and the unusual arrangement of them cause the mind to wonder what is being said. That's when it's hooked, because as soon as you wonder what is being said, then you know that what is being said hasn't anything to do with what you think! If I were saying what you think, you'd be very happy to be in a church! But how can you be in a church when you are the Temple? Of what? "The living God."[1] If you *are* the Temple of the living God, there cannot be any imperfection in Actuality. It is this state of realizing that God, or the Source, Principle, Life, Truth, and Love, Spirit, Mind, could never impart to a corresponding identity a flaw. The flaw is purely that which is perceived in the thing as it comes and goes.

Why have we moved, to-day, into such a level of indifference to the demand of life? is a great question and a great concern. Do you notice that as long as your attention is held by that termed "the television" or "the news," or the eyes are fixed on propaganda, you are entrained with the exact opposite of what you really are?

Fear only takes hold when we believe we are in a condition of being destroyed.

Being cannot be destroyed! The form can be because it was never meant to be eternal. The reason we can *think about* eternality is because we have, within the storehouse of our knowingness, something that relates us to the State that is termed eternal, which is a State that has nothing to do with time; therefore, it has nothing to do with thought. **Thought gives you this dimension and the continuum of time and space.** *Without* **thought there is no time or space.** So, what you hear comes spontaneously from the timeless and spacelessness of a continuum that exists beyond the mind! You know this is so because of the uniqueness that is a concomitant of the Authentic.

You should play with being a mortal, and fool everyone! Who would ever guess that right where the mortal is found enjoying himself or herself, the Divine is waiting to be seized by recognition?! Yes!

What is one of the marks of the divine Presence that everyone may carry?

Randle: Constancy.

Laurie M: The ability to alter?

Absolutely. It's the ability to alter. In other words, your comfortability with the seeming becomes *uncomfortable!* As soon as you become uncomfortable, you know that Something is present that is superior, and then you have to realize your "*inferior* state." [laughter] There is no inferior state! That's the way we try to describe differences in the realm of differences.

Our language is all conditioned to be utilized *according to the conditions,* and each one has a different condition. Then, how do you expect there to be peace, harmony, and brotherly love if everyone has a different condition? The only common element every one of you has is what?

Students: Awareness.

Yes. Which always points to . . . ?

Students: Consciousness.

[Dr. Mills points to a glass on a table beside him.]

The glass is filled with . . . ?

Students: Water.

Yes, but is it the well?

Students: No.

You answer a question without even seeing the well because you know there must be no limitation to the source of the water. Everyone present contains the water of awareness, even though they know not the Well of cosmic Consciousness. You don't have to know the Allness, for everything is contained within one element of the Divine. It is in this very fact that the trumpet sounds and the dead are supposed to be raised. If they can be raised, they can't be dead. If the dead are to be raised, then it must mean that those who consider themselves to be a corporeal entity have got to alter their identification and find their identity commensurate with the pristine state of That.

> *The whole purpose of Easter is to see how the corporeal body is transcended through the opening of the awareness to that of the divine Effulgence. The divine Effulgence is that which encompasses everyone to-day, and it is in **this** that you should rejoice!*

> **It is not that man has to die to find the Eternal; one has to die to the suggestion of false identity, and the Eternal is at hand!**

The horse of the mind must be trained. Don't try to ride two horses. That's for the circus! It's amazing, they only go 'round in circles; you never find them galloping over the plains.

The tangible nature of Being is as present as the sun, even though at times it seems to be hidden by a cloud of delusion. Dissipate the cloud and find the Light, but you never see the body; it would blind you! To describe anything defines its limits. That's why you cannot describe the words of the vocabulary that constitute Spirit, because the definitions are difficult to bring to Words that have nothing to do with "you." Don't define; *defy* the suggestion that you are embodied in clay!

> **Your Reality is a Conscious-awareness experience, and each vessel bears the common element of the refreshing awareness of All that IS.**

> **It all depends upon you, what you will choose: the sublime or the ridiculous.**

[Dr. Mills takes a piece of fruit from a plate beside him.] Now, talk to me. Yes, Susan.

> *Susan A:* Clearly, then, the vocabulary of the Infinite is not understood with the mind. You speak of it as "an impulse."

Yes. You must have the words that correspond to the impulse. Your mind can mimic the words. I can look-up in the dictionary words like "infinite" and "eternal" and "transcendental," but those are definitions that allow us to start to see the language that can only bear power when the words used are attributable to Principle, Soul, God, Spirit, Mind, Truth, and Love.

> *Susan A:* Is it that these undefinable words, or at least undefinable in terms of the mind, come to us almost like an electrical impulse?

They come to you with an impelling force for expression. **Remember, the repression of the Invisible is due to the mind of the visible.**

> *Susan A:* So, to say "the divine impulse to set the captive free," is that how the freedom comes to us?

The impulse for you was to come to Toronto to be with me, and you found that being with *me* was just like being with *you* until I spoke! That's what set the captive free.

> *Susan A:* Thank you, Sir.

Yes, Barry.

> *Dr. Barry B:* Last week you said that you *look* just like us and at that point it stops. I want to thank you this morning for taking us past that point, Sir. I also wanted to share something. Susan and I, in the car coming-up last night, were talking about a force that used to ride the New York subways that was called "The Guardian Angels," and we were contrasting that volunteer presence that was able to maintain a level of order on the subways versus what's happening now with armed guards at various places in the city. It caused me to consider this idea of guardian, that the guardian is not so much an offensive as it is *a presence.*

It's a state of presence in awareness that disarms the "robotery" of the mind. All soldiers are robots, and those who find it difficult to be in the army show that there is still hope because they are rebelling at the thought of forms like themselves being subject to destruction. *There's nothing more threatening to a dictatorship than those who are vigilant of the rights that are divine.*

> *Dr. Barry B:* Sir, **as guardians, then, what is it that is to be guarded?**

***Our Presence* so that nothing can interfere with the divine intention to recognize in form the appearance of those attuned to the Higher Way.** They can pass unrecognized and frequently they're only recognized by their disturbance at meeting you. Usually the people who are most attuned, who have found it difficult to incarnate and go on with life as they think it is — then they meet you, and their incarnation brings with it the recognition of something that happens, they know not how, but it brings with it a recognition that causes them either to respond or to reject what the Presence offers. I was once told, "The people who react most to your Presence are those who have been with you before and have been challenged by the Teaching before, and this time they came to get it all straight."

I was once told that I had quite a number (I knew the number at the time) of students who had studied with the disciples of Jesus and they had been badly taught and this time they were reincarnating. I had to be very aware of them because they were always trying to go through the adulterated because they were so affected by the lack of understanding of the esoteric messages that were given. Even the people who have written the Bible, it's obvious that they have never understood what was there, because it can be taken literally but most frequently it should be translated metaphysically. **The reason you use metaphysics is because it takes "the objects of sense and translates them into the ideas of Soul."**[2]

Yes, Bill.

> *Bill W:* Thank you for the *Unfoldment*™ to-day, the beauty of it, and for us beginning to be given some of the responsibilities of a guardian. I once asked you about the ministers of a state, how they would change and see what it is, and you said that the change would happen within.

Yes, the change happens within, but it's like the change happens within, say, a pot of rice. You put the kernels in the pot and then you add the boiling water, and they swell to a great size. It's the same thing with the "kernel appearing"! You add the water to the pot of reaction, and it will swell until they realize that the enhanced force-field surrounding their hard core-like nature is malleable in the presence of Love. That is how the people in high places can be changed.

It's so interesting, to-day the people in the high places are so unsure of their place — it isn't very high. People are reluctant to ever broach the subject of man's Reality, because we are being treated as if we were a part of an *animal* kingdom and we are being treated as if we were unable to perceive the subtleties of bondage. That will never last, but it's just as has been prophesied. It has always been said that there would be wars and rumours of wars. It will always be as long as a human is in the belief-system. He has to be freed from false identity in order to realize how man makes *a dent* in the armour of belief. **It's correct Identity that always causes the piercing of the shroud of incorrect identity.**

Isn't it amazing how many shrouds cover us? The mind just has layer and layer and layer after layer of beliefs that you *think* you have to clear. If you find that you don't like who you are . . . [Dr. Mills holds-up a grape and drops it], will you please tell me why you tear it apart and put it together and call it a grape, one of wrath?! Why do you take so long? Don't *consider* being Real; it's impossible! You think you have to change your thought. No! **You have to accept One!**

If I recognize a grape, all grapes are recognized. If I recognize a strawberry, all strawberries are recognized. Yes, Bill.

> *Bill W*: That so helps to close the apparent gap between the controlled and the controllers. The whole thing, even the apparent being controlled or in bondage, is an appearance, an illusion. It seems to me that not only are there the controllers to be changed but there are the masses that need to realize that they *are* being controlled.

Yes, but, you see, if we don't have this understanding within ourselves, then there is no way that you can move another. You can't bring about a change unless someone asks, but your presence can bring about a change. Just like when, in the early days before I could control the Force-field, some people would come and sit before me, and the side facing me would be burned. Like David facing me: he would be burned on this side of his face. He knew a Force was present; he had the mark of it. And that's what happens with people, but most people to-day are scared to death to alter their pattern because they are afraid to love. A woman isn't; a man is. A woman feels she has a right to be in love; in fact, she feels she *has* to be in love because otherwise what is she doing here? She has to love, but a man, for some reason, has been taught the exact opposite, when a *man* is Love! *Man* is Love. It's *men and women* who break it down into pieces. (Oh, yes.)

The highest initiations are given only when you understand the androgynous nature as an experience. This is what most of you men would never accept, only in thought.

Yes, David.

> *David W:* Sir, at a recent meeting you said that every question asked that evening was asked from the standpoint of person. If this is so, as I suppose this question is, how can one ask a question other than from the standpoint of person when, it seems to me, from the standpoint of Principle there is no question?

I know. This is what David was going through last night, too. Would you say it again to me, and I'll tell you as you go.

> *David W:* Yes, Sir. How can you ask a question other than from the standpoint of person — ?

You can.

> *David W:* You can?

Of course! I don't expect your question to be person, and if your question seems to come from the person, it's because it's to reveal *what-isn't*, and that revealed reveals *to you* that you are a Conscious-Being and not an answered being! The answer never appeals to other than your thought, but the Force-field of it is to *Essence*. That's why questions are asked even by great Teachers. The question always points *beyond* the questioner to what he really IS.

> *David W:* Thank you.

That's why questions are asked. Have you got that?

> *Students:* Yes, Sir.

Yes, Dorothy.

> *Dorothy M:* Dr. Mills, what you're saying this morning brings to mind what was discussed last Saturday evening about the corresponding identity, that there is the objective level of the idea. What you're giving is beyond that,

and how to ask a question without bringing the ideas that are so transcendent to an objective level —

I have done that all my life. There's nothing wrong about bringing them to the objective level, because that's only to *you* that it's objective; it's not to me. *You can't fall for this illusion of separateness.* **That's the challenge. You can't even see that with the nations of the world that are in turbulence. Your recognition of their turbulence comes to you to give itself up. You know it isn't true, and that's why you can expect to see changes, but I think we should expect to see changes right within our own environment!**

Yes, Andy.

> *Andre P:* Dr. Mills, you have frequently spoken of the redeemed imagination, and this week I was imaging Eugene attending the Wordshop, and he surprised me last night by saying he wished to attend. My question is, are the imaging faculty and the redeemed imagination the same?

They are the same. The difference is: the redeemed sees no impediment to what is seen; the imagined sees whatever appears to be. The redeemed imagination sees it as it is; the unredeemed sees it as it thinks it is. Got it?

> *Andre P:* Thank you.

Yes, Greg.

> *Gregory S:* Recently I was sharing with you the wonder and joy of sharing this *Unfoldment*™ with new people, and you had said, "You'll be amazed at how that comes back to you." It brought me to consider the Law of Reciprocity. At the end of classes we always say: "I pray that I have enough humility to have a new perspective from a given Standpoint. I pray that there be discipline, obedience, and the Law of Reciprocity a living experience." [Kenneth G. Mills] Can you articulate more about the articles or anything about the Law of Reciprocity? It seems such a wonder to me.

Let it remain that. Don't define it. The mind wants definition because then you think you have more of a hold on it — and, actually, it's a lessening of the hold. As soon as you're satisfied with my explanation of it, then you're at ease with it! I would rather leave you . . . "uncomfortable?"!

> *Gregory S:* Thank you.

Yes, Moira.

> *Moira D:* In considering "Mind instead of matter," it occurred to me that if you think it's Mind over matter, or just matter, life could be random, but when you realize that it's Mind *instead of* matter, that's when the responsibility for knowing that you create your experience comes in. Is that accurate?

Yes. **It's when you know that Mind is not in matter that you take care of the suggestion called matter.**

> *Moira D:* Another question: Is it simply the awareness of the unlimited Mind that opens the door to the flow that takes care of matter?

Yes. **It's the awareness of the Unlimited that provides the doorway through which you may enter as you drop the baggage of mentality.**

> *Moira D:* Thank you!

Yes, David.

> *David N:* Sir, is the awareness of the Unlimited, then, Wonder?

The door may be opened by Wonder. Wonder is a part of magic. It's Wonder that usually brings healing, and people term that "magical."

> *David N:* Wonder is certainly part of this morning.

Yes, Donna.

> *Donna C:* Sir, in one of your books, *A Word Fitly Spoken,* in the first chapter when you were talking about metaphysics, you said that the body itself is actually a *notion*.[3]

It is.

> *Donna C:* The body as matter is itself a notion, and it's actually *idea*.

That's right.

> *Donna C:* That statement starts to trigger one into unhinging from the body being material, because, in effect, the only way we even perceive it is as an idea.

Yes, manifested as a Word.

> *Donna C:* Oh!

Yes, Nurit.

> *Nurit O:* Sir, you often use the phrase "to magnify what we know to be Real." How is that done, and who is it that's magnifying?

The Self. The Self is always Self-magnification, Self-glorification. The magnification is also what you perceive, as a trait is magnified. You say a trait is under magnification, in other words, it's growing larger and larger; or it's under the law of diminution, it's growing less and less. Magnification and diminution are all part of the process of development, and it all bears relevance to the ideas that are associated with the various themes that you would consider relevant to what constitutes your composition of Life.

Yes, Jennifer.

> *Jennifer M:* Dr. Mills, in "The Newness of the Unchanging" you said: "Magnifying does not necessarily mean to enlarge beyond all possibilities. . . . To magnify a point is to have the attention focussed on none other."[4]

Yes, that's right. That's how you see through a leaf. Yes, Steve.

> *Steve M:* Sir, yesterday morning there was a long layover in the Phoenix airport, a couple of hours. Sitting there, there was such a strong awareness, at first, of all the diversity — a tremendous number of people coming through with all of their various conditions and afflictions

and the state of the world. I wanted to just leave and I realized at that point that it was more important to pick-up one of your books, so I started reading *Tyranny of Love*[5] until the sense of otherness and separateness disappeared. I'm wondering now, with this discussion of the guardians of the race, if that is —

That was part of your Work.

Steve M: Is there more to be done?

Oh, yes.

Steve M: Then, in that, once the sense of otherness and division disappears —

It must be a constant, not spasmodic. God is not in a spasm and God is not spasmodic. The Source is not spasmodic.

Steve M: No. The other component of that was to realize exactly that, that a condition or a state thought to be able to be assumed depended on conditions.

That-which-isn't will always present itself to That-which-IS, to be either recognized or given-up. Yes, Linda.

Linda P: Sir, in the *Unfoldment*™ entitled "Apprenticeship" you made a statement of which I'd like to ask the meaning. You said, "What is 'making an altar of Earth'? *Making the demonstration of an enactment of elevation.*"[6] What is "making the demonstration of an enactment of elevation"?

It's the actual perception that you develop in perceiving the Earth as your own projection. The Earth is nothing but your own projection appearing manifested to satisfy what you consider the perimeter of your actions at this time. That's how you make an altar of Earth because it becomes the very stage upon which you enact the drama of your growing awareness of Actuality.

Linda P: Along with that, then, you said something to me in January about perception. You said that "perception congeals and congeals and congeals." What is the value or the end result of that congealment?

Anything that congeals comes to a point of solidarity. When you become solid in your knowingness, it has ceased, and you will be treated to having to face congealing, congealing, congealing until it all jells and you suddenly realize where you are no longer and yet *are*. It's always pointing beyond the limitations of a mind concept.

Linda P: Thank you!

Yes, Terry.

Terry S: Sir, is the fundamental characteristic of Conscious-awareness the knowing that I am not matter or mind?

It doesn't require you to know or not know. The fundamental characteristic of what?

Terry S: Of Conscious-awareness.

You're asking from the standpoint of person, and Conscious-awareness doesn't know person. You're asking as if Conscious-awareness knows "you." Conscious-awareness doesn't know "*you,*" at all; it's there for your use! Conscious-awareness is what you're using to pretend that you have something you haven't, and that's why your awareness has to be redeemed, and that is termed, "in the Light of the Christ." That's the whole point of the Resurrection: you still have the body. In the Bible it tells you that Jesus was supposed to have said, "Father, Thou hast forsaken me," but then they found that was a misinterpretation; He said, "Father, Thou hast glorified Me."

So, when you think that you have an awareness that you are considering, you've got it backwards (you're capable of crucifixion), but the attainment revealed that Conscious-awareness is what you are using as a seeming mortal in order to gain your *immortal* nature. It's only through awareness that you can gain any semblance of the dimension that exists beyond this objectification. You can't *limit* awareness; it is. You can always limit your sense of awareness, but awareness can't be limited!

Terry S: Thank you so much.

Yes, David.

> *David N:* Sir, just in this interchange with Terry, you were speaking about the redeemed imagination, and it's caused me to see that in a completely different way. I had always considered the redeemed imagination as reconsidering individual components, so to speak, of the imagination, whereas what you're saying is, it is *re*-deemed. The entire imagination is deemed to be something other than what I thought it was! It's amazing because it's a total redeeming.

Yes, Randle.

> *Randle:* Sir, in the symbology of when "Jesus wept," you've spoken of His tear, and you mentioned just a moment ago that what He said had been misinterpreted biblically and that He actually said, "How Thou hast glorified Me!" What is the importance of His tear and why is that important?

You might say that He shed a tear, but it wasn't at the Crucifixion that He shed the tear, was it?

> *Students:* No.

No. It was at Lazarus' raising from the dead. It showed that *feeling* was present, and that's why it was termed "a diamond." **The Word is the diamond of brilliance, it's the diamond of clarity.** That's the symbol of a diamond. It's the Word, the clarity and the brilliance.

Yes, Blair.

> *Blair R:* Dr. Mills, I feel that when you speak about the mark of the divine Presence being the ability to alter, that feeling is what enables the alteration to happen.

It is.

> *Blair R:* The wish is that Conscious-awareness and feeling are *one*.

They are.

> *Blair R:* Yes. Why does it appear that they're not, sometimes?

Because of a mind that questions!

Blair R: Thank you!

Conscious-awareness-feeling is not a mind product; it's only an energy-field that you have *put* into thought. It's an energy-field that you have wrapped, encapsulated as thoughts. Mind-awareness-feeling: that is an energy that you have attempted to encapsulate as words, but they're always one. You can have Conscious-awareness, for sure, but when it is settled completely, there couldn't help but be feeling, because **full Conscious-awareness is not attained without the awakening of the Soul. The awakening of the Soul is the awakening of feeling, which far transcends the suggestion of an emotional encounter with divinity.**

Blair R: Thank you.

Yes, Dianne.

> *Dianne O:* Sir, thank you so much for giving this Wordshop. This morning was just incredible, what you gave. You said this morning that the mark of the divine Presence is the ability to alter. Should there always be the awareness, for instance, if one walks into a room, that there's any alteration?

No, you are just what you are.

> *Dianne O:* So, in Being, it doesn't matter if you know or not that something is altered?

No. The sun doesn't know whether the windowpane is dirty or not! Yes, David.

> *David K:* Sir, I feel there always must be a lesson to the stories you tell, or something that can be gleaned from them. *You've* never stopped giving, thank goodness! That's where your whole life is such an inspiration, because there have been so many unfortunate events, so much tragedy, seemingly, and you've never stopped, thank goodness. Thank you, Sir, for being here to-day.

Yes, Steve.

> *Steve M:* Claude and I were speaking this morning, and he used a phrase that I doubt if he's encountered in reading your books, and yet I know it's one that we have heard very often, and it's "the law of your Being." You've used the phrase, "You are where you are by the law of your Being." Claude was on the verge of a very important question that I'm hoping I can either prompt or help. The first way that it came-up was last evening when he was talking about how people who are on the Path, or claim to be on the Path, seem to adopt a posture of having to struggle, always introducing conflict. This morning, when he used it, he said he was wondering what they had accepted as "a law of their Being" that would incorporate —

That's exactly what happens, though. It's what they *accept* into their life that creates the law, and they *condition* Being. So, if the belief-system is such that it becomes the law under which you live, you have conditioned yourself so that Being is dressed in a garment unbecoming to It. So, that's why you are where you are by the law of your Being. It all depends upon how much you have discarded the shroud of suggestion and revealed the living body of the Realization.

Yes.

> *Claude C:* Thank you for the new perspective. This is my first time at an *Unfoldment*™, and in line with what you have just said, the question gravitates more around people having a personal law that obviously is the centre of their belief-system. This personal law seems to be a product of trauma, physical, emotional, and intellectual. How important is it to recognize what your personal law is, in the healing process? How important is it to address the emotions that are the cause of that? Can all of this be healed through the Word?

Yes.

> *Claude C:* It seems to me there are a lot of people working on their emotions to try and heal trauma that has issued from emotions.

Yes, that is so, but when you have, say, a disease, to know it by description because you're emotionally involved with it doesn't help you one bit in nullifying its consequences. An emotion may develop because it's part of the suggestion that you're "this," but the knowingness has to be maintained that this suggestion of a law of limitations surrounding a disease or an emotional state is not bearing any power of its own, other than the attention you give it. So, **you rest in the assurance that the essence of Being is undefiled by the suggestion that confronts the suggested ailing situation.**

It is not important to know what constitutes the disease or the emotion surrounding it. What is important is that one perceives the divine Nature as a possibility, and thus the error or the hold of the emotions on a situation is lessened, and the healing may take place. But remember, any healing of the material is only a lessening of the material confinement. It's not because you're more spiritual; it's just because there's less and less of the suggestion present.

So, emotions and the laws that you have built-up surrounding yourself are there to cause you to extricate yourself, but unfortunately so many people find that they need a confrontation of their own making in order to feel that they're accomplishing something, whereas to know What-IS is so simple if you are willing to deal with the confrontation as you would a snake in the grass. You don't pick it up and handle it; you let it slither away. That is just what the Devil is like, or error is like, or illness is like: it takes your attention until you say "Thus far and no further do you enter into my garden that is uncontaminated by the fetters of hypothetical disease!"

People won't like that, because everyone likes to have *a process*; they like to have a process because they think they're achieving something. It may *appear* processive, but you never accept process as an actuality. I was "in the process of becoming a pianist" but I never considered myself *in process*; I always considered myself *a pianist*. So, you don't consider yourself in process of being Love. Love IS, and you may be in the process of expressing it. That is why music is so important.

Yes, Bill.

> *Bill W:* You have spoken of the universality of Being, the wonder of that, and just now when you were talking with Terry, a fraction of a second before you mentioned the

Resurrection, it had come to my thought. Is there a universality to *awareness?*

Yes, awareness *is* universal. We have the awareness of the world, we have the awareness of the cosmos, and we have put it outside ourselves, but remember, **there is nothing in our experience that isn't experienceable from the Standpoint of the universal Consciousness.** This is why some people talk of returning to their home planet and returning to this galaxy or that galaxy. But we are not *mediums;* we are only *bridgework* between the different dimensions. **That's all my life is, is a Bridge.**

My Work is just a *Bridgework* that allows you to pass from sense to Soul in the Feeling of Being I AM.

Students: Thank you.

⌘

1. II Corinthians 6:16.
2. "Metaphysics resolves things into thoughts, and exchanges the objects of sense for the ideas of Soul," Mary Baker Eddy, *Science and Health with Key to the Scriptures* (Boston: The First Church of Christ, Scientist, 1875), 269–15.
3. "Consciousness is fundamental, and if consciousness is fundamental, you know that it is only in consciousness that you can experience body. You, I, or anyone does not really experience a physical or material *body* as such. We are actually, in fact, only aware of the *idea* body. The notion that the body is material is itself an idea. The body is a manifestation of a series of ideas, a conscious experience, and people mistake it and believe it to be material." Kenneth G. Mills, *A Word Fitly Spoken* (Toronto: Sun-Scape Publications, 1980), p. 15.
4. Kenneth G. Mills, *The Key: Identity* (Stamford/Toronto: Sun-Scape Publications, 1994), p. 293.
5. Kenneth G. Mills, *Tyranny of Love* (Stamford/Toronto: Sun-Scape Publications, 1995).
6. Ibid., p. 81.

Sound Investment

Chapter II

Realization is evidenced by mentality being altered and bearing the vocabulary of the Ineffable.

Sound Investment

Themes: Unity ~ Principle ~ the Christ Spirit ~ divine individuality ~ balance/androgyne state ~ talents/music ~ belief systems

Happy Easter!

>*Students:* Happy Easter, Sir!

Perhaps I can read you something that you might find interesting, something I said to The Star-Scape Singers (which I found this morning in one of these old books) during a rehearsal on November 24, 1991:

> If you enjoy music, it's because your mind is less than most.
> If you love music, it means that at that time you *lose* your mind.
> If you do not love music, it means that you have a mind that is calling out to be lost and to be informed anew in the Light of Wonder!

Do you remember it?

> *Dianne F:* I do now!

Then there's another one; I'm going to put it on the Internet.

> Age is what men and women have dreamed-up in order to dye the garment of life with the tint of sequence!

And this one is not to be forgotten:

> In politics stupidity is not a handicap! (Napoleon Bonaparte)

Let me see. On March 21, 2000, I was considering this. Jesus said:

> This people's heart is waxed gross, and their ears are dull of hearing, and their eyes they have closed, lest at any time they should see with their eyes and hear with their ears, and should understand with their hearts, and should be converted, and I should heal them. (Matthew 13:15)

I said:

> The above shows why Jesus often refused to explain His words, because when people are mesmerized by the virtual, they cannot comprehend That which is its antithesis.

Let's see what else I can find. There are so many good tidbits here. Hadrian said:

> Everything is always easier than to exercise common sense.

Hadrian said:

> I have no children, nor is that a regret. I have no special concern to bequeath myself to anyone. It is not by blood, anyhow, that man's true continuity is established.

Ramana Maharshi said:

> It is necessary to experience Reality now in *this* life in order to experience it after death.

This is the morning of April 20, 2003, an Easter Sunday morning, and there's an interesting remark I made, here in this notebook:

> What are the suffocating bonds under which you live and pretend you don't?
>
> What do you allow to cast out your comprehension so that the bonds are not recognized? (March 25, 2002)

[Dr. Mills picks-up the Tibetan bells from the table beside him.] Easter's every day, you know. Isn't it amazing, we only dress it up in these wonderful colours because we think it's not?! [Dr. Mills rings the bells.] They speak to us from three centuries ago. Isn't it fascinating, what speaks to us is not at all like the objects. What speaks to *you* is not anything like the object.

> Isn't it amazing, when you consider without doubt,
> The tantalizing experience of hearing a sound that
>   you call an attention-getter for those who
>   doubt?

You see, a sound bears no resemblance to the form
   from which it comes,
Any more than the centuries hold in suspension the
   wonder of the eternal Sun/Son.

It is in this glowing recognition that the object unto
   time
Is seldom ever equated with anything divine.
It's only when it's struck and opened to the
   wondrous trumpets of the Light
That we find the vehicle is saying, "There is only
   eternal Light."

You who have found in your peregrinations that you
   have wandered here and there
Have always taken with you a mind filled with
   thoughts of sometimes happiness and
   sometimes despair.
But it now comes before your attention, as never
   before in time,
That it is essential to realize the impossibility of
   attempting to have unity in a variegated mind.

The two can never unite and the two can never
   dance;
It is only the One that is divine that allows the other
   to seem to peregrinate and live by chance.
It's in the need of recognizing that from this point on
   in life
You should live, without doubt, the Knowing that
   we move from the Unity Standpoint and not
   from the fragmented parts of a mental strife.

Mentality is always equated with the mind of men in
   time,
But *know* within yourself that you have a purpose,
   and that is to find out: are you really divine?
Of course, there could never have been a resurrection
   if there had been doubt in the One who did
   succeed
In wiping away the shadow of doubt that One could
   pass and leave no deed.

He passed in the wonder of a moment; He appeared,
    in the astonishment of time,
To walk the sacred way of Emmaus and He blew
    away the mind of the disciples of time.
He saw within their doubting "Just how did this
    happen to this man?".
"Touch me not," He said. "That will not prove to
    you that I have ascended where I AM."

They thought by touching Him they would find
Whether or not He was materially felt as before.
But He said, "That is not where the proof lies.
It's where *I live now* and know the Father so
    inclined."

So, the Principle lives in everyone when Unity reveals
    this spot:
That you must live *out* from the Star of knowing and
    allow others to see what a sparkle you are to
    their thought.

The whole joy of Easter is *being freed from the catatonic state of suggestion.* You never can succeed in attempting to find freedom by utilizing the mind filled with beliefs. Remember, the belief-system is what has impeded the recognition of the Divine (or the Ineffable) in our lives.

When we say "the Divine," we are really speaking of a State that the intellect cannot comprehend. It is like the cymbals, the bells: when they are struck together, the tone is one. It's the same when we unify: the tone we exude is very different in the tonality of our voice than the tone of one who is still fettered in the intellectual realm where they are trying to gain, through progress and study, freedom. **Freedom is not gained by study; it's gained by surrender (to Principle).**

Remember, it tells you that the man that walketh out of the way of understanding is lost.[1] What is the *understanding* that is so important? That *the mind* that you have is in such a state that it can accept the divinity and allow you to think you've experienced it! It can allow you to think you have Enlightenment when *it* doesn't know a damn *thing* about Enlightenment; it's darkness itself! *The mind only deals with the suppositional, virtual reality.* This is why the High Teachings, as they say, are really kept from the mass, because the mass tends to consider anything new a challenge to its force-field. Remember, the mass is nothing but the ordinary people who are in a mess anyway because they don't consider that they are being slaves of a system that has evolved to make people susceptible to language that refers to their belief-system of virtuality and *not* to the Truth-aspect of their Actuality!

Every time you hear the news (or you read a newspaper) and you have to consider what is being heard, know that *it is coming to you so that you may stand porter at that door, and don't allow it to be re-enlivened by your expostulations about its seeming nothingness.* To you who know the Truth, that which isn't true doesn't need to be cognized. **Just knowing Truth obliterates the suggestion of its opposite!** Who cognizes (as of great interest) someone who thinks that two and two is five? It's when you know two and two is *four* that it's obvious you're successful, and the one who thinks it's five is obviously having difficulty. Only when they have *enough* difficulty will they ask you, "What makes you accurate in your configurations, and me inaccurate?" You can say, "Well, you're always attempting to get something for nothing! Two and two is four, and you're trying to gain *five* out of it."

How many of you expect to be paid for being nincompoops? A nincompoop is one who has never succeeded in climbing the wall of suggestion regardless of his or her attempts to jump over the garden fence! *How many of you have ever considered the need to really leap over the suggestion of any form of limitation?* It's only when you realize your possibilities have been hampered by a system of belief that everyone seems to sponsor and you have found inhibiting.

When you take a step out of the ordinary way of the populace, you stand out like a Madonna. Madonna, the pop singer, as you now know, has been struck, you might say, by the Light. Madonna has declared in an interview, as well as in the newspaper, that she now sees that her whole life of the past has been nothing but illusion. She is changing her whole stance in life, and her whole *new standpoint* is working from the standpoint of seeing the illusionary nature of her experience and how now she is so thrilled at what she has found. It's really quite inspiring.

Do you ever consider how your deeds seem to always be in limits, when **the Source of any good and perfect deed is not a** personal action; it's the evidence of the Divine or Principle or Source or Self present.

When it says "I of myself can do nothing; 'tis the Principle that doeth the work," then we know immediately that our activity is not given forth without the affect of power and the affect that could be called "an altering" to the situation. If you really are one of Knowing, no one will forget your Presence. If you know you are bearing the Christ Child invisibly in the state of Wonder, then you know others will recognize the whimpering of the heart that would be cast free. *You can discern the wish of another when you have succeeded in freeing yourself from the total encroachment of the suggested mind of limits.*

When you look at the world to-day and to-morrow, you will see it before your gaze every time you look because having eyes you see *exactly* what you are projecting. **The world doesn't exist without *you*.** When you go to sleep at night you rest because you don't have the world to populate, to have discord, and to have resolution. Why do you think you sleep?! Or have to take a pill to do so? The world is such an object of concern because you feel you are entombed within the sarcophagus of time and space and the continuing of mentality. You have to escape from this. This was part of the initiations of the past. The person was put in a sarcophagus and had to "die," and when the lid was lifted, they were to come forth, supposedly, bearing the realization that they existed beyond the time-space continuum because they existed not as a mental being *dying* but as a Conscious Being *birthing* through the encrustations of mentality!

It is terribly interesting to consider how to-day so few people (it's obvious from the few who are here) are really interested in being genuine. You who are here are blessed beyond doubt because you bear within you a surrender to a Tonality that bespeaks the wonder of your divine Selfhood. How many people want this Ejaculation to penetrate your womb and bring forth a new type of encounter with the Ineffable?! You can be assured no one wants you to birth anew with a sparkle, with a force that causes them discomfort. To the musically inclined, dissonance is very difficult to stand. This is why we have hoped, through the years, that the dissonant music of yesterday would pass because dissonance is reflective of the state of **mentality** that **doesn't know how** to resolve the chromaticism of time into the harmonic structure that would bear agreement.

We have all kinds of music. We have the rock and roll music, but as I said recently, that always tells you exactly where it comes from: the *mineral* state! [laughter] So, why is it so popular, if it isn't rolling *you* right into the gamble/gambol not on the hillsides with the One Shepherd but in the desert that bears no refreshment but the dust particles of yesterday?!

You are really gifted beyond doubt, not only in your artistic endeavours, not only in your musical endeavours, your painting endeavours, your photographic achievement, your singing accomplishment. ***You are talented beyond doubt***, which means there is no measure to your achievement; it's according to how you view your courage and your daring to refute the limits of even associates! Whatever you do, start to **have the courage and the fortitude that come from knowing and claiming your divine Individuality,** and take a stand with those who find you so comfortable to be with. Take a stand and let them see what it is like to stand next to a power source they never knew existed! What's it matter whether you're liked? What's it matter whether you're loved? That is looking for recognition from the outside. If I had looked for recognition from the outside, I would have passed years ago!

I still have not given-up that one day men will be men, and women will be women, and the androgyne will be at least experienced *consciously* so that the awareness no longer will be inhibited by the suggestion of division. We divide everything into black and white, brown and white, yellow, green. Some people are very yellow and they have nothing to do with the Orient! They don't dare to take a stand for the greenery of ever-newness! In the winter they think everything has died; that is when everything is *re-energizing* to break the encrustations of a seasonal sequence. That is all.

Everything you're doing tends to be sequential, and it's only in sequence that you seem to find comfort, when things *follow* things naturally. But it is not natural to have a sequence that follows a *limited* sequence. *You should break any sequence that would have you non-glittering!* [laughter] *Any!* Glitter! "All that glitters is not gold." That's what Shakespeare said, and it's quite true, but it's great when it *is!* [laughter] Of course, *your* glitter would be golden. Why not?

The Word is that which is likened unto the sun, and the sun still shines right through a dirty pane of glass. It can't be blocked by a clouded mind, but if you use the magnifying power of a lens, you may find you burn yourself by being careless with the sun that has only tried to embrace you in its warmth. **Magnify through personality the Light of Truth, and you may suffer the consequence of trying to unite the Mind that IS with the mentality that isn't!** They are not equal; they are totally separate. Therefore, what lies before you is the need to find the unity that divests the suggested mortal mind of any power to encroach upon your adventure in this life.

If the Christ is risen from the dead, it's obvious that State could never have been born. It's only something that has been born that dies. Therefore, the Christ Spirit could never be born or never die. What is missing here is *your recognition* that the Christ never lived nor died in the flesh; it was only — what? — the wonder of the coincidence of the human and the Divine. *That's* what lived, but it only happens so rarely that one dares to consider that eternity has had a mouthpiece in the Tonality of a cymbal/symbol that never was struck by anything but the Light! It is the Light that sets man free, because in the darkness he only sees his own likeness.

Don't be living on the face of time! Live *now* in knowing that no one can give you anything. How can you be given anything when the great Gift is not a *thing?* The great Gift is breaking through the mesmerism of your belief-system and allowing you to experience. **It's only by experience of the Ineffable that you *know* without doubt.**

The reason we use the word "Principle" is because it allows one to recognize the Source without giving It gender. The Christ is without gender, the Self is without gender, the Source is without gender. Now do you see why the balanced state, often called the androgyne state, is so called for? Until the mind is reduced to a point of wonder and surprise, it is not open to receiving the *blast* of the might of omnipotence. Why do we say it's a blast? Because it *blows apart* all your belief-systems, and you have to re-organize them in order to cope with your friends and associates, but it also allows an alteration to take place.

One of the greatest obstructions to peace is the personal wilfulness and arrogance that arises from a clever and brilliant intellectual attainment. An intellectual attainment is easily achieved by anyone — if they want it. The great fun is to have it and use it as the Sword of Truth with such ease and such dexterity that no one even sees its movements!

The whole value of the lilies of the field is to wonder, not how they grow — it's inevitable that they would grow because they are a miracle that you cannot acknowledge as *your* creation. But, just think, they are part of your objectification which, if you look closely, causes you to wonder "What did *'me'* have to do with *that?!*" Something happened that you did not seed that seceded to the wonder of "How did it happen?" This is why the Son of Man, or Solomon, the Man of the Sun, could not bear any of the glory of the lily, because he thought he was what he wasn't. **The lily has no thought other than to bear its petals to attract your attention so you can die in its fragrance. That is the whole point of fragrance. It is to allow the invisible to escape and verify its presence. Remember, you cannot have a fragrance without realizing something has yielded wonder.** That's the value of the lilies of the field. "They toil not, neither do they spin."²

We can say we have all these incredible rights. We do, and for heaven's sake, don't lose them. Don't be inveigled into the disillusioned acts of the present day. Stand porter and perceive how you can be lost in the avaricious nature of those who find the material wealth so important that they would sacrifice the glories of an objectification of people, to fulfill it.

Remember, perhaps you are precipitated from another dimension. You are only here as a coincidence of agreement: you all agreed to have this form upon cognition dawning of another. The lily knows of none other. What is the difference between you and the lily? You toil and you spin and forget that the natural condition of any creature born of Wonder is to blossom. You can't blossom if you confine yourself to toiling and to spinning and to passing on remarks that are not true about you, your associates, or me! God help you, or those who do, because the Truth is the very source of Life Itself, It is the evidence that Life IS, and a lie is the evidence of the living dead. The living dead: they are the mummies of yesterday. **You can't have eternal Life by trying to contain it in a skeletal framework.**

Do you realize there is no mentality to be found in "you"?! (If that isn't a "bulb" of suggestion!) Isn't it amazing how we are educated to believe that we have developed *our* mentality? "Mentality" is only the name given to a sequential order of beliefs that others call logical. Then a few start to agree with it, and what happens? They start to make the same addition and get the same deposit: salt, water, chalk, protoplasm or slime, all slung together in a bag in time. The same deposit! But what is your credit rating if you think it's your *personal* achievement?

Man has no *credit* rating until he drops the suggestion of being "this," and then "all that I have is thine."[3] But if "all that I have is thine," then it can only be had as a Conscious-awareness experience because the "I" is only a sound.

> **I is only a sound that bears *what* as its source? *The Holy Breath!* That is why the Invisible is known to be, and the Breath you cannot see, the Breath you cannot capture, but it is that which allows sound to bear witness to its life-giving Allness.**

You live and move? Yes, but you *breathe*, first and foremost. That is why I used to always say in meditation: "Always meditate on the breath because the breath is the Holy Visitor and when you breathe out, the exhaling should bear the grace of the Holy Visitor entertained without mentality." What can you say if you're not breathing? You leave it up to others to say it. If you're not breathing the Holy Words — in other words, the words of a vocabulary that the ordinary can understand, but it intrigues their limited intellectuality and causes them to wonder "What is the matter with *you?*" until you suggest you're not the least bit upset. Why don't they look to see what is upsetting *them?*

If you find it difficult to love, now you know the answer. "*You*" don't know anything about it.

> **Love is no respecter of persons; Love knows nothing of person.**
> **Love is the innate rhythm of expression undefiled by emotion.**

This is what enhances your God-given talents and your gifts, and this is why it is so simple to understand the meaning of "Do unto others as you would have them do unto you." Even if they don't do it unto you, you have no alternative, because *yours is not an alternative way.* There is no alternative in your life, and if you try to mingle with what isn't Real, there is nothing but discord, disharmony, and the need of resolution.

Error has tried to suggest so many things to so many of us, but, really and truly, we have to know that it is the mentality of time that fosters the inconsistencies that come from mortal beliefs bearing a form. *Remember to always protect yourself.* Mrs. Eddy said: "Clad in the panoply of Love, human hatred cannot reach you."[4]

Practise what you know to be true and allow yourself to think of concertizing in the future called "the to-morrows" of your objectified world. It's always a solo performance, it's always One. When the people applaud your action, remember, they have lost some of the inhibitions of mentality! The wonder of an artistic performance is that it stops the mind in its tracks. In Canada they criticize it because the mind doesn't want to be stopped in its tracks. In Europe they *beat tracks* right to the door of the dressing rooms to exclaim at the wonder of the artistic presentation. In the movie *The Pianist,* Maestro Tadeusz Strugala is the conductor of the orchestra, and when we sang *The Fire Mass*[5] for the first time at the Wratislavia Cantans in Wroclaw, it was Strugala who was there. He came rushing through the doors and threw his arms around me. This is a man who is so aloof that you'd never consider doing anything other than shaking his hand. He threw his arms around me and he said, *"Never in my life did I ever expect to experience anything like this! It's magnificent!"* They never stopped applauding. I think we made about nine appearances on the stage, and Chris and I by ourselves. It was just unbelievable! And yet, in Canada there was hardly any recognition of it other than it was broadcast on the CBC *once!*

You cannot understand the situation of the mentality that is only partially educated to *think* music. You can't think music; the only people who do are critics! A critic always thinks music. Perhaps they wouldn't be a critic if they *were* music.

Yes, Dianne.

> *Dianne F:* I remember so well Maestro Strugala, this very accomplished conductor and musician and yet so full of wonder that when he burst through the doors and threw his arms around you, he also looked behind you, trying to find where these other instruments and

voices were that were released by the overtones of our singing! He and his wife could not believe what they heard, and they were looking behind you, "Where are the clarinets, where are the instruments?" He was so full of wonder and yet so full of accomplishment.

Yes.

**Every day you awaken is an Easter.
It's up to you to see the turban of the tulip
burst forth and reveal its crown of rejoicing.
It's yours; use it, and perhaps the captive will be
set free.**

Always listen to your inner voice lest your footsteps stray.

Students: Thank you, Sir.

Let me see. I wish more people had the courage to come. Why is it that so few men have the courage to be the Superman that the world is waiting for? It has nothing to do with age; it has to do with the daring to be Real, authentic. There is such a need for people who *have* presence to wrap it up and die and be born again in the realization of a correct Identity.

You women have been so wonderful in supporting this Work all your life, and the men here have done the same, but always obvious is the challenging aspect that must surround mentality with the *thought* of being Real, that keeps people away. Because there is a responsibility. As soon as you realize that Love, Truth, Spirit, Source, Self, is all there is, then you have not only a responsibility to massage the kinks out of people and the "what have you" out of people but the responsibility of knowing, as you plough through the various levels of avoirdupois, that something will be done to the appetite so that you can really feel the fibre of their Being! That's your responsibility: **feel the fibre of Being actual in spite of the flabbiness of flesh.**

Is there any serious question that is bothering you to the point where you are discomforted? Now, not everyone put up their hand, please! This is the point of everyone being so content, having heard the flow of Sound Investment.

Yes, Else.

> *Else L:* Your Presence is so wonderful, so great, so unbelievable! I can't say all these words that are beyond our belief and beyond our concepts, actually, and I thank you so much, for all of us, because you have given us this most wonderful Easter gift this weekend.

I'm so glad you're here, Else. You look marvellous. It's great that you are here. Yes, Stephen.

> *Stephen W:* Sir, you said that we have many gifts, and I just wanted to say that *you* have gifted us this morning and always. I thank you for that, Sir.

Yes. You asked otherwise you would never have received. You can't give to somebody who hasn't asked. You have no right to intrude upon the mentality, because up to the point of realization, they believe that *mentality* is the way to realize, whereas mentality is a way to *evidence* it. **Realization is evidenced by mentality being altered and bearing the vocabulary of the Ineffable.**

> *Students:* Thank you, Dr. Mills.

⌘

---

1. Proverbs 21:16.
2. Matthew 6:28.
3. Luke 15:31.
4. Eddy, *Science and Health*, 571–18.
5. *The Fire Mass*, Latin Ordinary of the Mass with additional text by Kenneth G. Mills, music by Kenneth G. Mills and Christopher Dedrick; recorded by The Star-Scape Singers conducted by Kenneth G. Mills, Sun-Scape Records compact disc KGOD26.

Overview

Chapter III

We cannot arrive at any place of significance if it isn't realized from the start that the mind, indiscriminate, unknowing of anything it's fed, might as well be fed the Truth!

Overview

Themes: God-Presence ~ Standpoint of Unity ~ awareness ~ acceptance/ understanding ~ mind/intellect ~ sensorial data

This is the morning of April 21, 2003, Easter Monday, and I'd like to read you a couple of things. It's a good way to start because then we all can consider the one idea here. I failed to write down the name of the person who said this:

> The greatest mistake and the greatest injustice we do in regard to one another is to imagine that everyone is conscious.

That was one, and the other one:

> The shaman's initiation is a journey into chaos, a plunge into the primal realm where things are not what they seem, where rules and guidelines governing conduct and belief fail and are no longer appropriate.
>
> Shamans know that the Real and the unreal are merely opposite ends of a continuum on which Reality can be stretched to include what is normally considered unreal — like a circle, where end and beginning meet and become the same point. It's like the serpent. So, the serpent can be seen, depending on point of view, devouring and disgorging the universe of its own body. (Tom Cowan)

This is a wonderful paradox:

> When you give-up everything, everything is yours. (Rumi)

Dr. Munir Graham said in 1975:

> The test comes when there is a choice between the personal will and the divine Will.

I said:

> This Work is not annihilation; it is a celebration of the totality of Being in a garment of praise.

Anything that can bend is alive; that which cannot is dead!

Henry David Thoreau said:

Without visionary imagination, no theory nor any facts have much meaning, but who the real wizard is remains a mystery.

G. K. Chesterton said:

If a seed in the black earth can turn into such beautiful roses, what might turn the heart of man to become in his long journey toward the stars?

I said:

You are a human alarm; your role on this plane is to be that which awakens.

A philosopher, a lover of wisdom, is one thing, but if wisdom doesn't find a lover, what is the value of it? It's just talk! (January 13, 2000)

Everything is temporary by the duration of mesmerism. (August 18, 1998)

Ramakrishna said:

A pundit who doesn't know how to discriminate between the Real and the unreal is no pundit at all.

Does the magnet say to the iron, "Come near me"? That is not necessary. Because of the attraction of the magnet, the iron rushes to it!

I thought this was very interesting. This man, Dr. Maxwell Multz, said:

It usually requires a minimum of twenty-one days to effect any perceptible change in mental image. During this time, do not argue and do not debate. Persist in playing your new role.

I wanted to read you what Madonna said:

I'm a speck, an atom. Everything physical is an illusion, but it's there to guide us or test us or deter us. Our job is to navigate through this world while understanding the only thing that matters is the state of our Soul, and that's very hard because I'm in the entertainment business which is completely based on illusion and physical things. Any success I have is a manifestation of God; it's my ego that wants to claim ownership; it's arrogance and greed.

I said:

People are willing to follow the Golden Rule as long as it doesn't interfere with their own tarnish!

This is interesting:

The virgin gold of respect would be too soft without some alloy of fear. (Hadrian)

This, I found, is applicable to some people in the Group, in Proverbs 23:2.

Put a knife to thy throat if thou be a man [or a woman] given to appetite.

Did everyone hear that?! [laughter] In other words, walk *past* the refrigerator and take *half* of any serving that anyone offers you, and watch yourself regain your figure.

As far as you can, be a slave, not a monarch. Let yourself be struck. Be the ball and not the bat. (Rumi)

Very few people quote what Rumi says that really has to do with you!

God has said, "Like an ass laden with books, knowledge that isn't from Him is a burden. Like a woman's make-up, it doesn't last!" (Rumi)

I said:

A disharmony is always a result of the incompatible thought-structures colliding in a stream of energy. (January 2, 1998)

I said this in the Salle des Etoiles:

> It is a universal fact that man is One. It's a universal myth that he will *become* One. (January 2, 1998)

On September 12, 1996, I said:

> The breath is unseen. It is obvious you cannot live *without* the Unseen!

Yesterday it was mentioned that we had to deal more with wholeness than with parts, we had to deal more with unity than with parts. The jigsaw puzzle is a good example up to the point of realizing you have to find the *centre* to achieve any *view* that another might comprehend. Everything exuding from the Centre always reveals a picture that is new, because What-IS is never known by what-isn't. **What-IS is never known by what-isn't, and yet we try to make What-IS known by what-isn't!**

The only value of study and of using correct language is to treat the indiscriminate component named the mind to a sound frequency that cannot interfere with the frequency that IS. When the mind thinks it's achieved, it will not interfere with your attempt. This is why it is often said that we do an injustice to others (by imagining that everyone is conscious), because so many are not conscious. They are not conscious if they are not aware of two horses (or of a mind) that are being ridden. *You have to arrive at that state where you are spontaneously in the saddle of service without the burden of an imbalanced state.*

You cannot bring about a balance or you cannot bring about a healing or you cannot bring about a releasement from suggestion if you are constantly attempting to juggle the spiritual with the non-spiritual. We say the spiritual is intangible and we say the sense data is so tangible. Remember, it is always the sense data, or the sensorial data, that draws us to associate with conviction that we are "this," where **it is the spiritual that reveals there is an existence that is not bound, circumscribed, or limited by the *suggestion* of "this."** Now, that State is one that is Unity in itself. You don't try to work from the standpoint of division; you work from the Standpoint of Unity.

It's so interesting how we have given our lives to the logical sequence of beliefs, and if they weren't logical, we would always say we're confused. But really, we cannot arrive at any place of significance if it isn't realized from the start that the mind, indiscriminate, unknowing of anything it's fed, might as well be fed the *Truth!* This is why you study, this is why you read, because the mind that is fed the Truth doesn't regurgitate it when it actually happens. The mind is only confused when it is put into a position of having to assimilate incompatibles. It never does assimilate them; it arrives at conclusions that allow you releasement from the disturbance of incompatibilities. This is why you have to be so very alert when you are walking down the streets of time, caring little for what you are considering and just going along with the picture.

The picture is always objectified because the mind has the objectification as the evidence of the conviction of its creativity. The mind's creativity is a counterfeit, because the *Authentic* never changes. What do we conclude? That the counterfeit does change and it's so "new" that you forget that it is your remembrance pattern that is not interrupted that is continuingly engulfing you with *what-isn't*.

You attempt to remain courageous and strong and filled with conviction, and it's well that you should, but you must realize it is necessary to feed the mind "I AM" food. I don't expect my cats or the dog to start declaring spiritual statements![1] [laughter] They do have a tremendous capacity to appear stupid, and yet we know their intelligence is so present. They (the animal natures) approach What-IS, and when What-IS attempts to reduce their "withdrawal" habits, they go like the wind; they want to be *chased*. They may feel the divine Magnet but they don't rush to it. I feel that they must consider the difference between a furry coat and a skinned one.

It's amazing how the animals have so much fun or are at perfect peace just watching what is going on around them. It never destroys their focus; they are aware. *Are **you** aware of what is going on around **you**?*

You have to cease expecting the mind-that-isn't to reveal the Mind-that-IS. The mind-that-isn't can be fed the most incredible meals, and they're all well cooked, but it *never* can do anything but *ape or mimic* the Divine!

You know how you've talked to people in the office or on the subway, but it's rare when anyone responds. They may want to but they may not know that they *need* to. That is the problem to-day: **the mass doesn't know it *needs*.** That is a very important point. The people to-day do not know they *need*, because they feel satisfied in being slaves of another's endeavour! If you become so entangled with your endeavour that you cannot extricate yourself from it, you should put it at arm's length until you can, because that is the very entanglement that would keep you so engrossed with making a success. To be a success is fine and dandy but not at the expense of being a failure. The purpose for which you came was to — what? — evidence, for others, the naturalness of being liberated, but you can't be liberated if you have portions of your considerations tremulous and not purified in the knowing that *all* **will be made new if you only surrender to What-IS.**

If you've noticed over the years, most regard a change in associates with a bit of scepticism and certainly a lack of understanding because there is a tendency to expect everyone who is really sincere in their actions to remain the same. Do you realize how every morning you expect the people around you to be the same because if they're not, you have to say "What is the matter with *them?*" In actuality, you should say, "What is the matter with *me? They* seem changed, and I don't know why they're changed, but I certainly don't understand them." It's obvious that you haven't budged *and they have.*

Don't misunderstand change. It takes work. I always remember reading (what I read to you) about taking twenty-one days for a trait to be changed. You should *not* spend time hearing What-IS and then dissipating that energy-field right after it. This is one of the things I notice so much. A few people can come upstairs in the morning and talk to me, but I wonder how quiet they are when they *leave* me. What has been given would never have been given to them *downstairs,* because *I was upstairs.* Yet, you go downstairs and only get involved with what it is like down there — instead of remaining upstairs and allowing everything that is "downstairs" to be taken care of because you have developed such an overview and you perceive the required movements. This is what you should do.

Do you notice after an *Unfoldment*™ (or at home when you get there) you will start being so frivolous and so energized, and before you know it, it may have dissipated? It's very important until you've contained it. There's no point in meditating if you are the same when you come out. Your energy-field should be different, your outlook should be different. That's why I stopped meditating after *years* of meditating; I realized that I was always so different after the meditation, but it changed after an hour or so, and then I was ready to meditate a few hours later. I thought, "This is ridiculous! If I can enter that State in meditating, why not make it constant?" That's what happened, and my goodness, I didn't realize it had really happened until I started to speak the Word, because then I realized it was a constant Presence. I only had to flick my eyelash to alter the perception of this dimension. It didn't happen all at once; it used to take me some time to do it, but to-day it's very difficult for you to know *where* I am! You don't know just what you're talking to!

When you ask me questions about Identity, you should really make a point of studying what I have said about Identity. Don't try to understand Identity; trying to understand Identity is impossible!

Be aware of what is said to constitute Reality. Don't try to *understand* It. "Understanding" is one word that should not enter the vocabulary until you're close to a hundred, and then you perhaps won't say it; I'll tell you. **Understanding is not necessary; *acceptance* is, because if you accept what you are given, you will prove to yourself immediately whether or not you understand.**

It says in Proverbs that "the man that wandereth out of the way of understanding shall remain in the congregation of the dead." It just came to me now (it's so fascinating) that we were talking about, on Saturday, the *mummies,* the congregation of the dead. Anything that is being factually passed from one to another is great, but you should attempt to do it as a result of *living* what is passed.

When anything is *past,* what do you have? The *residue.* We have the residue of a log in the fireplace: ash. That's what happens to the intellect in the fire of Love: the log of intellect is consumed, and that's why we have an Ash Wednesday, Thursday, Friday, Saturday, Sunday, Monday, Tuesday! [laughter] The only thing is that on Wednesday you usually *advertise* it! It would be wonderful if it were considered this way. It's so amazing to think a log could give you warmth. It can't as it is; it has to be *kindled and fanned,* and then when it catches fire, the warmth is exuded.

That is the same with *you:* when your intellect is burning as a result of the risen Fire, what you give is the warmth and you reveal the hearth of Being. It's always the *Home* sense that becomes present — you've *arrived.* If there is no warmth and there's no *feeling* of warmth, you can be assured it's sensorial data waiting to be experienced.

Are there any questions? You should ask whatever you wish because I'm going away this week, so I won't see you again for several weeks. I don't want you not to have your prescription filled if you need it! Yes, Barry.

> *Dr. Barry B:* Sir, you mentioned this morning, and you've mentioned many, many times, this idea that the mind will accept anything that you give it, so why not give it Truth. Clearly, there is a discriminatory element. It's the same thing as "behave as if": in order to "behave as if" something, you have to *know* what that Truth is or what that Ideal is. That clearly is not mental, am I correct?

No. That clearly *is* mental.

> *Dr. Barry B:* What is it? The Truth?

Purely mental.

> *Dr. Barry B:* So, even the discrimination is mental?

Oh, totally! Discrimination is totally mental.

> *Dr. Barry B:* Then, how does one learn to discriminate properly, so to speak?

What does the sun know of what-isn't?

> *Dr. Barry B:* It just shines.

That's right. That's all you need to do. But you try to have the mind having an ability that you think is essential; in other words, you're trying to say that the sun has to be known intimately in order to appreciate its rays! You see, the mind is capable of discriminating between what IS and what isn't, only because the mind is not in control; it only *appears* to be. That which IS doesn't know what IS or what isn't. What did I say? "Love *allows* you to embrace the objective" and have *fun* with it!

Yes, Ross.

> *Ross M:* I have a question about the first statement you read this morning, which was, "The greatest mistake and the greatest injustice we do in regard to one another is to imagine that everyone is conscious." I wasn't exactly sure how to view that, where to go with that.

I'm not sure, either. I'll tell you, though, in a minute. [pause]

To be conscious is to be God-Presence.
To be aware is *your* presence.

That's where it is. So, you know those who are not conscious, because they're not perceiving God-Presence, Truth-Presence, Love-Presence, in an active state.

> *Ross M:* Thank you, Sir.

Yes, Chris.

> *Christopher D:* One of the blessings of this weekend or this Wordshop for me has been the clarification, more and more, of what an impasse the intellect is — being able to see where it *doesn't* go.

Yes.

> *Christopher D:* You've made it very clear how it could be intellectually active, talk about the Truth, "know the Truth," and not be conscious. What comes with that clarification is this enjoyment and appreciation of that which makes *no sense, at all,* to the mind!

None!

> *Christopher D:* Certainly Love, certainly the breath, all the things that we can't really describe in any way, are coming into so much more a feeling of being aware that that is *there* and that it's great that the intellect can only talk about or represent it but can't —

It can only talk about it. It can only talk about it but *can't* experience it. **The intellect *never* experiences God. Never! When it *appears to,* it's God-Presence, and the breath allows the Holy Word to be spoken.**

The intellect is somewhat like water. You can contain it and you can look at it and you can describe its various states all due to different conditions (heat and cold and what have you), but *describing* it is not *experiencing* it. If I were to throw what is in the glass at you when you didn't expect it, you would say, "Oh!! What did you do *that* for?!" ***That's* God! It alters your response entirely!** You can't expect to remain in the same use of words in expression when that has happened.

Yes, Claude.

> *Claude C:* I don't have a question, Sir, but I wonder if it would be appropriate for me to share with everybody what I have perceived on the weekend?

Oh, that would be wonderful!

> *Claude C:* I pale in eloquence in the beautiful language that I have seen in the last few days from people who grow under the wing of such a divine Container as Dr. Mills, but hopefully this will not become the babbling of a crazy Frenchman and hopefully you will be somewhat lenient in my use of your language.
>
> I just wanted to communicate to you that I've known Dr. Mills for four months, and this is my first Wordshop. I was lucky enough to recognize who Dr. Mills was, instantly, and he seemed to acquiesce at this. When I was invited by Chloe to come to this Wordshop, I really was elated with anticipation, and it's hard for me to find words for the transformation that I went through. I basically felt like a spiritual sponge that needed to be filled, when I left Montreal, and thereafter I felt like a cocooning caterpillar that was following a road to a new experience. But I have to say that as soon as I crossed Dr. Mills' threshold, or portal, I became like a *budding butterfly!* It was a reflection that was a tying of a knot.
>
> I had this experience seventeen years ago that was so beautiful in its simplicity. I had to go halfway around the world to live it. I had this bird come to me and walk across my body. It had never happened before and it's never happened since. This bird really reflected to me that he was willing to sacrifice his life to show me the perfection of

what I am, and he was really telling me, "If I can recognize the perfection of what you are, why don't you get it?" So, the tying of the bow happened when I was greeted by Dr. Mills, and that's basically what he's telling all of us.

I was privileged to witness the extension of this divine Container by seeing the unbelievable beauty, the artistic beauty, in his household. Never before have I seen such a concentration of creativity, but there's something beyond all creative endeavours, and that's the unseen Reality. Everything spoke with the same voice because they are all gifts that you gave to Dr. Mills, and they all say, "Dr. Mills, we love you." And so, this unbelievable beauty really pales with the content, the divine content, of this divine Container that is trying to teach us to be container-*less*.

So, I thank divine Principle that Dr. Mills is here, and wish that this sharing will become an affirmation for the *Now*. I feel that I've come into Dr. Mills' life to share that with him, or to allow the mentality to accept such a Principle. He stated yesterday that when Jesus raised His body (let us be reminded that He also went through a process of transfiguration), it was out of *spiritual coincidence.*

I hope that you will rise right now and join with me (please rise) in the affirmation that whether this concept is Truth or delusion, **all of us together here right now wish and want to nudge divine Principle into focussing on *you*, Sir, whatever degree of incorruptibility physicality can bestow upon you.** This is the inhale of a breath, an action, an affirmation that will become for all of us a *surrender* to the results. But it is important that as a group and as a focus of unbelievable energy, we recognize that *we are needed* by this planet right now, and Beings of the like such as Dr. Mills are of utmost necessity.

Students: Hear! Hear!

Claude C: So, Sir, I raise my hand to you in the hope that your physicality will remain with us during this Easter and for as long as the Divine will allow, because, Sir, *we need you very, very much* and hope that you will be with us for a very, very long time! Thank you very much.

Students: Thank you.

Thank you.

[Dr. Mills picks-up a blueberry from the fruit plate in front of him.] What is it?

Students: A blueberry.

You know it as a blueberry because you only see it at this stage of development. If you knew it from its beginning, it was a little white flower on a bush very close to earth, and when it first appeared, as the flower died, it started to gain a form that others expected, and it was pure white. When you looked at the pure white *acres* of these berries, the blossom was being transformed so that you would see the stages of its development. Then it turned a pale green, a lime green, and as it grew in power and gathered its forces to contain an enzyme that only *it* contains, it grew into a pale blue and then into a dark blue, which said, "I am ready to be consumed and bear *for you* the apparent process of sense to satisfaction."

The blueberry contains the sacred enzyme of Venus, myrtillin; it's the *only* berry that does. It's delicious for its flavour, but its unseen power is an essential constituent for your objectivity to be able to point to the bush so lowly, transferred in power to a blueberry so succulent. That is like the progress that time performs as you witness growth. But if you can perceive without all those steps and do not understand how the blueberry became a blueberry but you can assume the *wonder* of the berry and what it has to offer, *you don't need to know all its stages*. All you need to know is, you can't put the greater into the lesser, but the *lessee* has a possibility of offering to you the instantaneous succulence of its body if you are willing to take it. Then you may understand how it grows and toils not, just like the lily. And yet, Solomon in all his glory was *never* as one of these. [Dr. Mills eats the blueberry.]

It's amazing, when "indifference" strikes the bush of blueberries in the fall and the atmosphere becomes cold, the bush turns the most incredible vibrant magenta. My uncle had acres, thousands of acres, of blueberry plains that he could only see by being in his plane, they covered so much!

It's so interesting how people flock to the blueberry if they like it, but boy, do they pay the price! Why do you pay the price? Because somebody else perpetuated the idea for *you* of the unseen promise in a bush of humility. **Humility in its final stages dons a robe of the Ascended.**

It's so fascinating, you don't have to have a whole box of blueberries to know the flavour. *One* reveals the wonder of all the acreage! That is termed *"the overview."* You will always recognize blueberries because, essentially, you are attracted to it.

Out of the small bushes of the mind, you are planting the seeds of Wonder! You have to tend them and let them grow, and don't allow others to dissuade you from the experience of change. If the blueberry were expecting to be liked or disliked because of its colour, it would never have reached fruition. This is the way we must look at the world. You can't go by the colour, for the fruition is the overview of God-Man and the cosmic splendour beyond the grass, beyond the changeable, beyond the short-living. **Life is Self-sustained.**

You could rake all the blueberries you wished and pass them through the wind machine at the end of every row. Every row of blueberries was maybe one mile long, and you'd go to the wind machine at the head of each one. Every row was marked by twine, and people stayed right within that row; they weren't allowed to go over that line. They'd take rake-fulls of blueberries, drop them in the wind machine, and the wind *blew-out* all that was unbecoming and left the berries just needing to be washed in the purity of water, and they were ready for consuming. A very interesting thing: it was after two years that the *entire acreage* had to be given to fire, for then they would be cultivated, they would grow to great dimensions. **It is always the fire that quickeneth the spirit of Fullness, Allness.**

It's amazing how a plate of fruit can point to the wine and the dance of the Infinite.

> Just remember, they appear on a plate in order to be served. Your offering has to be placed the same; it has to be *ordered* and *contained* within the dimension of your serving.
>
> If the cosmos wants you, always remember the strawberry.

> If it expects a demonstration, always know the grape, and if they demand more, always remember the ballet of the pineapple!² *That's* how you dance!

Okay?

> *Students:* Yes, Sir!

It's been a beautiful three days.

> *Students:* Oh, yes, Sir!

I am so very grateful to have been able to do this. I *appear* to do it, but I of myself can do nothing. I am so very grateful that the vehicle has been capable of doing all this. I am just so sorry that *thousands* didn't hear it.

> So, it's up to you to bear such a Song within your heart
> That others will hear it whene'er we part,
> And may it be found on the harp strings of the mind
> To reveal the Tonality that is simply divine!

> **You can always name a note, but remember this fact:**
> **You cannot name the Tone, for That is That!**

Thank you.

> *Students:* Thank you, Sir.

⌘

---

1. Iams is a brand of pet food.
2. Referring to *Pineapple Poll,* a ballet.

Resist Ordinariness

Chapter IV

There is no solution to the problem of "this" if you aren't willing to abdicate from the throne room of mediocrity termed "your mind."

Resist Ordinariness

Themes: The Realm divine ~ energy ~ elegance ~ mind ~ fear ~ otherness ~ evil ~ stooping to ordinariness

This is the evening of June 21, 2003. It will be an evening of variety. Kazantzakis said, in *The Last Temptation of Christ,* that the greatest temptation is whether or not you will resist ordinariness.[1]

> As we look over the horizons of time and perceive in
>   the wonder of the moment called "Now,"
> We see with direct perception the purpose of
>   why we are here and how.
> We came in, in an attitude bearing perspective; we
>   came with an intention that would be cleared
>   in Fact.
> It was the fact of Truth that brought meaning to the
>   irresistible, termed "the Soul of That."
>
> We move in a rapid action, for creation never stands
>   still,
> And we move as a service to mankind in order to do
>   and present the Father's Will.
> In the glad tidings that reach the ear prepared, we
>   find in this time of doubt
> That it's only necessary to step beyond the time-
>   space continuum and find the Eternal is there
>   without doubt.
>
> We come to perceive the event of meeting the
>   struggling mass of time.
> Do you suppose they struggle in order to perceive
>   something that they know is buried in mind:
> An ember of an unknown state of Glory that is
>   dressed in the yearning of the heart
> That they would come-to and be present in the
>   wonders of the creative art.
>
> The joy that comes with knowing gives us confidence
>   to face this fact.

The struggling masses struggle because they have
    refused to accept their struggling act.
They refuse to see the condition, which is this,
    there is no doubt,
That they have to face themselves — the source of all
    the struggle in this world of doubt.

It is this point of consternation that fills the heart
    of men;
It is this consternation that seems to have no end.
But remember in this moment, *Now*, that the fact
That deals the blow of death is to speak the truth
    to a logical mind and see it rebel and act
In defence of something that doesn't exist other than
    a logical sequence of thought,
And you are there to bring the struggling masses to
    their knees in the act of wonder, for which
    they did not know they had sought.

'Tis in this act of knowing that man takes this place
    and finds
That the joy of knowing the Eternal bears the
    fulfilment of all of time.
Every Age that we look over from the Standpoint
    beyond this history-making time
Reveals this fact that is glowing, that the human and
    all mankind
Must see without doubt the evidence that springs
    from this Fact divine
That thou art now a beloved in the heart of the
    Cause divine.

You look upon the creation and you say, with
    unbridled glee,
That the joy of emancipation is what has come from
    the Truth that sets the captive free.
**So, rejoice in the simple statement that the great
    temptation of time**
**Is to *stoop* to impress the ordinary instead of
    elevating the ordinary to the Realm divine!**

You walk among the people and you talk and chatter
    all the time,

But is your chatter really conversation or conversing
  that would convert the mortal of time?
Your speech should be seasoned with salt, and your
  heart overflowing with love
Because it is the sign that you have not stooped to
  temptation but have offered what is termed
  "the Grace from above."

Every nation, every century, has a promise, and they
  look for it always slated for time,
Other than the moment *Now* when it all can happen
  that it's fulfilled in the divine Afflatus which
  comes as prophesied.
You can only give to the fatidic that which would
  entice your thought
To reduce itself to wonder and see what beyond the
  Ages has been taught.

What is beyond the Ages that man has numbered?
  'Tis the agelessness of Being divine;
It's all wrapped-up in the knowingness that I could
  not have created the mind
That could entertain a Mind superior, when the
  inferior chitter-chatters all the time,
Conversing about the madness of the mundane —
  while the language of the Divine

Does not appeal to the common man, does not
  appeal to the ordinary of thought,
For in the bosom that beats with surrender lies the
  wonder for which the Ages have been brought
To kneel in expectation and develop *some kind of
  feeling* that resolves the situations of time.
But, you see, if they look and face them*selves*, they'll
  see there are multiple and many resolutions
  but they're not divine!

Man makes his own conditions and thus creates his
  problems to evade the fact
That Man, in the divine Estate, knows not of trouble
  but only knows this glowing fact
That you look, and you see with wonder what
  appear to be the wonder*less* in time

> Are only waiting to find they stumble and say, "My
> God, where art Thou? I am now inclined."

The whole purpose of *our* gathering is in the realm of learning how metaphysics is able to resolve things, to resolve thought, and have a corresponding identity called "thing"; and then also, to perceive that this is just *an exercise of the intellect*. The more advanced stage is philosophy, but it is not the philosophy that is tinged with psychology; it is the philosophy that in essence deals with perspective. It is the perspective of the higher realms; it is not the perspective of your prospects.

The perspective of the higher realm is very, very different than yours. You can measure *your* perspectives, but the higher realm's perspectives cannot be measured. You know they're present because they alter your perspective, and they alter it via the use of a vocabulary that is not ordinary. That's why, in *The Last Temptation of Christ,* it is said that the great temptation He had to resist was to stoop to ordinariness. How often we stoop to it — the ordinary way of greeting people, the ordinary way of making others feel comfortable in their ordinariness. I usually make people feel uncomfortable and never intentionally do so, but it always seems to be so!

It is very important that people be jolted to consider: **where they are is a result of their thought, and every problem they have is a result of their own making.** In other words, all your problems should point to the fact that they can only be solved by *evaporating* the problem. You don't have a problem that seduces you and causes you to fail *unless you stoop!* Why do you think so many people have backs that bother them? So many people *stoop* to pick-up a problem of their own or of someone else as if it were Real. **You would never have been given the ability to consider something greater than yourself if it wasn't more actual than what you** *think* **your self is.**

This is why the Grace of the Source, the Grace of God, the Grace of the Christ, is so important, because it is always present in the recognition that you are *not* "this" in actuality. So, what do you do? **You have to delete from your index of mediocrity the statements that are untrue.** Metaphysics allows you to do this and still have your sanity. Metaphysics, remember, is helpful only in training the mind to consider a different perspective. That's all!

Metaphysics allows you to "exchange the objects of sense for the ideas of Soul."[2] The very elementary state of this is when you find a chair that is comfortable. You say the chair is so comfortable (or what have you), but the chair doesn't know anything about being gracious to you; it's *you* who say it is comfortable. So, therefore, the chair is there as the evidence of that condition that suits your frame, termed "comfort." Your car is the evidence of immediacy; your elevator is the same; your airplane is the same. *It is really renouncing any condition that is in support of a limited state.*

The newspapers, I guess (I never read them, but from what I hear), are filled with a lot of fearful statements. The news on the radio and the television is the same, but if you look at it, don't believe a word of it, because it's all being brought to your attention in order to capture your thought because it can only live like a vampire — not taking your *blood* — a vampire of *energy*.

So, don't give your thought to and don't bring feeling or anything when you look at the news. *Take this stand that it comes to you to give itself up.* Only you can annul the jurisdiction of this propaganda that is causing the Age to have the black death, which in this Age is what? Fear! (These statements are all leading to something I know is going to unfold over the next few days.) **Remember, fear is only the suggestion that there is two; it only arises in the belief of otherness.** That is why it is so important to see your creative ability, because your creative ability allows you to look at one another and see the magic of your ability to create an object that bears perspective, dimension, and mass to your experience. When you close your eyes, *it doesn't exist.* If what appears before you doesn't exist with your eyes closed, then it can't be Real, **because the Real never changes!**

How can evil live if it isn't supported by ignorance?! The ignorant don't know, but it doesn't mean that the ignorant are devoid of energy. Remember, the Divine is always an energy-field, it's always a frequency, and it always bears frequent visitations in order to spike the interest of those who are dismayed with their mediocre creativity. It always comes before you so that you can add unto your credit that you were able to take the seeming and find the Essence immutable and immortal.

There is no process to manumission or to freedom. Remember, it's up to you whether you *dare* to be free! For example, I wonder how many men in this room would dare to wear this bolero[3] and I wonder how many *could* wear it, because sometimes you look so uncomfortable in what you *are* wearing! And you wonder sometimes where in heaven's name you got it!! **You have to sustain a plane of elegance because that is the evidence of being beyond stooping to ordinariness.**

People who scoff at being elegant and living elegantly — it doesn't mean you have to be very, very wealthy, but why not?! You *can* be if you stop considering yourselves *not* to be. Where does the lack of wealth exist in the root beginning? It exists in *false identity* and what? The way you were taught as a child, to believe that you are going to be great or not great. *There are not two ways!* Everyone should know that the only course is upward if you consider there is a downward one.

This dispensation is dealing with the Word that comes perpendicularly to this horizontal yet curved plane. It's very interesting, It is always perpendicular to the curve, and in Its essence, It is always bearing a point of force because it is this point of Light that becomes the centre of the divine attraction that allows each and every one to know, without being told, they have met another experience from a different dimension.

Recently I said to a couple of people in the room: "You will always have the body that you need." So many people are concerned about death and "What's going to happen? Am I going to lose my body?" Well, you wouldn't be going if this one were still functioning! [laughter] So you're going to pick-up a new one if it means that much to you. You will always have what you need. I said here [Dr. Mills reads from his notebook]:

> You will always have the body that you need, whichever dimension you go to. No dimension is difficult other than this one because in this dimension you are dealing with choice, and as soon as you have a choice and you make the wrong one, it is very difficult to change your way. Why? Because you have such secret compacts with ordinariness.

Do you realize, you feel at ease in the mass because they're *just like you*. But isn't it amazing how comfortable you *are* in the mass?! You spend most of your days in the mass! How much time do you spend being holy without the thought-structures of the mass?

What is the connecting link between here and There? *Thought!*

I want to read you something else I said: "We create our own problems and then torture ourselves trying to solve them." This is what happens! The reason you seem so self-satisfied in being where you are is because you have no difficulty in creating situations that are problematic, just for the fun of having to resolve them in order to prove you still have an ability to create something different! But how about trying to restrain from creating these problems and see what there is to solve?! There is no solution to the problem of "this" if you aren't willing to abdicate from the throne room of mediocrity termed "your mind." You exalt the mind and allow it in its belief endowment to guide you and strengthen you, but this is a marriage that should be annulled; it is a marriage that holds you in a position of inferiority.

If you are going to be a pianist or a singer, or any musician or an artist of any type, it means you have to come out from the world and be separate. Why do you have to come out from the world and be separate? Because as long as you're in the world, you have to chatter an empty chatter, and yet you say it's conversation. Have you ever realized how difficult it is to have *a dialogue?* You see it in these people who ask others all kinds of questions, and you sit there and listen to them in the talk shows. Some can be very interesting, but it's a dialogue that someone prepares. It's usually not the one who's being interviewed; it's the *interviewer* who has to prepare because he can't dialogue with his guest unless he prepares himself.

How do you think you can prepare yourself by thinking about *yourself* that can never be prepared to meet its doom unless you gear the mentality to a fundamental basis that is termed "Principle," and out from this Principle you move and live and have your Being. What do you do? How much of your time is spent that is not principled? It's not principled in the fact that you're not *using* what you know that is of a Higher Order and transcends the mundane!

The world, they say, is filled with evil. It always has been filled with evil. Have you ever seen a time it wasn't? No, there's nothing historically that isn't evil. It must be! History is nothing but the coding of the memory of forgetters, and it is nothing that can bear testimony to your actuality; it can only bear testimony to your *unreality.* The historical past testifies to the unreality of the objective world.

The reason the name Jesus lives, Buddha lives, any of the great spiritual leaders of the past lives, is because what they gave had nothing to do with the time in which they were living; it had to do with the Timeless out of which they emerged as Conscious Being amidst those of ordinary attainment! That's why it was said that He chose fishermen. But what did He say? "Drop your net and follow me." "Oh, He didn't really mean that!" Of course, he did. You have to drop your net. Why? That's what's catching all these erroneous thoughts, and you cook them up and have them all the time!

Do you realize that evil cannot live if there isn't another?! **Evil only lives when there is otherness.** Why does it only live on otherness? *Because evil has no energy; evil is energy-less. It's your energy that is misused that becomes the fuel of evil.* How does evil get your energy? By injecting *fear!* And fear does what? Causes an uncontrolled releasement of energy. It's wild, it's frenetic. The energy can only be present from those who live, just as Dracula can only exist on those who live.

Have you ever become afraid of your own thought? You should because it is your thought that generally is the cause of so much of your disharmony and discontent. It is *only* thought. The only reason you're here is to have your thought challenged, because I am not thinking.

What is allowing the fear, if it isn't your imagination? This is part of your perspective. It is the imagination, and that was linked with Nathanael. Nathanael is from the Bible, and his characteristic was imagination. It has to be redeemed, otherwise you think the Christ is personal. That's what some Christians think, that the Christ is personal. **The Christ is the *degree* that one attains in reducing the suggestion of personality and thought so that the Divine can have an entrance into the midst of those who are ordinary.** The ordinary may have the purity of spirit more easily at hand than do the cultivated intellectuals who find the High Way so challenging because they can't argue against it. They try to. I have never seen one intellectual win, and the atheists are the best because you can really challenge them in a minute! In other words, they think they create themselves. Now, tell me another!

What recognizes that the body exists in an environment?

Dr. Barry B: Mentality.

The intellect. Mentality. Mentality is what is your servant. How easily we can say "mentality," but it is the servant! That's why you can alter your thought. That's the God gift to you: you have the ability to alter your thought and adopt that state that is open to receiving. The direct reception only comes, usually, to one who is able to stop thinking when speaking.

Does the body know anything about environment?

Students: No.

Isn't it easy to agree with it?! So, guess what is declaring that you're living in it? The intellect. Now do you see why it's important to stand porter at the door of thought, admitting only those thoughts that you want to entertain in keeping with your Ideal.

A lady by the name of Mrs. Elaine Pagels said, "We are all born as sons of God, and Jesus is the Example which can be attained as the Son of God." I think that's very interesting. In other words, *that state of thought or Conscious-awareness is attainable by everyone who declares they have an intellect. But do you want it?*

I'm going to read to you something I said just the other night, because you should have it. It is really marvellous. I'll just give you the first paragraph:

> Evil lives on the residue energy of otherness. If it doesn't have enough energy of others, evil will always know how to receive it by injecting fear into the stream of thought. Fear causes an uncontrolled releasement of energy. Evil latches onto it because it is flowing from those who live by the injection of a capsule of fear as thought. Fear is nothing but the work of evil because it is the energizing of a creation that exists only hypothetically as long as man lives in an imaginary world unredeemed from the standpoint of the eye/I of God or the Source. (Kenneth G. Mills)

Sometimes it doesn't seem that a very high *Unfoldment*™ can be given until everyone is attuned to receive it. It is very difficult to give an unabridged Emanation unless the people present are qualified to receive it. This is what is waited to be felt, and this is why the first two or three Lectures of the Summer Festival with so many people are as this, because each must attune to a non-personal attitude in listening.

Whatever you do, don't try to correlate. Don't try to say, "Oh, that's exactly what somebody else said," or "This is exactly this or that," or "You said it ten years ago, you said it thirty years ago." To that which has been said and is saying, it isn't in time anyway, so thirty years ago I have no idea what I said; in fact, I have no idea what I said a few moments ago! If I knew what I said a few moments ago, I would have to hear it again; I only get tidbits of it. Although I look like I'm just conversing, I'm not. So, you just be receptive and receive it all. But you can't receive it if you are correlating.

There was a most interesting statement that somebody sent to me, and I think it may be just the evening for it because of one of our guests.

> A sick man turned to his doctor as he was preparing to leave the examination room and said, "Doctor, I am afraid to die. Tell me what lies on the Other Side." Very quietly the doctor said, "I don't know." "You don't know? You, a Christian man, do not know what is on the Other Side?" The doctor was holding the handle of the door, on the other side of which came a sound of scratching and whining. And as he opened the door, a dog sprang into the room and leaped on him with an eager show of gladness. Turning to the patient, the doctor said, "Did you notice my dog? He's never been in this room before. He didn't know what was inside. He knew nothing except that his master was there, and when the door opened, he sprang in without fear. I know little of what is on the other side of death, but I do know one thing: I know my Master is there, and that is enough."

Isn't that beautiful? We'll talk some more to-morrow morning.

⌘

1. Nikos Kazantzakis, *The Last Temptation of Christ* (New York: Simon & Schuster, 1960).
2. Eddy, *Science and Health*, 269–15.
3. Dr. Mills is wearing his custom-designed, chartreuse-coloured jacket.

The Freedom of Love

Chapter V

The essential feature of the God-Mind is the love of freedom and the freedom of Love!

The Freedom of Love

Themes: AM-ing of the I ~ Truth ~ Love ~ intention ~ mind/matrix ~ projection ~ world ~ objective ~ time, space ~ education ~ belief

This is the morning of June 22, 2003. In all our comings and goings we are always bound to some degree of intention, and it is obvious that this intention has manifested in your presence here at this time. It behooves us all to consider without doubt and to bring to our attention the great number of speculations which have arisen as a result of our state and our confinement mentally within the environs of a *conjured* world and universe.

It is well to consider *all that can be named is conjured,* and the only way of hope remaining alive within the hearts of each and every one is to question with rigorous and vigorous enquiry into the whys and wherefores of this hallucinatory (and yet great) experience of being contained within an environment, which for our own reason must have a reason to become surfaced in order for it to appear before one and all that their intention is to be fulfilled. If they have tasted the fruit of emancipation from the material confinement, they are at once contented and encouraged to move along with courage and rapidity into the ever-flowing Stream that exudes from beneath the throne of the Invisible.

The great demand of to-day is not so much to come out from the world and be separate; it's to be that state *within yourself,* separate from the world as it seems to be and holding it as it truly is — as a divine Idea — and we thereby are not confined by the perimeters that mankind has set upon its condition. We are encouraged to come and to bring to this plane what we have found to be on the escutcheon of our Soul and to perceive within that the need of our presence. You have found the need of your presence either you wouldn't be here. It is to re-awaken yourself by the hearing of the Sound to the invincible words of Truth and the forcible execution thereof.

When one has transcended the belief of the confines of their conjecturing, then one has attained that moment of blessedness that allows the force-field of Truth to bring to the so-called masses *a hope,* because they who are attuned and who have forgotten to look within are, by your very presence, moved to do so. They say, "What is that glow? What is that vitality? What is that happiness? What is that joy? What is that evidenced expression of wonder that exudes from your appearance?" This is a sign that they themselves are awakening to the wonders of being more than "this," and thus a Philosophy may be engaged — not the philosophy you study at a university but the Philosophy that springs from beyond the mount of revelation. That Philosophy deals only with the peregrinations from sense to the highest considerations or the Ultimate, and from that Point we can bring cessation to the struggling thought-fields of confusion, which *must* exist, so it seems, for mankind to have a reason to use their energy. You see, as long as confusion reigns, you are constantly trying to solve a problem — when you yourself have constituted it!

The great "problem" of being is not that of finding your beingness up for consideration; it's finding *what Being means!* "Being" is the name or the sound that we adopt to indicate activity. The great I AM is totally a static condition; it has no power whatsoever. You can say it a thousand times, and the only thing it does is lull the mind to a sleep state where you feel you've attained something! The sleep state is not a state where *anything* is attained; the sleep state is the opposite of the wake state.

Man was told and given the command to awake from the dream. This dream has always constituted the purpose of belief, because a dreamer cannot exist without some form of belief that triggers some sort of response, no matter how mundane or how elevated, because he has to have a reason for being and he invents what is necessary to enhance that inner longing. This inner longing can never be grown and nurtured to any degree without some system that would bind him, and *that's* where we have dreamed and given authority to what is termed "the matrix."

We can never have freedom as long as we are in the matrix — unless we have entered the matrix to offer freedom to those who are caught in it. That's what *you* have done. You have entered the matrix, or — what? — the mind-projected scenario. The entire world is a mind projection, and the incredible part of it is that we have the ability to project objects into time and give them a spatial reference to one another. But you have *assumed* that just because you see an object and experience an object, you have *understood* the object. Remember, the object is not of itself capable of *naming itself* an object! *You* do that by your invention, and when you have invented something, it becomes your intention to name it. **You cannot perceive any object without surrounding it with a mental consideration that gives it a viability.**

Objects, such as "you" and "me" and the lamppost, all exist as a result of our own creative ability. When you stop and consider what is actually happening, it's quite startling because what you say is an object is nothing but the description of a sensorial experience. First and foremost, it is an *eye* experience, and the interesting part is, it's received upside down by the cones in the eye, and we have the ability within the matrix to turn it right side up. And what do you say? "Oh, there is an object, and I bumped into it." You certainly have because you have failed to perceive that without the incredible mechanical contrivance within the matrix, the neuro-interactive system, you would not be able to perceive an object or have the experience of an object — *but it is all within the mental realm!* **What the object is remains only described by the state that has projected it! It has no intrinsic value whatsoever.**

No matter how much we describe a table, a horse, or a man, the description is all arrived at as a result of the stimulation of the eyes sensing an object that we attempt to feel at ease with. We attempt to describe it and leave it entirely in the hands of the present moment. If not described or searched for and considered, it becomes a thing that you buy and you place in your home or you place in your bed — and it's unfortunate that so many seem to be carrying the bed with them invisibly most of the day! They're asleep to the wonders of Actuality!

The bed is never meant to do anything but hold the seeds of promise, not the evidence of a failing system. [laughter] The failing system is our mesmerism with the seeming projection and the required need, constantly, for re-evaluating and altering the stage upon which we live. We are constantly trying to move things about without realizing what is the value of it if you haven't moved that which is *essential* about.

The matrix would have you unaware of what IS actual. Remember, the Philosophy that we speak about is really pointing to the Ultimate, which means what? That relativity ceases to play a part in the adjudication of that which confronts us as this experimental experience called living in this world on this Earth. You sometimes, perhaps, never consider that you may not have any vibratory frequency at ease with Earth. *The Earth is a vibratory frequency only from the standpoint that you give it the energy to exist as long as you are consciously aware of it!* When you lose your conscious-awareness of the Earth, it does not exist, but that doesn't mean that *you* do not exist. That which comes with the Earth goes with the Earth, but Conscious-awareness has never come with the Earth or gone with the Earth!

The Conscious-awareness is the evidence of what our language attempts to describe as "the Eternal," but the Eternal can never be considered in the framework of time. Eternality has nothing to do with time, because it is only a Sound-wave of force that is freed from the impingement of thought-processing, which limits it to something that you can entertain and, thinking about it, feel you have attained! You can't attain this at all, because you really don't know what it means other than it hasn't to do with time. You see, it (eternality) must be the opposite of time because you dare to create a word for it when you don't understand what is beyond time! What is beyond time is eternality.

You are living as a result of false education and false belief-systems in a dualistic world where you must have time and space in order to have and to define *objectivity.* And you must have time, and hopefully are *on* it instead of *in* it. When you see that the time is only that which measures the limitations of the mortal activity, then you'll see why the mortal activity under the jurisdiction of the Eternal is never ceasing; in fact, it is always on duty because it never knows what it is to be inactive. It is the evidence of *Being,* the activity of the static state of I AM brought into practicality as the AM-ing of the I.

This AM-ing of the I is the practicality to your life on Earth with the realization and the acknowledgment of your at-Onement with That which can only be sounded as "Conscious-awareness." The Consciousness is uncontaminated and unfettered by your mentality, but the awareness is what allows you to experience what you came to this plane for, which was to experience choice, and it allows you to navigate this realm and extract from your experience that which is necessary for the enhancement, perhaps, of your own invisible vehicle, as well as to bestow as the Light-confetti the wonders of the emancipated state to those who seem bound in "body, mind, and soul."

That trinity is not fecund. The only hope of body and mind is Soul, and the only hope of fecundating this triad is to see that it must birth to something higher. We say, then, it is what? Body, mind, and Spirit. We say it is Spirit, Soul, and God. You can name it anything you wish, but as long as it remains in the formation of a mind object — just think, that is a *mind object,* and you think it is what? It is nothing but a mind object, but what is not the matrix is That which allows the birth of such a concept. Nothing that is evidenced in the matrix as constructive is really, therefore, bound by the matrix provided you find a Teller, a Messenger, or Someone who can alert you to the entanglement that arises from belief-systems based on your unrealized state.

There is no belief-system for one who is aware of the impersonal and, you might say, *spiritual* **State.** "Because God made thee mine —"[1] I prefer to say "God made thee *Mind.*" This Mind is what lies beyond the door. Remember, the Oracle said to the doubtful one, who was doubtful of his mission, "Let me see your palm."[2] She didn't need to look at his palm; she did that *for him* because he doubted. She looked at his eyes and perhaps realized, if he were really seeing, he would be seeing the non-dual state in spite of the one who was making cookies. He was in doubt, and she said, "Oh, do take a cookie and enjoy it and go through the door, and you will feel *wonderful* because you will have no remembrance of being confronted by your true Reality."

He went through the door and he did not feel wonderful, but anyone who has been touched by a "Cookie" who bears the wisdom is moved *just by taking it!* This is why if you are given a gift of even a cookie, the Cookie that made it may very well have imbued that gift with a feature of force that will cause you to be curious as to why you have such a strange feeling.

One of the situations that arises upon hearing the enunciation of a Message that may stem from above is that it always disrupts the present state of thought because it doesn't have anything to do with it and takes no care or concern for the condition of it. It just says, "Get rid of your thought as 'you' think, and expound as I!" From that Standpoint you see the possibilities are limit-less.

Drop the parcel of your thoughts. Why do we say "parcel"? It is something that means we have collected in a bag. Look what you have collected in your bag! You have collected, through the wonders of a creative Spirit that is beyond our comprehension, this form of salt, water, chalk, protoplasm, and slime, and yet you seem to consider it is the means to salvation. Not one of those elements can reveal the actuality of Being. **Your only hope is to restore the kingdom of Light to where it belongs: available to those who are willing to surrender to the wonder and the need of understanding how the objective seems to be and is reduced to the wonder of a Light creation.**

> What is the greatest gift you can give to anyone?
> A sound that bears sincerity,
> a sound that evidences freedom,
> and a sound that is an invisible treatment
> to your disordered belief-system.

Isn't it amazing, as a child — all you have to do is look at your childhood — what is taught. It's wonderful to be taught in the way that is strict. When we "belonged" (so-called) to England we had a system of education that provided education. To-day the system is really up for question because we have withdrawn from the discipline and from the classicalism that once imbued teaching. We have adopted a low standard in the system, and people are passed-through a schooling or a disciplining period of thought-structures and how to create and reduce them and elevate them before they even know that they are the custodians of their future, with no thought of how to propel it to the arms of Light. They think by *thinking* they will attain.

How can the mind of matter ever be equivalent to the non-spatial omnipotence of the Invisible? The only link we have with that concept, which is purely of Earth, is that we can put the Earth and everything on it into question — only from the Standpoint of being *beyond*. That "being beyond" means that you have the ability to enhance what appears as your experience, to enjoy, to offer to everyone, but everything you do and appear to do will be done with such a graciousness and such an *amplitude of Force* that people will say, "Who and what are you?!" As soon as they do that, you know you may have taken a step on the ladder, but remember, it isn't going up. You're not going to go up to Heaven and down to hell. The mind has to make-up *both* in order for you to have some idea which way you're going! Certainly, you can't go sideways without meeting yourself eventually, because no line can withstand the pressure of the Infinite resting upon it.

The magnitude of the Infinite is such that only the circle can point to its incredible dexterity in dealing with every horizontal suggestion. The circle and the line can never meet, but, my goodness, the line can certainly be drawn as to what is found within the circle that points to the availability of that which we deem so needful for our present time. A circle cannot be drawn without a centre, and the radiant energy of your radius of activity may extend in so many directions that those who see you may attempt to find you "on line" where *they* are. But this is an assemblage of points; it is not other than a way of causing those on this line of horizontalization to look to the Centre and thus the circumference of their Being. From the Centre exudes This; from *your* centre you exude "this."

When children (such as you) have been educated, they have been taught to think. We were taught to mimic sounds. When those sounds were put together so that another would understand, then you started to have a language. But remember, that has been given to the *mind* or that faculty which can imitate. Every belief-system is based upon the need for something greater, and when this was discerned centuries ago, guess what came into experience? That which was termed "the priesthood." The priests had some inkling that there were gods that would bestow that which was necessary to satisfy the questions of the mass, but they would never reveal to the mass what was considered only essential for the few. In one way they were right, because it behooves every one of us to be very cautious in sharing the Truth to those unprepared for it, because it can be very shocking. How is it shocking? It disturbs the comfort you have with systems of belief that comprise your present "state." **The Truth can alter your present "state," and consequently it's disturbing because your belief-system cannot cope with what isn't a belief.**

That's a very important consideration! **Your belief-system cannot cope with what is not a belief and, therefore, it moves into a shocked or agitated state.** This is very important because if the Truth were like you are at the moment, there would be no need to bother speaking to *anyone!* It is obvious it isn't like many at all, because if it were known in its fullness by everyone, we would have what is hoped for by those in belief, termed "Utopia."

Utopia is a fabled place that we all expect to go to. I suppose it's like so-called Heaven. But Heaven is *here* and *now,* because as soon as you are capable of entertaining the thought that "this" is not Real, you are moving to that harmonic state where you may be open to hearing a fundamental Tone upon which all your scales are built. That is termed "middle C," in other words, the C that exists in the centre for the lowest and the highest.

If you know where C is in *your* life, that Consciousness divine, then you can scale any octave and know where you are when you leave the assurance of the centre of your keyboard, because every step you take higher you will find is an octave of the Realization that is fundamental and enables you to appear capable of sounding, on *this* plane, octaves above that, which are necessary for those who have vigorously searched for the irrefutable wonder of Truth.

> **The magnitude of Truth is what draws us all together.**
> **It's the magnitude of Love that embraces us all,**
> **and it's the wonder of the Invisible that incites**
> **manumission and a Light Force of incredible promise.**

You are engaged and, actually, if you have surrendered to something beyond your understanding, then you may more easily grasp the Fact. Go beyond your understanding! A Fact is a Fact whether you understand it or not and whether or not it agrees with *your* philosophy. A Fact is a Fact, and that allows a fiction to be novel! [laughter]

The classical event is divine Love, and its robe trails in a train of sound that allows each and every one to respond according to the openness of his heart, his soul, and his spirit to the wonders of the Unseen. In this we rejoice and in this we live and move and have our Being — *Being,* uncontaminated and unfettered by any suggestions of belief and emancipated in the midst of those who cry "Sahib, food!" You have it.

Reduce the object to what it is — your own invention — and see how all of your objectified world is nothing but the evidence of the wonder commensurate to the magic of the White Christ or the Light, the Self. It doesn't matter what name it is, because It knows no name other than to be recognized as Fact. What a novel experience it is to experience It as Conscious-awareness freeing the belief-system from bondage and allowing the believer to exude the wonders commensurate with a free state and to be no longer a slave to the matrix that has been perpetrated in order to create a serfdom of humanity.

We are so endowed with magic!

> Look at the magic of a smile,
> Look at the magic of an embrace,
> Look at the magic of a child,
> And look at the magic of a smiling face!
>
> Look at the wonder that it can wear,
> Look at the joy — there's no despair!
> Look at the joy of being found
> Embraced in the arms, unlimited, unbound!

It's quite a species you belong to called "the *human*kind." They got it quite close — the *hu*mankind — but they spelled it h-*u*-m-a-n. They should have called it the h-u-*e* kind, the huemankind. It's a man really existing in the *hue* of the Light. It is a *radiant energy*. When you "speak the Truth" to others and they are challenged, it's not your words of Truth that are challenging them. What is challenging them? They're only looking at you as an object, and it's their own hearing, their sensorial apparatus, that is translating what you say according to their belief-system! But when you speak to them and they react, it is the radiance or the radiant energy that surrounds That which we call Truth, being present! It's an energy-field and it appears as words but it isn't words. You write the word down that upsets you, and it doesn't upset you! [laughter] But you *say* it, and it really can upset you. "You" is like this [U]; it's a sack, it catches everything! [laughter] The U should be this [∩]. It should be the Rainbow Bridge.

The Rainbow Bridge is a concept that many entertain. Why do they entertain it? Yes, Barry.

Dr. Barry B: It's a sign of hope; it's a sign of promise.

Yes. They leave it in the realm of symbol and a sign for something, and they name it "promise," perhaps, but the Rainbow Bridge is much more than that. The Rainbow Bridge or any bridge is that which has been erected to allow passage, and that's what I've walked over this morning. What I've walked over this morning is that Bridge, and I met you on the other side. As soon as we have lunch, I'll be right where you are, on *that* side. What we have done is walked over the Rainbow Bridge and met you on the other side. The reason it's a *rainbow* bridge is because it describes the *hues* of the fractured Light and how it is minimized as it approaches the terrestrial plane. As it approaches the terrestrial plane, it becomes more and more opaque. This is why a Messenger cannot bear the White Light as His action, because It is too pure to withstand the density that exists on the other side, on the material side.

Now, if everyone is marching to Truth, you cannot possibly pass over this bridge in step, because it has to be what?

David K: Syncopated.

Syncopated, because it has to be a rhythm that will not destroy the thunder of the density that surrounds you until you cross over, if you haven't received the Teachings *before* crossing. You mustn't destroy that bridge by ignorance. Just like an army: they only cross a bridge in syncopated step. They tell you, "Out of step!" I know! Why? They don't want the bridge to collapse by perhaps a false rhythm. That's what's happened! Many people have aligned themselves to a false rhythm of humanity and have created a bridge and have destroyed the bridge that was so easily crossed with a clear intention. That is why the world is waiting for the so-called Reappearance. They call it "the Reappearance of the Christ," in some cases, but they're all waiting for the reappearance of a Messenger, the reappearance of Lord Maitreya — someone! (These are the aspects of their attainment which are given names. You can't bring a thing to you without naming it, and it is by naming it that you will bring it unto your cognition.)

What has happened to-day is, due to ignorance and such poor education, people have destroyed even the inclination to find the Bridge. If you asked, I'm sure, many people what they're doing here, they would say, "Well, I have a mother and a father and I look after them, and I have a wife and I look after her — no, she looks after me! And I have several children," or "I don't have any children, but I'm having a good life." They're having their thoughts of what life should be. That isn't Life at all! Do you know Life isn't in the body?! Truth isn't in the body! Life, Truth, Soul, Spirit, God, Principle, Mind, Love: they're not in the body. *That's why you contemplate them.* If they were in the body, you would not consider contemplation, you would not consider meditation. Those qualities are not in the body!

As I told you, Dr. Wilder Penfield said, when he made his discovery and announced it in the newspapers way back when I was young, that there was no trace other than perhaps a slight marking that something had happened in the process of thinking. I mean, you could have a slight marking for many things in the process of thinking, but certainly the process of thinking marks where you are! You can be assured that isn't the Mind that is one with God, the Source.

> **The difference between *your* mind and *God*-Mind is only that which you activate as a disciplined action that frees. The essential feature of the God-Mind is the love of freedom and the freedom of Love!**

Love is certainly one of the characteristics we all long for. I wonder why. Isn't it amazing how we dream of being loved? If we're dreaming of being loved, where did that dream originate? Only in the belief-system that didn't tell you (because you weren't ready for it) that that was really all you are! You *are* Love . . . not "to begin with"; it's your eternal nature! If the eternal nature is Love, why do you limit it just because you have a body to tote around? It's a wonderful sack and you should *wonder* at just the magnificence of the form! Could the Maker of every perfect gift be flawed?

Student: No, Sir.

So, if the body is flawed, you know right off the bat that it's not of the divine action. Which is more powerful, your action or the divine action?

Students: The divine action.

Yes. That's it! Isn't it amazing the divinity of Man?

Students: Yes, Sir!

**Now you know why you are divine — not *"you,"*
but your knowing of the Divine *is* the Divine.
Your doing is the evidence of the Being,
and the Being is the evidence of the AM-ing,
and the evidence of the AM-ing remains static
until one is able to vigorously look into the puzzle
of *being human* with the wonder of emancipation!**

The centre piece of every jigsaw puzzle is Love, and that is Life's Omnipotent Verities Eternal, an actual Fact! It's novel to the fiction of to-day and it is so disturbing to the well-educated! It's so wonderful to have an intellect that is well educated and capable of surrendering to the Invisible. It's the Invisible that allows all of this to happen, and that is the miracle of miracles: *it becomes visible!*

The reason the world has need of you is because you support the world, and you, knowing the answer to need, supply the fullness. Look at the families we, in the past, took care of who didn't have means, who didn't have food, didn't have a place to live. What did we do? Food was given to them, clothing was given to them; they were right with us, and we supplied it, and look at what happened! Some of them became movie actors; they are in Hollywood. I wonder, we never have heard from one of them, but they'll never forget, because **the bestowals of Love are not in the realm of remembrance; they're never in the realm of remembrance!** There is that incredible saying on the licence plates of Quebec: *"Je me souviens."* I mean, **it's so important to remember that you're not a memory! You are an actual actuality in the presence of Conscious-awareness.**

There is no hope for this world if there are not more people like you. There's no hope for it. If you are interested in the mass (we are because we're *here*, we're not sitting in caves meditating), **then you must be servants, but you must only serve from the standpoint that you have *actual realization* because otherwise you may be entering a fire and get burned.** Don't ever enter a situation of doing good when you think you are the do-gooder, and don't enter a situation that you are unprepared for, just because you think it's necessary. If you aren't prepared for it, don't enter it, because you may be burned.

All good should be involuntary. You shouldn't say, "I'm going to be nice to Rachel to-day because she looks so nice." That's good, but you don't say that with the hopes that she'll smile back at you and say, "Oh, you're wonderful!" You say it because that is the appearance. You all look wonderful, but why wouldn't you?! You *are!* You are wonderful. You are wonder-*full* otherwise you wouldn't be here, truly! If wonder wasn't really present as your experience, you wouldn't be questioning "What am I here for?" and "How do I know I *am* here?" You create a tremendous assumption when you say "What am I here for?" Prove to me that you know you *are* here! Yes! Prove to me how you know you *are* here.

Remember, it was said, "Not by your words but by your . . ."

Students: Actions (shall you be known).

Yes. It's always a great challenge to everyone. I was raised in such a strict fashion, and the belief-system was well set out, but as I started to break away and see it for what it is and for what it isn't, it was so interesting because when the shackles started to fall, the minister wanted to speak to me to find out how I could know what I knew!

It was interesting, the priests did the same thing. They would call my father and they'd say, "George, when is Ken coming?" Then, Father Gillan, who was very aloof but a very wonderful man (and here *we* were, not Catholic, but there was never a better catholic than *I* am! Ha, ha! [laughter]), he'd come-up on a Saturday night. Then Mum always offered some of her newly baked breads and cakes and pies and cookies. Friday and Saturday were her baking days, so there was always plenty for the weekend, because we always had so many people around. He got to the point where he'd say, "Now, if Mrs. Mills invites me up on Saturday night, please serve it before midnight because I have to do an early Mass to-morrow morning and I can't eat after twelve!" [laughter] We'd be sure he had his "lunch" before twelve, because we'd often talk later.

Love has nothing to do with name; Love has nothing to do with denomination. It can't be degraded by thought. Only when you think that Love is within your jurisdiction can it be degraded by action. It can't be, in essence. God doesn't know anything of the degradation, anyway; it's only you who know better. God is not a condition of serializing how much you attain and don't attain. You create your own experiences for greeting the Master, by your attitudes, what you have done, what you haven't done, and the resolution of suggestions to their native nothingness.

> **Don't deal with a problem as if it is true.**
> **Don't deal with a loss as if it is true.**
> **Love is never lost and It never *can* be!**

Don't deal with the suggestion as if it is true. Be much more intuitive, because as soon as you become more intuitive, you realize that there's something more than your five senses.

I always use as an example that is so practical the man who's on the radio, the announcer (you remember him). We had done a rehearsal, and he was sitting there. There were about fifty or sixty people at the rehearsal in my music room at home, and the Singers, and it was very exciting! (This was just a few years ago. This man, being a radio announcer and knowing of the Singers, wanted to come to a rehearsal.) To hear back what they had done, I sat down beside him on the sofa. It's a large sofa so there were ten or twelve people on it. I sat with him and I put my left hand on his right knee. Now, I don't know why, because I never *thought*. I had no thought of it; it just was there. When we listened to what had happened with the Singers, and that had finished, he turned to me and he said, "What did you do?" I said, "I beg your pardon?" I didn't know the man very well at all. He said to me, "You have healed my leg!" I said, "I beg your pardon?" He said, "Seventeen years ago, I hurt my knees so badly, I have been in pain for seventeen years, and this morning, after you put your hand on my knee, it's the first time I have been free of pain in seventeen years! How about putting your hand on my other knee?!" [laughter]

So, you just don't know. You don't go about *doing*; you just don't. But it's fascinating because you wonder how it happens. I did this with Mum once — not with the intention. She came to visit me at my house on Argonne Crescent and she was sitting on the sofa beside me, and I took her hand, which I seldom ever did but I wasn't thinking about it. I just picked-up her hand and I ran my right hand over her hand. I said, "What are these bumps?" Huge bumps covered her hand; they were all over it. I couldn't believe my eyes because I hadn't seen them. She said, "They're very painful, dear. Don't press on them." And the next morning, they were all gone! She wondered what had happened. They never came back or anything else. There is your wonder!

"I of myself can do nothing."[3] 'Tis the wonder of the Invisible that doeth the work! That's what happened with *the singing*. I had lost my voice and couldn't sing, and the doctor said I never would sing, and for thirty-six years I never did sing, other than six notes in the bass. In 1976, thirty-six years later, I opened my mouth and out came a sound that was beautiful, and I said, "Chris, it's yours!" And Ellen said, "Where's *mine?*" And then Sandy. That was the beginning of realizing I could open voices if they were willing to be opened.

Why is it important to have an open voice? Because the sound that you hear falling upon your ear is really the evidence, the most non-material evidence we have, of That which IS. This is why I always meditated with the consideration before entering meditation that the Breath was my Holy Visitor and I was taken on the Holy Breath; then when I came out of meditation, when I exhaled, it was the Message of that visitation. That's why I realized I can talk naturally and be at ease with anyone, but if I'm asked, then I may speak.

> Your vocabulary can't be the vocabulary of the ordinary. That's the temptation: to use the ordinary language. Ordinariness is the last temptation that has to be resisted.
>
> *Resist ordinariness.* Just be the uniqueness you really are, and you find yourself levitating in the thought realm to the *Conscious* realm where the infinitude of Being pulsates with the grandeur of eternal Man, eternal in the heavens, the sphere of harmony, rhythm, and sound!

Thank you.

⌘

1. "Because God made thee mine, I'll cherish thee," from the song "Because," words by Edward Teschemacher, music by Guy d'Hardelot.
2. Referring to a scene in the movie *The Matrix*, Village Roadshow Productions, U.S.A., 1999.
3. John 5:19, 30.

The Code of Your Unreality

Chapter VI

The Earth as you experience it objectively is a figment of your imagination.

The Code of Your Unreality

Themes: Actuality ~ Conscious-awareness ~ Tonality ~ Creator ~ imagination ~ perception ~ Earth ~ space ~ senses ~ cherry

This is the morning of Monday, June 23, 2003. To grow-up the way we grow seems to be so natural, but then, as you start to question how is this a form, you realize how *unnaturally* you have grown-up. (This is very important.) You have taken the basis of your experience as natural to be this human, as natural to have a mind, and as natural to have senses (how often they're used, you sometimes wonder!); as natural to feel (but how many really feel?!); as natural to like and dislike; and as natural to feel "I will" and "I won't" ("You've got to develop your own personality"). So, you allow a child to have leeway to do any damn thing he or she pleases "because children can't be suppressed; they must develop their own personality." My goodness, it's the first thing that should be *stopped!*

A personality is our biggest hang-up. We get hung-up on this idea for centuries, and it's by being hung on this idea that you become what is known as "a hanger." You hang onto everything you have been taught that is natural, becoming a human form. After all, the human form is really an incredible, magical feat of constant presentation — it seems constant but it isn't. There are so many gaps between each frame that we fail to see how it's reconstructed every moment!

Every time I look at you, there is a new frame. Every moment I blink my eyes, there's a frame and hundreds of thousands of frames that constitute the images, and there's the tremendous speed with which our computer, the mind, can assimilate the information, transfer it by the nervous system and the sensorial system to that part of the brain which encodes what has been seen. The eye, having taken the picture through the cones and the rods, passes it onto a film of the retina. This is immediately sent to the mind, and before you know what's happened, you've got a picture that's upside down, right side up! It's developed *that quickly* that you don't realize you're doing nothing but creating the expectation of your teaching! But they have never told you *how* you do it, and that's how we trap ourselves on this plane.

We trap ourselves on this plane by *believing* the simplicity of what we have been taught as being human and a child growing-up and everything else. It isn't that at all! The development of the picture is so fast that we don't see the gap between the frames, and that's why you feel it's a constant! That is a Grace that the Engineer provided, that we don't see there is a gap creating moments when there is no existence. But, of course, we have misconstrued *the objective* as constituting existence. It isn't the objective that constitutes existence; it's the objective that verifies that it is a creation of an invisible Source. That's why you have confidence, in the beginning, to question what you have been taught.

What you have been taught in the second chapter of Genesis is that you were a clod of earth and the Holy Breath was breathed into it and you became a living thing. That had to be accepted because no one had the skill to penetrate the subtlety of how this happens. This is why, I presume, that a few of Us have come over the years to try to clear this, because it's one of the most demanding adventures you can enter upon.

We have come to try to clear this acceptance of mortality, in other words, of being a mortal. This has to be given-up, now that eternality has been found to be a constituent of freedom. Immortality is the exact opposite of the suggested mortal. A mortal cannot become immortal; matter can never enter into immortality, because matter is what?

Students: Changing.

No! Matter is what you project to satisfy, without knowing it, a creative aspect of your Source-dom. You have mistaken the matter world and the population and the Earth and everything that constitutes it to be the Actuality; it isn't, because *it can't bear existence without your Conscious-awareness participation!*

Without everyone agreeing, you would never have this planet. You would never have the conditions on this planet if it wasn't for "you." Then, what is your purpose? What is my purpose? One of them is to alert those who have moved, graduated, from the neophyte level (which you have) to a higher level, to bring into their cognition the possibility of looking at everything with a new meaning — which is the evidence of what? Attainment.

It's so exciting, because there is not one object — a cherry, a grape, a blueberry, a raspberry, a fig, a lychee fruit — there is no way that one of those things tells you what it is! But you say, "Oh, I want my cherries. Oh, I want my grapes, and I want my vines to be abundant." Do you realize what you're doing?! [Dr. Mills laughs.] It's so funny! It really is; you'll see the humour of it.

Nothing in the objective has the ability to declare its presence. The body can't declare its presence without a component that isn't in it!

This information gives us a sort of inward consolation about all our faux pas in the sensorial world and how we cope with the sensorial data that is fed to us by what is termed "experience." Now, where the power comes that is so important is this: it is termed "the power of discrimination." This power of discrimination allows you to detect *that which isn't actual*. Now, the reason we say we are all in a virtual reality is because it is sustained not by the Self but by the false sense of selfhood, which is termed "the mind" — the name for that state of registering whatever information is sensorially imprinted upon its system; and it retains this in what is termed "the memory bank."

The memory bank does not retain the actual experience, and that's why it becomes termed "memory." It's only the partial fragrance of an experience, which sometimes can be relived if you do what? If you are hypnotized. But tell me something: isn't that rewinding a tape?

Students: Yes!

Or if that isn't going back to your floppy disk and pulling forth something you've forgotten?! [laughter]

What is so important is, since nothing can tell you of its nothingness — because you have made something that really doesn't exist without your senses, without the operation of your eyes, without the operation of the incredible engineering feat which underlies the fact of a Creator that we do not comprehend through the mentality with which we have been encoded! Now, it is due to this perceptible situation that we have got to accept that the Creator, then, must not exist within the coding given to you as a natural child. The coding doesn't exist there. **The coding of your Actuality is brought forth by a vibratory frequency that is not of**

Earth, because what I am saying is creating the Earth for you . . . as it really IS. The Earth as you experience it objectively is a figment of your imagination.

[Dr. Mills takes a cherry from the fruit plate on the table beside him.] To see this cherry and to realize it is an object as a result of the incredible engineering feat of the Divine and given to you as the capability of creating and identifying the creation . . . ! Yes! If it were not for you, you could not identify the creation. Now, stop and consider that. If the creation is identified, it must be because the Creator gave you the ability to perceive it and to use the engineering feat of the sensorial data to register it upon your awareness; it is nothing of itself, but the wonders of the Creator itself allow you to perceive it and name it. *Without your perception and awareness of it, it has no existence!* But it doesn't mean there is *no existence.*

When "this" can be seen through, I am still here. I know. I have seen through it and I'm telling you it and I still exist! I exist in a way I can enjoy it and have great fun with it, just like I enjoy David and have great fun with him. It doesn't deny "it"; it *frees* "it" from the impinging force of limitations that go with a superficial awareness of objectivity!

Students: Thank you, Sir.

Got it?

Students: Yes, Sir!

Now, the next step. (These are huge steps; it could take hours going from the cherry to how you *actually* perceive it, but we could spend a week just on getting through that one sentence.)

The great factor that we appear to have is the ability of cognition. When we cathect a thing, what do we mean? Yes, Erika.

Erika Z: To invest something with an emotion.

That is right. To cathect a thing, you imbue it with an emotion it does not have, but it affects it. That is what's happened to you with your parents! They cathect the object and create an emotional link! This is what a husband and wife do; this is what friends do. Do you realize that what you are emotionally cathecting upon another is really an aspect of *your* creativity that is funnelled through as an emotion, which is what? A degraded form of feeling. Feeling is with *Soul;* emotion is with *person* because emotion is the result of the senses.

You can look at a hot plate on a stove, and it's quite harmless, but if you put your hand or a finger on it, you scream because you say it's burned. It isn't the finger that has screamed; it isn't the finger that has even felt it. It's the sensorial data that reaches the mind or the brain, and when all the senses and the nerves react to the situation, then it's described. Before that happens, the finger hasn't registered it. **It's only by registering the sensorial data that you have a burned finger, but the finger was not burned; it was the senses that described it as burned. The finger is *an idea!* It can't be burned.** ***The object can be hurt, but the divine Idea can't be.*** So, that's one of the digits to remember! [laughter]

Yes, Claude.

> *Claude C:* I imagine that this is the reason why some people can walk in fire and not be burned, because they don't surrender to this idea.

That may be so, I don't know; that could be the case. That, perhaps, is the very foundation of it. Firewalkers: it's amazing how they'll walk on coals and don't dare to face the Truth! This is what happens. They don't dare to face the Truth. I've known some who have been with me and then gone and done firewalking to prove that they had attained something and that they had a right to prove to me, who didn't think they had attained anything (I don't know how they knew that, because I never said so!) — but they go and walk on the coals to say, "You see what I've attained, Mr. Mills! I didn't *need* you." Of course, you never needed *me,* any more than anyone needs a "me," and that's why we have so many screaming "me-me's"! What happens is that they mistake mental control for attainment. The only way mental control is of value is when you cease to create co-ordinates that allow you to escape the Fire of transformation.

Do you realize, if there is some injury to the spinal cord and the information of the burned finger can't reach the brain, the finger doesn't know it's burned. It has no road to reach that organ or whatever facility it is that translates the "experience" and names it and conditions it and describes it. That's why when the nerves in my finger were cut and I had the neurosurgeon put it back together and I said, "Is it necessary?" he said, "Oh, yes. If you don't, you could break it so many times without even knowing it's broken!" Thank goodness he put it back together, because I can bend it and I can still play when I want to.

> **Godliness is that State which modifies the creative spirit and reduces the god-like nature of mortal mind to its rightful place in the service of the Most High.**

Yes, David.

> *David N:* Sir, I wanted to say that what you were saying this morning really highlights something that I had heard of years ago from the medical profession, from somebody who was coming from China. They were describing how in burn units, in this hospital they visited in China — I know here that there are special beds and fabrics and everything else developed for people — people were just lying in ordinary beds with terrible burns from fires, et cetera, and they did not experience any pain. As you were describing how the emotion is passed from generation to generation, this had never been embedded in them that this would be a painful experience, and it wasn't.

That's unusual, it really is. I had only one experience of it in my life. Once my wife and I were cooking lunch for some guests coming. During the preparation, this container of boiling oil went over my right hand, and my wife screamed. I said, "There's nothing wrong!" I didn't even feel it. She never forgot it and I never have. It was one of the highlights of my marriage! [laughter]

> *Robert M:* This morning you mentioned that the memory banks would give a partial fragrance of an experience. I've noticed that when it comes to the sound of a tune or a smell of, say, grass, that seems to have a more vivid experience than a normal thought would. Is that a different kind of memory?

Every time you experience *anything*, it's new. It's only *your thinking it's old* that it doesn't impress you with the discovery of it being created every moment! That's what I've tried to show

David, that being with me and me being with David, *it's always new*. I can't imagine he's been with me "so many years," because every moment with him is as if it were for the first time.

> *David K:* It's very true.

Looking at everything *in a new way* brings the *meaning*, which is a component of the higher awareness. It brings much greater meaning to everything you do. When you look at anyone in the room — I look at Claude, I look at Suzanne, and I look at Lise — everything has a different meaning when you know this. And they will look at me the same way. It's this different meaning which brings what? The fruition of an ability to bless what appears as "the struggling masses who know not they struggle."[1] This struggling of the masses who know not they struggle creates the sulphured cloud. That sulphured cloud is the cloud of unknowing, because they have been taught not the facts of their sensorial, emotional encounter with a body. Just because they're grown-ups doesn't mean very much, you know. You have to love your mum and dad. It doesn't mean that you don't love anyone wherever they are at, but it does mean that you can only go along as far as you can still maintain your clarity in the whirlpool of suggestion.

Yes, Moira.

> *Moira D:* Sir, you once read from your notebook — and I believe it was from the time when you put your hand on the stove. You had written a realization that you had from that: if you raise your vibrations to the level of the fire, you won't be burned.

Yes. I remember a passenger in my car closed the door on her hand. It was dreadful. I grabbed it, and the Presence was there, and there was no evidence of the door having closed on it. There was nothing.

> *Jo-ann V:* That was I. To me that was a great miracle!

It *was* a miracle!

> *Jo-ann V:* You grabbed my hand, and my pinky was completely flat. You held it for a little while, and we went

into the car and we drove off, and by the time I got back home, which was an hour later, there was no trace, no pain, no bruise, nothing.

I am so glad I said that, because I don't remember when these things happen to most people. I haven't forgotten *the experience,* because it was wonderful.

Yes.

Jo-ann V: In an *Unfoldment*™ from 1997, you spoke about the art of meaning, and I've been wondering about what the art of meaning is. What you just said, that you create every moment, the awareness of a new creation every moment, that would be the art of meaning?

Yes. In other words, it would be the meaning of *art.* Your creation is your art. And you, through this present, may be the growing awareness of what it really IS, and this proves to you you can bring *meaning* to it. Does that register okay? Everything that you create now has a meaning instead of just a sensorial reference — as that cherry. I don't think of it just as a cherry; I know everything that goes with it. That's the meaning of the art of your own creativity. I appreciate every feature that constitutes this abundance, because all that abundance is the evidence that I AM, present in order to cognize it! I could not have the cognition of the wonder of this plate of differentiated fruit if there wasn't the wonder of the Invisible present. Your simple teaching would never allow you to appreciate your creative ability; you are taught that "this is a cherry, this is a grape, this is a blueberry, this is a raspberry" — your ordinary teaching. There is no art to that; that is rote acceptance.

Jo-ann V: And art would fill your words with meaning.

Yes, and your *world* with meaning, because you are not really of Earth; what you really are is not at all in relationship with Earth. You in essence are not an Earthian, not at all! At this very moment the essence of you is what is termed "non-spatial." It is not found anywhere within the environs of mortality. **What you are in essence is a vibratory frequency or an energy-field that has been lowered in intensity to engage what appears as your bodification.** You know all of this because the energy has met a resistance of what is termed "object," and that resistance is termed "the lowering" of the energy so you can cope with it, and it appears as the energy encapsulated as a thought. It has to be lowered. What do you call it electrically?

Michael G: Either a transformer or a resistor.

I like "transformer"! [laughter] Don't you dare resist!

That's how it works. It's more complicated to the mind than it has appeared to be at this moment. It's very simple to put it this way, but to arrive at it may be a little more subtle because you have to just assume, whether you understand it or not, that basically you are not Earthian. I know we're not.

This is why if you were *really* what "this" seems to be, "this" would be eternal. It's amazing, we know "this" isn't eternal, because we know the fact that eternality is. What is eternality? The opposite of a timed experience. So, you suddenly realize that you do what? You live in a dimension of perspective and masses all because you experience *one* dimension of *time*. So, we say the Timeless is the closest we have to the State where it is instantaneous creativity happening! (That's it.)

Yes, Nancy.

> *Nancy M:* I'd like to check an understanding that I have gleaned from your *Unfoldments,* particularly from this morning. When we agreed to come here, we agreed to take on the thought called a body. Did we agree to take on the limited belief-system only to have to learn to translate it from a higher perspective, such as to-day? This is the Teaching happening now. Did we agree to do that? As a child I would wonder about "things," and no answers would come, only other thoughts about "things." It's only having met *you* that I wanted the code broken to see things in a new way. Is that part of the agreement?

That is accurate and it is part of the agreement. Let me tell you the story that is given for this. It is said that you are a traveller or a voyager and you decided to come to the plane, as we apparently all have done. We have decided to come *with bodies* to the plane. We decided to take on an embodiment through our own manipulation. We asked for a vehicle that could translate what we were experiencing into a new mode of conception, which was *matter,* with a vehicle that was registered to cope with the information as it was sensitized as a mortal into your experience. This sensitization happens continually and has happened — since the world was created? They don't know when the world was created, because there had to be one viewing the world to say when it was created, and the one viewing the world who said it was created could not have succeeded in coming to the plane and leaving the plane successfully.

The plane is so seductive by objectification and emotion that people forget what they came for. What they came for is to try to find out if they have the skill *to come and go at will!* This is why you (and all of you, I say) are here as servants, because you will have the ability, eventually, to allow others to perceive that they have forgotten their original intention, which was to explore, through the graciousness of space, the experience of moving it apart and allowing objectification to enter its body. An objectification entering the vibrational body of space allows us to have a place to sit, but it's all due to that incredible daunting, powerfully daunting, force-field called "space." It is not at all empty; it only seems empty to correlate with your ability to engage the energy of the Higher Way. If you engaged too much energy you could not occupy this space; it would limit you.

Yes.

> *Nurit O:* When we say we're not of Earth, there is an inner knowingness that that is so. I know that I'm not from this Earth, and I know the agreements, some of the agreements at least, that I came here with. In spite of that knowingness, there's absolutely no memory of having made those agreements.

They are instilled within the escutcheon of your Soul. They are *written* upon the escutcheon, and this is actually a Grace of the Creator of the Divine because if you had a memory of all that, you could not cope with the rush of input that you receive every moment you exist in form.

It's unfortunate that so many people have not perceived the subtlety. You have no idea, in the past, the density of the mentality that was present, and it was partially due to all the drugs that were taken. *And yet, people appeared to be healed.*

Many of you remember the men who came to me — no woman ever came to me with a drug problem, but there were men who did. Sometimes people would come, and I wouldn't even know who they were. I never asked their name. I was living alone at 283 Hollywood. They'd knock on the door after I'd finished teaching at ten o'clock at night, and then I never knew whether I'd be going until two o'clock in the morning or not. There would just be knocks on the door, and no one, seemingly, knew anything about me other than I was a piano teacher. And *I* didn't know anything about me, other than I was a piano teacher! I didn't know what I could do until it started to happen before my eyes, and I think it had to happen that way for me to realize what I was about. Because I had no one to talk to.

I wouldn't speak to anyone without recording, because I found that the mind is treacherous. It would say things that I said — that I didn't — because the mind altered it in order to escape the result of what was said.

Yes, Eugene.

> *Eugene M:* Sir, one of the words that you used earlier was "cathexis," and that always implies possessiveness.

It doesn't imply possessiveness; it implies giving.

> *Eugene M:* Giving an emotional —

That's what *people* do, but there can be a cathexis other than an emotion. The dictionary refers to "you"; it doesn't refer to the higher meaning: focussing on a situation and cathecting it with the Force that IS. It's a very different thing, and that's what you must do. **You must be able to cathect the object in front of you with the impersonal, divine Gift that presents itself.** You have no way to know what it will be.

> *Eugene M:* That is the answer to my question. I wanted to see how it would be redeemed.

It is redeemed by the motivation within the individual, whether your motivation is personal or impersonal.

Eugene M: Thank you.

You can see how practical this is in your world because you start to perceive the need and the want of others. You can't say a word unless they're open to questioning, but you can minister unto them in the silence. You don't have to talk to them. What do you think I do when I talk to people? I often just listen, but that doesn't mean that's all that's happening. I learned that a long time ago. This is why so many things happen after a meeting or in a meeting. It is amazing.

Some of the people are still with me who remember the incident. One man, a philosophy student, came to me. He was one of three brothers — a fine looking fellow — and I said to him, "Why don't you wear contact lenses?" I said, "Take off those glasses. Go and get contact lenses." He said, "I can't wear them, Sir." I said, "Go and get contact lenses." I said it three times. He made the appointment to get contact lenses, and in a week or so he came back with contact lenses and with the most amazing story.

Due to having taken a lot of cocaine as a young man — he was still very young (I was stunned when he told me) — he had found the salts of the cocaine deposited upon the cornea of his eyes, and the verdict from the ophthalmologist was that he would be blind by the time he was forty because nothing could be done to remove them from the corneas. He went to have his eyes tested, and the doctor said, "Of course, you can wear contacts!" He said, "But, doctor, I have salts on the cornea of my eyes!" He said, "Your corneas are perfectly clear."

> *Blair R:* I heard him attest to that himself on your diving board at Arinaka, standing-up before a whole Wordshop. He had told the story himself.
>
> *Robert M:* I've heard the story from his mouth, Sir.

Yet, guess what happened? He left. *That* is the sadness, because it was just another one who leaves the choir, the choir of sponsors. The people who have experienced should remain because they know from experience what to offer to one who asks for "Food, Sahib." You see? Yes, Barry.

Dr. Barry B: Yesterday you spoke about the non-spatial and omnipotent quality of the Infinite, and what you've done over the past couple of days about shifting the entire perspective of what is space and what isn't has caused me to reconsider a phrase that you've used as long as I've known you: "the centre and circumference of Being." How can one entertain that without being spatial or referential?

The Centre is always that Point from which you have originated, and that must be from the Conscious Identity of being Actual, either you couldn't be returning to it. You would never have attainment if you weren't going to return to it! That Point, reclaimed and experienced, is termed "Principle," so you won't lose your direction in your celestial navigation. So, you then have the radius, and your circumference is only defined by the extension of your ministration. The circumference is only the evidence of how far you have extended your "ministry," which is what? Your involuntary offering.

Yes, Judy.

Judith M: It's so amazing what you're offering this morning! When you began this morning you spoke of the gap between the pictures. You said that we make it seem like a continuous happening but there is a gap between them.

Wouldn't it be awful if you knew it and didn't know what it was? The gap isn't *emptiness;* it's the Force that allows the continuity to continue! **The purpose of art is to express the artlessness of Being.** The art of Being is artless, and that's why art can be such a means of presenting to a viewer the wonder of his ability to translate the colours into a meaningful response within his uncontaminated Selfhood.

You would not have a colour if it wasn't for a background and you wouldn't have a colour if it wasn't reflected light. Every colour we have is a result of refracted light, of a prism breaking the light. Just think of what the experience is. You're dealing with the isolation, the individuality, of responses of the cones and the rods in the eyes to an energy-field that is represented by colour! *That's* what you're responding to.

Yes, Angela.

> *Angela W:* If every object is projected and we are here to bring light, we are bringing it to — there is no separation. It's the Self.

How do you know it's an object? The only way you are able to perceive an object is by what?

> *Angela W:* Awareness?

Yes, it's the way the light is fractured or broken. The only way this cherry stands out is because, you can say, it's against a white background, but it *isn't*. It's because this cherry is a part of the spectrum, part of the *red* spectrum, and you cognize it and *give it colour* by being the Light that is unbroken. You couldn't conceive colours if the Light within you wasn't unbroken. It's not within you; It's *without* "you."

That's enough. I think there is almost enough given here. You can get drunk on it.

> *Gregory S:* Eugene reiterated the idea of cathecting emotion, and you said earlier that emotion was a degraded form of feeling.

Yes. Emotion is sensorial. Feeling is that which arises within the Heart.

> *Gregory S:* So, the question is, would the act of cathecting be imbuing with emotion and . . . ?

It's exactly the way the mind control of to-day works. The people who are mind-controlled, you can tell them in a minute because they have no originality, they have no energy-field that can transform, and the awful part of it is they don't know it. There are schools of mind control. They say there is a huge one in London, England.

> *Gregory S:* The question is, can you cathect feeling?

Of course, you can. Yes, you can from the right standpoint. *You* perhaps might cathect emotion, but if you transcend it, if you have the realization that goes with it, you could cathect feeling.

> *Gregory S:* Would that not create a quality of binding?

No, no, feeling doesn't bind.

> Feeling the Being I AM
> Rescinds all suggestion of bondage to man,
> As he isn't in Mind
> What he is in time.

Remember, what you are talking about as man is the way you have objectified a concept of individuality. Yes, Chris.

> *Christopher D:* Dr. Mills, you said this morning that the body can't declare its presence without a component that isn't in it. Is it accurate to say that that component could be called awareness or Conscious-awareness?

It would be called *Consciousness*. Consciousness IS. Awareness is included with Consciousness, because it is the awareness that identifies the objective to satisfy your need at this time, as long as you are on this plane.

> *Christopher D:* There seems to be a habit in language that tries to individuate that awareness, and that awareness does appear individuated, in the sense that my awareness might appear in a moment to be somewhat different from Barry's awareness. But the Consciousness that is supporting that awareness is not individuated.

No. The water in this glass seems individuated from the well from which it came. But this glass is Waterford. That's what it is, but it hasn't affected the water. You name it "Christopher," but it doesn't affect the Consciousness, the Consciousness that IS. Nothing can affect the Consciousness that IS. It's your *awareness* that belittles it . . . by ignorance. The awareness belittles *What IS* by ignorance.

> *Christopher D:* So, the Path to the Centre, the Non-differentiated, is the Path of losing ignorance, then.

Yes, it is.

> *Christopher D:* That's what we're doing here. It's what we're doing here by hearing you.

It's "the Path of Losing Ignorance." It's a very good way of putting it! [laughter] You said it! Yes, Lucille.

> *Lucille J:* This morning you have used the phrase "coming and going at will." Is this image of the movement along the radius from the point of the centre, Principle? The question is, **What does it mean to come and go at will?**

It means the ability to be what appears in the objective and out of it at the same time. That's how you can travel anywhere. That's how you can bless somebody in China. By the time they have asked for help, the thought is already there — before they have finished!

Yes, John.

> *John A:* When you were speaking about the frames and the gap between the frames, the frames seemed like discrete units. What I'm wondering is, is there an underlying rhythm that allows us to be synchronized?

There couldn't be creation without a rhythmic structure. Remember, the whole experience is a dance of the Divine: three-four time, a waltz! The trinity or the power of expression over squaring all your deals is what allows man to waltz.

Yes, Laurie.

> *Laurie M:* You spoke earlier this morning about agreement, and there are a number of questions about our agreement upon coming here. You also spoke about agreement in the sense that we agree to maintain the consistency of the appearance of the objective, and that is based on agreement.

Yes.

> *Laurie M:* Is part of our service to break down the apparent reality of the objective?

That's one purpose you're here for. Remember, as I said earlier, you are here because many people who have incarnated, in other words, taken on a body — if we can say somebody has reincarnated, there must be a point where they are discarnate. So, those who have reincarnated have taken on the body, and they have done so with the full intention of not being seduced by the wonders of nature and the environment and the people who are in like position, all visitors to this strange planet. They perhaps forget that they came here to experience differentiation; they came here to experience different forms of choice, *knowing that they had no choice in actuality.* That's what they've forgotten.

You have no choice other than to be what you really are, and you will come and go until you realize that.

Thank you very much.

⌘

1. Kenneth G. Mills, "The Sulphured Cloud," *Embellishments* (Toronto: Sun-Scape Publications, 1986), p. 115.

How to Reconstruct Your World

Chapter VII

This wondrous work of appearance (the three-dimensional objective world) is never denied; it's only re-identified in the Light of Actuality.

How to Reconstruct Your World

Themes: The Word ~ Principle ~ Energy ~ mind ~ language ~ receptivity ~ understanding ~ practice ~ space

---

This is the morning of June 24, 2003, and we are meeting once again in the vestibule of time where it is being opened in order to perceive the wonders of being able to *stand* on it (time). In this respect, we are reducing all the underground entanglements of beliefs to their proper condition, that of being reviewed with the assurance that from the standpoint of Truth, that which is extruded from this system will bear fruitage unto the future of men and women found caught in the matrix. For those who have qualified themselves to receive the higher understanding of what this whole experience is about, they will find that the beliefs are that part of a system that no longer forms a force-field of entanglement.

The tendency of all belief-systems is to bring into control the multitude who would ask for but receive not the fullness. They are not taught that they have to be prepared to receive; they are not taught that their great adversary (and yet their great companion) to be recognized and yet subdued and trained is the mind. It always goes where you go. It is in the adumbrations of our experience; it is always there hiding, waiting to try to influence us in a condition so that it can remain superior in its actions.

However, you have perceived now that the matrix is, without doubt, the condition of the world to-day. It is the *mind,* and as long as the matrix is in existence, we will never have freedom; and as long as freedom is still felt to be essential to life, then we are at the foot of understanding what it is that has confined us to this plane of limitation and yet this plane of such wonder because we of ourselves could never have created it!

We come to a realization that the underground system of the everyday world does nothing but bring us into contact with other systems, and the tracks are so numerous; we are always searching for that Brakeman or Trackman who can alter them and bring to view the frustrating experience of duality. The tracks never meet in actuality; they only seem to with a long distance view! **Duality will never allow you the experience of unity. Either it is Mind or it is matter.**

The mind that we find as our shadowy companion is the mind that we have accepted from the moment we received instruction. It was never given, as a form of instruction, that it was an instrument for navigating the plane of objectification; it was never given that it was to be trained, it was to be disciplined, and it was to be like the horse, ridden and capable of dressage. It was never thought other than that ability to think logically and to construct thought-patterns that would be logically united.

All of the logic in the world could never unbind the fetters that systems of belief have engendered in the lives of mankind. Of course, those in high places of power are always trying to keep from those who inquire the actual truth of what is happening, and there is nothing more insidious than to have *partial* truths. Partial truths, frequently, are those statements that seem true and are convincing until they are brought to the Light of Principle, and in the Light of Principle their fallacy is quickly perceived. Unfortunately, so many people do not know what to do when a fallacy is perceived, because it does what? It creates disturbance in every logical statement that has been formed around it. This is why Truth is so feared among so many who have attained by using logic.

If you are to become as a little child in order to receive the auric splendour of Presence, then you can't have your mind filled with the dullness of doubt, the dullness of fear, and the dullness of selfishness. There cannot be any form of gratitude from the standpoint of person. Ingratitude is always the evidence of mortal mind being present. Always! Ingratitude is always the presence of mortality running rampant, and it so exists to-day because so many people are loathe to give gratitude for something received; they are afraid it minimizes their achievement.

We are living, or appear to be living, in an Age inundated with all kinds of entertainment, which does nothing but take the attention and the energy that was meant to be used to escape from the planet and to build a vehicle of Conscious proportions that would allow us to move from this planetary experience to our Home Base, if we only knew enough to reduce the impinging force of materiality to its place as a hypothetical structure — not imposed but *self*-imposed.

You have seen from yesterday's expcrience that there is nothing in your experience of which you are not the creator. You have seen the power of thought, and Jo-ann, this morning, showed you the various photographs taken with different states of attention.[1] This is why it is so important for *you* to consider the state you are entertaining whenever you participate in an activity in which anything is happening that is creative, because your attitude supports the artist, it supports the performance, it supports everything that could enhance — what? — the *listening* factor, which is such a sensorial need. Most people cannot listen for more than two or three seconds to-day. You should be able to listen with the greatest of ease, with no time bearing upon it.

Perhaps you have forgotten, and most people have forgotten, that the core of the community of otherness is language. You'll notice how degraded the language is. The vocabulary is very small; it doesn't have the words that can exude wonder or magic. The first time that you have to look-up words, it's a form of wonder. It is, because looking-up words is *an adventure out of limitation,* because **it is *words* that have constructed your imprisonment. It is your words that constitute the limitation of your life.**

This is why "words must be fitly chosen, and words fitly chosen are like apples of gold on dishes of silver."[2] Silver is a *reflective* state; gold is the *direct emanation*. We all know that the direct experience of a tonal baptism is very different than a recorded one. Reading scripture, reading catechisms, learning catechisms, is very different than experiencing what prompted them.

The reason there have been outstanding figures in the realm of the objective world is because they have been precipitated in order to alert you to consider states that are questionable, and you know it must be so because the world of the Sublime is not one fettered with restrictions. **That is why unconditional Love is the basis of life living abundantly.**

Life confined to the vehicle of sensorial data and controlled by it is a life that is waiting to be set free. Knowing what you know, you are in such a prestigious position to offer the beneficence becoming one who is acquainted with authentic Being. We say this is a virtual reality because it is constantly changing, but so, we know, is the *world*. Therefore, we know that it cannot possibly be authentic, because anything that changes bears the stigma of "unreal."

Now, when you can love one moment and hate the next moment, you are right in the whirlpool of the underground system of entrapment, and as long as you allow your thought in any way to be in agreement with an edict that is not divine, you are supporting the riotous mass. The mass is in riot when it comes face to face with its counterfeit nature!

When you viewed *The Matrix* last evening, you undoubtedly saw yourself in most of it and you saw the men in black, that aspect of your "adumbrational" self that doesn't want to face head-on the mechanical nature that you have clothed and have lived in all your life. It was so interesting to perceive, in some of the frames, where all was reduced to numbers. What would you say had happened when all the numbers appeared?

Dr. Barry B: Neo had seen through the matrix.

Yes, that could be. Jon.

Jonathan S: He doesn't see objects anymore; he sees the energy of the actual objective.

I don't know if that is so. Perhaps he really saw that the code under which people are imprisoned was detectable and that no one's life could be numbered. I think he perhaps understood the encoding, which was such a threat to the shadow, and when he saw that coding he knew that he had perceived how others had been *encoded* to react to mechanical stimulation. That's why the people appeared so mechanical. They were without what?

Students: Soul. Feeling.

They were without feeling, the evidence of an unborn Soul. It was *buried* because it was not in their concept of life.

When Neo would go through the wall or through the form, what he was pointing to was the ability, on knowing What IS, to see how they're all thought structured. Remember the cherry; there's no difference to *the wall*. Every brick in it is your product . . . of imagination. It is first sensed, "nerved," "spinalized," "brainized" and structured with your attention for precipitation. Every being in this room is structured this way every moment we gaze upon you, but it is so lightning fast that you forget that the description of an object is not the object; it's only *pointing* to it.

The description of the object is really only pointing to what appears. **The essence of the object is what?** *Energy encapsulated as thought.* **Don't forget it! It takes practice. If you don't practise you will not develop the discipline that advanced study requires. You have to have such independence of thought that you can face the complex passages of notation with dexterity, in other words, the complicated passages of the communication art appearing as printed language.**

All language is devoid of meaning until you give it meaning by translating the code. **If you translate that code you start to perceive that the ink on the paper bears no resemblance to the sound full of meaning. Everything has to be** *sounded,* **and you can't sound it in an uncertain way.** *When Truth is known, it never is timid!* It says, "The trumpet shall sound, and the dead shall be raised."[3] The trumpet blown by an insecure trumpeter would perhaps give reason for the dead to be glad where they are! [laughter] However, the trumpet really is the *Word,* freed from the thought-structures that would be brass. The brass is always of "this" level; that is why *gold* is always the symbol of the Higher Way. That's why anyone who has been close to me, I've always given them some gold, because it always carries, whether *they* know it or not, a frequency that is totally unexplainable.

Remember, the gold doesn't tarnish. It does need *washing,* but it doesn't tarnish. Remember, in its pure state it is soft but never loses its quality, and to be used as an ornament, it has to be mixed with another substance in order to be hard enough to hold shape *for time.* Remember, if it is going to hold shape for time, either it can be just a plain gold setting or, usually, the gold becomes a stage for a setting for the appearance of a brilliance of some sort: a diamond, a sapphire, a ruby, or an emerald. This is rather important because out of what appears to be the mundane is the setting for the Transcendental. That is what's happened: Out of what appears to be the rawness of materiality, it becomes moulded to receive the impelling Force that is always present *provided the setting is ready to receive it.*

This is, perhaps, why you have received what you have received. I know the *Unfoldments* are very important and *they are showing you how to reconstruct your world.* This is the genesis that is promised for the Coming.

Everyone is waiting for the divine Afflatus. Whatever that is I'm not sure, but I do know the offering of newness and the emergence of something new is that which can stir the stew pot of your mind. I think that's why it has to be so well seasoned with herbs; in other words, your belief-system *sounds* good as long as you're talking to people who eat the same type of food! But *the Truth* is very different. What is the Truth? None of you know! *No one* knows what the Truth is. It's so elusive; it's as elusive as Life.

What is Love? My goodness, you don't *make* it! That's why most marriages flounder! Some of them survive. They're like the fish: if you skin it, it's sole! [laughter]

Then, what is **Truth**? What is **Love**? What is **Spirit**? These are all words of a higher vocabulary. In every language, they're always pointing to a different consideration which is not earthly. It's so fascinating, without that force-field of words, this framework of reference termed "humanity" has no meaning other than karmic involvement with its own thought-field. Karma is only the result of an incompleted act.

You must always reason from cause to effect, *never* to find the cause from effect. **All reasoning should be from cause to effect, and if one part of a statement is right, you have to accept the rest of it being true.** This is induction. Do it this way; it is simpler. If you accept something that you don't know is true, *try it on* and then you'll see whether or not it is, *from your own experience.*

We had such an incredible conversation this morning. I gave an *Unfoldment*™ on the deck at home before I got here!

David K: Yes, Sir.

Unfortunately, none of it was recorded. Can you tell me what I might share with them?

> *Randle:* You've covered some of it already, Sir, but you mentioned about space.

[Randle reads from his notebook:]

> "Space" is only the name given until Consciousness is perceived as fundamental. Upon the realization of the Ultimate, space is an aspect of creation that is utilized to evidence objectification.

> Space is really "the void" (in terms of the mortal) in which objectification takes place, which allows those in the objective to question how it came about. This somethingness, the objective, upon pursuit, returns to the Nothingness or the Void from which it sprang, and all that is left is the feeling nature of Soul; that's the Feeling of Being I AM. You never lose the Feeling of Being, with or without the form. (Kenneth G. Mills, June 24, 2003)

I'm so glad you got it down! Did you have anything, David?

David K: Yes. You said, "No one understands space, because it exists without objectivity."

Yes. You see, you only understand space because of *objects,* but space is not that at all. Space is objective either it couldn't be named. It's objective and it couldn't be said to be devoid of objects, but it *is* an object either you wouldn't have the object needing it for observation. It is an energy-field that is so great that it takes such density to hold it apart, and it's the graciousness of space that allows the object to be held apart provided you equal it. In other words, you have your space of being one hundred and fifty pounds, which is exactly what it requires to hold that space apart. *Every form has what space requires to be seen.* It is a energy-field that is blasting you constantly with its presence, because all the time you're moving through it.

Why do you get out of breath when you run? You're forcing it out of the way. It's not the fatigue of the legs, because the legs, if you really *know,* are a figment of thought, objectified. You create very bit of it. The only reason the legs ache is because you have allowed the thought to go to that state where it's dealing with the objective. Even if I find it difficult to do something, I know why; it's because the thought is present that seems to be inhibiting the movement. In actuality I know it has nothing to do with me as I AM. So I don't ignore it, but I don't allow it to limit me. Just like the suggestion of fatigue or anything. But I've been so apt at that that I've been advised not to do it anymore, because I'm overriding the sensorial data (that has been my experience) in order to fulfill my mission, and if I override it, it might terminate it more quickly, and I shouldn't. So, it's very interesting.

Yes, Michael.

Michael A: Sir, from what was said this morning and what you've just said, it really left me wondering, is space *alive?*

Oh, yes. That's why we appear to be so magnetic, why you appear to be so electrified. We are in essence *electric,* which is the essence of space. It's an electrical force-field, but on this plane we can't describe it other than without it we cannot pass information or any form of communication. **Space is really what carries our words, supported by the Holy Breath. Words can only be uttered as they move space apart.** It's quite a marvellous magical experience. Yes, Chris.

Christopher D: Is there an aspect of space that's not in time?

Space isn't in time in essence, any more than Consciousness is in time. Awareness is in time but *Consciousness* isn't. Consciousness allows the awareness. Awareness is almost an emissary of Consciousness, like Saint John the Baptist was the emissary of Jesus, the harbinger of Jesus; in other words, he said, "... greater things that He would do," you see. He wasn't the one they thought he was, but he wore skins, he wore furs (that was always pointed out in the stories about him). He was waiting for the appearance of the divine Afflatus to appear manifested, and he knew it would be when he saw Him. It was *the seeing* that brought the cognition! That is exactly what happens to-day, because when you see another with whom you feel a rapport, you know that there is something *beyond* you that has caused this to happen. That's exactly the predicament of Saint John. Upon seeing Jesus, he realized His auric field and knew *He* was the one to bear the *real* Message. Saint John was the harbinger. And that is exactly what *space* does.

Space is the harbinger, in a way, of that State that is termed "Divine" or "Consciousness." We only call the Conscious-awareness of the Ultimate, "Consciousness" because we have no words for God, for the Ultimate. We can say "God," we can say "Self," "the Atman," all these things; they have evidence only in the mortality range.

So, space is a thriving body of power and force, either it wouldn't be so hot to re-enter it! It's not the *friction* of the speed;

it's the *density* that *is* space. Look how, as the capsule re-enters the space, they have to cover it with tiles that are heat resistant, either it would burn-up. It's the resistance of the atmosphere or space that is encountered. The *rarefied* atmosphere would not have that, because you would be in — what? — neutral buoyancy with it. That was the value of the "Neutral Buoyancy" Lecture,[4] because that can apply to space.

> *Christopher D:* Sir, what is the meaning behind what astronomers are in agreement about in terms of "outer space" and the expansion of what to our minds has very little meaning — because where, really, *is* that? We can only know that as a projection of thought.

That's all it is.

> *Christopher D:* But they are approaching the boundaries of infinity, as you call it.

You're right on it with *this* Work. You're right on the edge of it. The astronomers are only projecting what has been *dreamed* constitutes the cosmos. That's *all* you're seeing! As long as they have an object to analyze, they have a reason for viewing. It's just like the people who were searching for what constituted the body and they found the atom. That was the big find, and then the bigger find was to find that the centre of it wasn't solid; it was a vibrating mass, *a tonality!* When Dr. Donald Andrews brought that out at Johns Hopkins University, it was a tremendous discovery, because he said a very frightening thing. He said that if the entire human race could be put in an atomic press and all the holes squeezed out of it, it could be put in a bottle that could be easily carried in the hip pocket.

You see, we *are* filled with hot air! [laughter] Then, again, if a hundred and fifty pound man, he said, were placed in the atomic press and had the holes squeezed out of *him*, the residue could rest on the head of a pin. Isn't it wonderful, we're spending so much time being educated?! But no one's telling you to see *through* the education.

> *Moira D:* You are!

[laughter] Yes, Moira.

Moira D: The big discovery right now in physics and astronomy seems to be the idea that when they look at all the matter in the universe and all the space, it doesn't make-up enough mass to explain what's going on with it. So, they're looking now, and they've discovered this thing they call "dark matter," which is making-up the rest of what's called the universe, and they're finding that it's actually *more* than all of what appears to be visible or what we call space. What would that point to?

It would point to the density of the *observer!* [laughter and applause]

Moira D: That's brilliant!

Undoubtedly the dark matter that they can't identify is their own thought being manifested; they know not how it manifests. This is why vision is so frequently *clouded;* you can't *see through* the matter and, you see, you should be able to, in other words, *penetrate* the seeming somethingness to perceive its nothingness.

Space is only being defined in the hypothetical way by astronomers. There is no proof. I have told you how I sat there, pondering, and I argued with my roommate at the time. He was a spectroscopist, a very brilliant spectroscopist, and he would disappear for days in the microscope! [laughter] (I know what I'm saying!) It was an electric one, very potent. This night he came home (I hadn't seen him for seventy-two hours), he came in very late and he said, "Ken, wake-up! Wake-up! I've got something to show you!" I woke-up, it was around three o'clock, and he pulled out this little piece of film, about one and a half inches long. I looked at it and I saw an inclusion in it; I saw a streak! He said, "See that?!" and I said, "Well, yes." (How could I help but see it?!) He said, "Well, do you know what it means?!" I said, "Well, something's wrong with the negative." [laughter] He said, "I've sat-up seventy-two hours to watch this. It has changed the whole basis of a formula for a gas that has been accepted worldwide, and I have the proof that the formula is false!" It did change much, and I can't tell you now (it was some time ago) what it was all about.

This man became famous in his research. He was about my age and he was my piano pupil and very gifted. He was at the initial launching of the rocket to the moon and travelled all over Europe, lecturing. He was a guest lecturer at universities. But the arguments we would have! I would always say, "But what would this be if you didn't have this viewpoint of limitation?" It was interesting because he could never accept what I was saying as so, because if he did he would wonder what he was doing with his life's work.

One very outstanding woman in the field of education and in the Mysteries, as you know (some of you had the pleasure of meeting her; she's from Venezuela), she and I dialogued at her request several times. One night we were driving up from Manhattan to Connecticut, and she was in the car with me and she said, "I have to tell you something: I cannot do any more dialogues with you." I said, "Oh. Why?" She said, "They are influencing me so much that if I continue, I will have to find my life's work of no use." I haven't heard from her for years.

Why are people so afraid of Truth?

You know why:
It alters how you view everything;
it alters how you view your life.
But the big demand is how you view *others*.

You know? *How you view others*. Yes, Barry.

> *Dr. Barry B:* Sir, as we're sitting with you here and you're speaking to us, the space is clearly a *charged* environment. Yet, when we return to the world or we leave the space with you, the space is different somehow.

Yes, it is; it *seems* different.

> *Dr. Barry B:* Is there an environment where the language of Spirit and Soul can be the most empowered?

Yes. You're experiencing it. You're helping to do it, but that only is to the *appearance*. Don't let it go to your head! It's all hypothetical.

> *Dr. Barry B:* How can we carry that to another space?

There's no other space. Space is not other than infinite, but what do you know of the infinite? Space is as infinite as

Consciousness is infinite. How can you carry it? You can't carry the greater by the lesser; the lesser is carried by the greater. That's why it *behooves everyone to realize what is the greater,* because then the Greater is always with you *no matter where you are.* So, your environment of the Greater is always with you whether you're in Manhattan or in the subway.

I know this was known so much when we went behind the Iron Curtain. No one knew how we got behind the Iron Curtain to sing in Russia or in Yugoslavia or in Czechoslovakia. How did we get there? everyone asked, and I said, "I haven't any idea! We just came." But we had to carry that, and believe it or not, we met far more courteousness on the borders of those countries than we've ever met crossing the border in the United States. The border in the United States is just far from anything we met under communism.

> *Christopher D:* Very true.

You remember.

> *Christopher D:* Oh, very true. They might have machine guns but they were absolutely respectful and welcoming.

And they're not, in the United States. So, you see, the environment, the atmosphere, is well within your jurisdiction. Why do you think that when you go to somebody's home, it's prepared just so? Because anyone entering it enters it for the purpose of being enhanced, either you wouldn't have invited them there. It's a mutual recognition of the oneness of the environment, of the Divine.

You mustn't forget how everything you're viewing, everything you're touching, everything you're seeing, happens. Yes, Lucille.

> *Lucille J:* Dr. Mills, an amazing example of the undivided State: this morning, while we were listening to the *Unfoldment*™ from yesterday morning, I wrote in my notebook "Is space objective?"

Isn't that interesting? Yes, it *is* objective; it is because it would not *be* without the subject. As long as you question, there is an object. That's why Mrs. Mary Baker Eddy said, "Understanding is the line of demarcation between the real and unreal."[5] But she didn't tell you the secret, and I don't know if *she* knew it, but the point is: *as long as you have the object, it is subject to question.* Like space: is it an object? It is because you are the subject, questioning it. That's why it always is present for you until you realize; and then when you realize, it's there to be *utilized* — but not with contamination!

That's why the environment is in such a state: people are contaminating the body of space. One of the worst contaminants is the way you think it doesn't matter. It's the most illusive form of matter there is! It goes hand in hand with *sound,* and it goes hand in hand with *the Word.* That is why it tells you in the Bible that the Word was with God and the Word was God; in other words, when the Word is sounded, the Source is known — either It couldn't have been heard and It couldn't have been sounded!

Yes, David.

> *David K:* Dr. Mills, are there experiences within the objective that are closer to what is Real?

Oh, yes.

> *David K:* So, sound or space, for instance, is a gift from the Source?

Oh, yes.

> *David K:* Because they point to something that's Real.

Yes, if you *know* that, they do.

> *David K:* It's still an illusion.

It's still an illusion; *everything* is an illusion, but it doesn't mean it *isn't. That's* the point. The illusionist knows you're an illusion either he couldn't make you believe what didn't happen; it only seems to happen. That's what *we* are. We forget, though, that what we create is only an illusion. We are given the ability or the grace of the Creator. Of course, it's His (the Creator's). That's how the love I feel for you and the love you feel for me is present, and that is *a great blessing.*

> *David K:* Yes, Sir.

Student: For all of us.

It is, because it is verification living that it's the same for anyone if they see the undivided Garment. Yes, Rick.

> *Rick F:* I wanted to share with you a small experiment that I was present for, this last week. As you can imagine — I've been studying gems — the study of gems has a lot to do with the study of *light*. A clear transparent stone was taken and dropped into a glass of water. There it was, the stone, in the water, because the water bends light at a different speed than the stone does. Then another glass was taken, where the water or the liquid bent light at the same rate of refraction as the stone did, and the stone was dropped in and absolutely disappeared!

What happens to your world? It disappears but it is still there in the "liquid state" of Consciousness! It can embrace *any state;* you can drop your world in that state of Conscious-awareness, and it becomes one with it, but it is *still* what is, serving its purpose of brilliance to one who knows how to set it in a ring of gold or platinum.

Yes, David.

> *David K:* Another statement that you made this morning, Sir, while we were studying was: *"The mind, or the matrix, is the womb of the illusion."*

Yes, it is. The matrix is the womb of the illusion.

> *David K:* My experience, and I think for many, also, of being in your Presence is like a slowing-down of the thoughts or perhaps even, hopefully, the *suspension* of thought completely. That's somewhat like perhaps the *code* being slowed down.

That is right. The code is your thought, and when that slows down, if you don't know What IS, you're in a pickle.

> *David K:* Yes, Sir.

If you know What IS, you're in the state of receptivity and superiority, because *without thought I AM* either you would not cognize there was *no* thought! That's why it is *never annihilation;* it's never denied.

> **This wondrous work of appearance (the three-dimensional objective world) is never denied; it's only re-identified in the Light of Actuality. That's all!**
>
> **The biggest thing we try to do is to jolt your considerations that surround mortality and its trends.**

You can't *convince* the mind of anything; you have to realize that *it's always going to stand in the way until it's awed by the wonder that is beyond it!*

Yes, Marshall.

> *Marshall O:* An awesome experience that we had lately at a rehearsal was how you played a few notes on the keyboard and transformed the space.

Yes, oh yes. It's so fascinating, if you go to the keyboard, you consider that middle C is the starting point, it's right in the middle of the keyboard, but that is *never* the note that I used to teach, because middle C has no identity to a new one. I always taught what was in the middle, and that is sort of like the middle Path. You can always see D because it's always the white note between two blacks. The blacks are always clustered in two and three, two and three, two and three. A child sees eighty-eight keys before him, and he just feels at a loss, but at the first lesson I show him, he can know the *whole* keyboard! It was the key of showing him the two black keys and asking him to find them. He found them, and I said, "But you must find what's *in between* them because that's your friend." So I told him to call it "Dee-Dum-Diddle, Dee in the middle," and that's how he came to know *every* D on the keyboard and he felt immediately he knew the keyboard was not a mystery. I asked him what came before D, and he said, "C." I said, "Well, what do you think your playmate is? What's *his* name?" I said, "Middle C." I said, "Find the other Cs," and he did, just like that!

That's how you taught them to read so quickly, because you showed them that middle C was "the baby in the cradle." The "mother" and "father" were separated, so that's why sometimes the baby was in the cradle close to Mrs. Treble Clef and sometimes spending the day with Mr. Bass Clef, and it would be closer. Suddenly the child was not bothered by the movable C! I had this whole lingo for them, and it was wonderful for them.

Yes, Jennifer.

> *Jennifer M:* Recently you said that if there aren't others like us, there's no help for the world, and this morning you spoke of the way we view others, and the importance. It brings to my consideration that I don't seem to meet people who are really questioning. I know there must be thousands like us in the world who *are* like us, and it really makes me question, "How am I viewing others?" and "Am I viewing others correctly?" This is why I would like to ask you: What is the correct way to view another?

As your Self. Talk to another as you would talk to your Self. You don't have to say how *wonderful* you are, but you can find what talents *they* have, because you have the talent. You can ask them if they like art, et cetera. There's always a way. Just remember, I was a piano teacher and I only knew my piano pupils, and I just agreed to speak if I were asked — and God help me, because I didn't know what to talk about! I just always took the stand that "the words of my mouth" would be manifested — you know, "May the words of my mouth and the meditations of my heart be accepted in the sight of the One altogether lovely."[6] That's what happened. I used to be just sitting there *waiting* for what to say to these people. They'd sit there in front of me, and then it would start to flow. There was never any advertisement, because I didn't know what I was supposed to advertise: I *talk!* So does the parrot!

It started happening; it was happening all the time to the point where what appeared to be one or two people grew into, at times, four hundred, and not one person came to me that hadn't heard from another. That's how fast it spread. I was still teaching piano! I taught piano right up until February of 1975, and yet I had been speaking to people since 1968 — paying off mortgages.

Yes, Rachel.

> *Rachel O:* Sir, what is in the sound of the high words, like "Principle" and "Mind" and "Consciousness," that

gives them this Life-force that can be felt even by those who speak a different language? And where do these words come from and how did they come to lose their force in the language of the street?

Because they're not used. They *can't* be used by the street people. Those words only are used scientifically; "Principle" is frequently used: "the principles" of this and "the principles" of that. Those words carry power because they *aren't* used. They carry power because very few people know *how* to use them. People worship, supposedly, Life, Truth, Love, Spirit, Mind, and Soul in every religion, but what has it meant? Look at the *wars!* Look at the wars *everywhere.* It's hypocrisy, because those words are termed "sacred."

The *sacred* word means *it is set apart,* and anything that is set apart means that it can only be known by instruction of how to say it. The only way you can say it with power is when you know the state of your Self. When you know the state of your Self and the intentions of your heart, then those words start to be imbued with the power, as every word of your language. Those words will always carry special power because when your heart is right, the frequency of the sound of those words takes on a different tonality. You know you listen to a businessman say "principle" — what in hell does he mean by "principle"? Then *you* say "Principle," and it sounds *totally different.* It's not because it's a male or a female voice; it's because you say it because it has meaning for you. To another, it's a question. As long as anything is a question, it's only a stumbling block to them until it is answered.

So, they become part of the higher vocabulary because they are usually only spoken with power when you have realized that Power *is* in the lap of the Infinite.

Yes, Michael.

> *Michael S:* Dr. Mills, it is so apparent to me that you are giving what appears to be information, but the tricky part is that it can't be taken in as information unless it is activated with *the authenticity* that your Voice carries.

Yes.

Michael S: It is apparent to me, even in listening to myself or others speak, that words in a certain way are like objects —

They are!

Michael S: — and what is encapsulated is very different for each one, and I don't mean this in a judgment sense. I am not sure that this is really a question, but it is an observation certainly of myself, but everyone, to really respect that what is happening here is not moving in a linear way of progressing from "Now we're going to tell you this next point; you're ready for this next point because you've taken . . ." I feel that sometimes we tend to start questioning what is said, in the spirit of going to school and making sure that the information is understood. You said something that was an amazing key this morning: "If you just accept the statement, then what follows can be experienced." I feel that what we are being asked to do is to accept what you are saying without perhaps putting it through this questioning process.

Yes.

Michael S: I know that Williams and Harvard (thank you very much!) gave me this technique, and I sometimes feel that sharing a laugh with you breaks it. But I do feel in rehearing it, myself especially, that I just don't want to see what's happening broken by a tendency, in a certain way —

It can't be questioned by the *mind*. If anything at all, it should be questioned by the result of *your surrender to it*. That is the only way you should question.

> Your surrender to the Fact
> Allows question to become an act
> And the answer the dancing partner
> And the rhythm simply divine.
> Then it's answered.

There has to be a rhythm created with a question and answer in order for it to be secure. If your question is right, the answer can be in one word or two; if it is not, there has to be a lot of words because you have to create the condition, you have to create the backdrop, the background, for your painting. It's the same thing with the words: you have to create a *sound* background for your words suddenly to have meaning.

Yes, David.

> *David K:* I feel it stems back to what Barry was asking (that everybody seems to be struggling with): how is this higher state maintained?

You didn't maintain it when you got it! It's *always* been your state. Your mind, with the underground entanglements of belief-systems, has *clouded* it from your own interior view. There is nothing to be attained; it's *already* yours! To think that you have to progress up to it is the way you have an excuse for not being actual *now!*

> *David K:* That's the part of the program we have to break.

Yes. Programs to Enlightenment are all programs of progress — and there is no progress; *it's instantaneous!* If I pick-up the grape and it is attached, I have to break it apart from the vine. That's what you have to do. If you pick it up, it doesn't take any effort to drop it. But it's difficult if it's attached to a belief-system. Don't I know! Belief-systems don't satisfy . . . only those who don't want to *inquire*. **Inquiry is essential.** Yes, Greg.

> *Gregory S:* You said earlier that the core of the community is language. In the topic of this idea of maintenance of the Higher Way, I think the bigger question is how do we maintain it with *each other.*

That's the way it's maintained.

> *Gregory S:* Yes, Sir. That was the dinner conversation last night, your statement that "Perhaps one of the reasons that people do not want community is because they do not wish to affirm another's meaning; they do not wish to allow another's expression, if the one dares to express."[7] Our dialogue was bountiful, and it became apparent that there perhaps are some opaque views that still exist in how we do view one another.

I'm sure of it. That is why there is smallness of number. (Your answer, Jennifer.)

> *Gregory S:* My question really is, How do you address those views, and similarly with the analogy that Rick had brought up, can you literally listen to the words that someone is offering and drop them into the broader idea of Principle and see if they are opaque or transparent?

You know *instantly* if they are opaque, because they have nothing to do with Principle. "Words without works are dead," and if there isn't the radiance and if there isn't the feeling, you know something's missing. If there isn't the joy, if there isn't the happiness, you know *something's* missing.

I would certainly watch the language, for sure. You mentioned you should converse with one another in the best and the highest way possible. **Don't use words that are going to limit your expression or your Life.**

> Why is it that we can't consider the possibility of Being divine, in other words, set aside with a language that reduces the world to a divine Idea held in the untarnished state of the Ultimate?

I think it's one thing to talk about our joys and our hobbies and what we love to do, but if you'll notice, that's the only thing that most people talk about. They can't talk about their experience of Being; they can seldom talk about it even after hearing it. I'm sure the *Unfoldment*™ was discussed at dinner instead of *evidencing* what unfolded. I think *that* may be one of the features that is very, very important to consider: *how much chatter goes on that eliminates the possible empowered speech?*

Chatter is often called conversation, but how can you converse with *chatter?* I find it very difficult and I don't enjoy it at all. This is why I don't go out very much. The ordinary is okay for a time, but the importance of language and the importance of what is said — you must, perhaps when you're with others, see what *their* wish is, even if it's in a hobby or in something they love, but contribute from *your* storehouse an idea or something that will *enhance what they're doing and cause them to consider their hobby or joy with a different facet of the Light.* That keeps the conversation somewhat on a different level because you're *actively engaged;* you're just not offering chatter.

Yes, Ken.

> *Ken B:* Sir, it has come to me many times that the reason we aren't able to access the information that you gave yesterday (I mean, the miracle that you have been following this theme!) is that we don't seem to have respect for *the time* or for *the work* that you've done to have realized that!

Yes.

> *Ken B:* Unless we are prepared to undertake the work that you've done to make that our own experience, then we won't hear, and therefore you won't be able to give what you gave. It's sort of a correspondence here. If we could mature to the level where we could even come to *the threshold* of what it took to do that — I mean, I can't even conceive of how you realized all those details of how it's actually working and its most incredibly addictive science or however you would call it! Unless we are prepared to see that what you gave us yesterday and today and the day before was the result of an incredible amount of consideration and watching, it can't continue; you won't be able to give more.

I'm very aware when people get what they call "high," because you don't want to be drunken *without wine,* in this case. Yes, Ellen.

> *Ellen M:* Sir, I feel that a wonderful parallel or a way of looking at what Ken is speaking of is to look at the Star-Scape Singers' rehearsals. You would give the opportunity and the experience of a tremendously elevated performance during that rehearsal, and the next day, if we didn't do all the homework of staying with all of the points — we had taken every note of what the instructions were, practised those instructions, and then came back to the next rehearsal with you to perform at that level — we learned the hard way, you might say, how much that took to start to, as you always said, "rise and set" and then "rise and set." It's quite obvious, what *you're* saying, Ken, is not possible without that same attention and focus and

intention to be able to come back and perform for you, Sir, or at least be able to receive from you, beyond what was given the day before.

I think this is what Jesus perhaps meant in part when He said, "You have to come out from the world and be separate." You separate yourself from the common by your language. That's why I brought out that the language is the core of society. But is our society cultured?

Students: No.

Not to-day at all. There's very little culture living, and when it does, it's usually set apart. It's very set apart. That's why when Mr. Murchie asked me to make a promise to him, when I didn't have more than twenty-five cents in my pocket — we were sitting in the library this night, and he said, "Ken, I want you to make me a promise. You having experienced this luxury and this elegant way of living for all these years, I want you to promise me that you will keep it alive in your life so that the future generations will know that there *is* this way of living, because it will not live for long." He said, "This Victorian house and this way of living is almost past, but I want you to keep it alive for future generations." I laughed and I said I would, and I thought, "It's the most ridiculous thing to ask me to do when I have twenty-five cents in my pocket!" But I did attempt to keep it alive. Every time I bought something, it was the *best* that I could afford. I never put it on Visa.

I never bought anything until I'd saved enough money to buy it — just like you! That applies to-day, too. I have not bought anything — other than the mortgage on my home when I first started, and on any house, because sometimes it's wiser not to pay it all off. *You should save before you buy anything.* You should tear-up your plastic cards, because that's all that the hierarchy of time wants: to eliminate the medium of exchange. That's why I will write a cheque and get some money from the bank and pay for things, and I'm sure the bank doesn't like it, but I do it because I don't want people to forget that there is that medium of exchange, which is an impersonal way of saying thank-you.

Money is used as a form of mesmerism. Do you realize what you do for *money?* Whereas, in former times what you did, if you wanted anything, was *barter.* You made a beautiful piece of sculpture or you painted and you exchanged it for woodworking in your kitchen in your home. No money was needed because that was the way you said thank-you.

The bank manager always said, "Why do you come all the way in to this bank when you could just do it all by phone or by your bank card?!" I said, "I never use bank cards. I don't accept them. I want to come to the bank to see if there's anyone still intelligent enough to answer a question!" and she would laugh! Ellen and David were with me. I'd say, "No, Marie, I won't do it by phone or by a card. I want to know there's somebody still alive here!" [laughter] She said, "Well, just put it on your card," and I said, "No way!" I don't put anything on a card unless it's absolutely necessary; I never put anything on a card that I know can't be paid for. That's the difference! It's not wise to spend the money you haven't got, because you can't expect exchange to happen if you have nothing to give, and you're asking somebody to give you something when you have no exchange.

Money is so mesmeric. Do you realize, you alter your life because of money? But you *should* alter your life according to money because you've got to look after yourselves in the future. You know, all of this Work is marvellous but it is extremely practical. It's not airy-fairy; it's right down to the ground for tilling . . . and telling. You know, it's wonderful to go to the bank and have a teller who knows enough about your account that they can say it exists! [laughter]

It's a very interesting thing when you try to hold a standard as a result of a promise. Promises to-day don't mean a thing! The people who have promised and they break it! **Don't break a promise whatever you do. It really is the weakest chain in the continuity of our experience. Don't break a promise. Let your word have substance.**

You can talk and I can show you very easily a lot more, but what is the point of it until you make *this* practical? You won't make it practical by *talking* about it. That is the wonderful "high" you get. It gives you a feeling of having attained it, to be able to talk about it. What I've said yesterday and to-day and years before is something I never talked about; it only became part of the language of sharing when I was asked.

That is the way: you don't impose at all; you wait to see where another is at. If they're not with you, you know they're against you. I think so many of us have too many relationships with people who are not on the Path at all. One Teacher said, "If you're not with me, you're against me."

Isn't it fascinating, I thought of what's happened in the United States. [Dr. Mills reads from his notebook:]

> They that take the sword shall perish with the sword.
> (Matthew 26:52)

That's why I have such concern for the States. David made a very important point. He said on June 10, 2003:

> The note can bear a name but the sound cannot.

I also said:

> Remember, What-IS cannot be experienced by what-is-not.

Underline it! And don't forget, "Put a knife to thy throat if thou be a man or woman given to appetite,"[8] and you will lose weight very quickly! [laughter]

I just opened to this by Rumi:

> As far as you can, be a slave, not a monarch.
> Let yourself be struck.
> Be the ball, not the bat.

James (4:4) said:

> Whosoever therefore will be a friend to the world is the enemy of God.

What is the most outstanding characteristic of your experience? *You can be aware of being aware.* Just consider, you are the only animal that can question itself.

I like this:

> The robot mind depends upon a virtual reality.
> The authentic Mind *is* Reality.

That's in *Food for No Thought*.⁹

> *Randle:* Dr. Mills, there was an aphorism you gave last night. You said: "Know nothing. Fear nothing. But *do something.*"

On April 12, 2003, I said:

> Problems always arise when one type of energy is being replaced by another more powerful one. Only by people learning to sing in harmony could they relieve the discord and dismal events.

We found that out in Lithuania. That's what they told us. David Kennet said on April 12:

> The ultimate drug is fidelity to the illusion.

On April 12, I said:

> Love allows the object to think it has an existence.

I said to a piano pupil in December 1966:

> All that I have told you that is personal cannot be remembered. But all that I have told you that is impersonal cannot be forgotten.

I said:

> The whole purpose of nature is to caress the senses.

The author is anonymous:

> God tries to get our attention until he has to use the megaphone of pain.

I suggested:

> Don't leave anyone with a confession needing more confessions.

I thought Anton Nemeth said a wonderful thing on March 1, 2003, over the telephone:

What you don't give can't come back to you.

Interesting. I have French here:

Les paroles s'envolent. (Spoken words fly away.)

Claude C: "Les ecrits restent." That's the counterpart of it, Sir. *"Les paroles s'envolent, mais les ecrits restent."* I think it was written or uttered by a poet, but I don't remember who. He said that the words fly off, but the written word remains.

"The written word remains." It's fascinating, *the written word never carries the tonality.*

Ramana Maharshi said:

Experience gained without rooting out all predispositions cannot remain steady.

So, it goes on and on. This is just my twenty-first book of notes. I said on June 18:

Evil lives on the residue of otherness.

Potent. Vasishta, an ancient Indian Sage said:

Better the rock-bound toad,
the crawling earthworm,
or the blind cave serpent,
than the man without enquiry.

Students: Thank you, Sir.

⌘

1. Referring to photographs taken of someone's aura, each photograph varying with the state of attention of the subject.
2. Proverbs 25:11.
3. I Corinthians 15:52.
4. "Neutral Buoyancy," Kenneth G. Mills, *The Golden Nail* (Stamford/Toronto: Sun-Scape Publications, 1993) and Sun-Scape Records KMOD-059-2 compact disc.
5. Eddy, *Science and Health,* 505–21.
6. Psalms 19:14.
7. "The Pleasure of Resistance," Kenneth G. Mills, *Change Your Standpoint ~ Change Your World* (Stamford/Toronto: Sun-Scape Publications, 1996), p. 136.
8. Proverbs 23:2.
9. Kenneth G. Mills, *Food for No Thought: a book of aphorisms* (Toronto/Stamford: Sun-Scape Publications, 1999).

Re-minding

Chapter VIII

The redeemed imagination has allowed you to see where you are the monarch of all you survey! You are not the slave of the objective.

Re-minding

Themes: Source ~ recognition ~ redeemed imagination ~ perception ~ language ~ bendable space

This is the morning of June 26, 2003.

> As we move beyond the periphery of the mental and
>   find within the encompassing Grace of Light,
> We find that the moment is a moment traced,
>   offering to us an opportunity of Flight.
> We move in the recognition that all concepts
>   are there for time
> And all edicts are pronounced as official, but the
>   official One is beyond the mind.
> It pronounces that Light is eternal and that
>   Consciousness reigns supreme,
> And in this wondrous world of Wonder may you
>   find how it is in your land and yet beyond
>   that of dreams.
>
> We never deny the object, we never deny its place,
> But we do know now, from having listened, how it's
>   possible to trace
> To see it as an appearance, but that appearance is
>   illusionary, you must see now,
> For in this act you become the one superior to what
>   appears as the plight of objects as they show.
>
> You are taught mind-constructs of confusion,
>   a farrago of thoughts not divine,
> And thus you mix them in this state of . . . "wonder"?
>   No wonder you become confused in mind.
> You must see in the moment of reception that what
>   appear to be the actions of time
> Are all seemingly "pencilled-in" for your cognition.
>   Are you going to accept them or reject them
>   as they seem to be, in mind?

> Every offering is given, as you see, in the action of
> yielding with grace and ease
> What is never *thought* to be a fulfilment of a
> promise; yet, some have called it this in deed.
> But the action is never one of *considering* — just the
> grandeur of Being the Fact . . .
> That this is now the opportunity for everyone to
> glean the magic of That.

You have all seen without doubt the incredible panoramic views that confront you each morning as you awaken, in *this area* particularly and in the everyday world of life. It is so wonderful to see the grandeur and the magnificence of it all, and we constantly exclaim how beautiful it is and how wonderful it is, but it could never be there if it were not for *the sense perception of it*. The sense perception of it, as you now know, is what? *Mental.* Therefore, in essence *everything that you perceive in the panorama of your life is all mental*. It appears as objective and it is not denied, but it is realized as *illusory.*

You're saying "uh-huh," but look at the gigantic leap you have made if you can *live* this way!

Students: Yes, Sir.

That's the key. It is said by the Masters that that which is known to be of greatness can never be given to the multitude, only to those who are capable of perceiving it and accepting it as the very means of life. There is no way that success can come to anyone with the mixture of entertaining the subdued plights of emotions and desires, because these are beneath the very surface of your thought and seemingly unpowerful, but they are extremely powerful because they cause you to be enamoured with the following episodes of your creativity.

When you start to find fulfilment happening as a result of your wish or desire to precipitate, never, never take it as a personal greatness, for anything you precipitate requires the ensuing responsibilities, and what you precipitate is what you render *by attention* into an object or into an experience. Therefore, what you have precipitated is always under the jurisdiction of your clarity of concept.

When you consider the power of imagination, you now, perhaps, see it in such a magnified way. From the initial moments of our togetherness one of the five Lectures given was the one on imagination. I said, "Look what imagination has done *to* you. Now look at what the *redeemed* imagination can do *for* you." In the past few days you have seen the redeemed imagination as *an experience,* and that's what it means. That early Lecture has been experienced, the past few days.

The redeemed imagination has allowed you to see where you are the monarch of all you survey! *You are not the slave of the objective.* If you are monarch of all you survey, then all your objective situations are your *feudal* components, and according to the way you view them will you receive the offerings that the feudal state offers. The feudal state is not a *slave* state; it's a state that's recognized as yielding what is essential for the object to be satisfied, because at the essence of satisfaction rests the total wholeness of divinity! "Satisfaction" is only a word that "you" would use; you cannot imagine the Source saying "I am now satisfied."

The imaging faculty has done an incredible thing: it has given us this entire world experience and this entire group experience or this entire organization experience. But **the only value and the only hope of any organization is to realize what constitutes its basis, which in essence is the** *culture* **of it.** This is the very basis upon which anything can be successful. You have seen the obstructions to the form of community which have tried to parade. It's been "lack of money," it's been lack of this . . . It's been "a lack" of *that.* Everyone has considered their experience in such a *minimal* way — every one of you! I do not know why you are satisfied with so little.

I remember, as a child, hearing the minister say, "All that I have is thine," and I used to consider, "What, then, is this impoverishment I see *everywhere*? Why is everyone so poor?" The minister would say, "Well, not the poor in *spirit.*" Fiddlesticks! We were poor in the grade of understanding what constituted freedom. Religion binds. What's the root of "religion"?

Students: To bind.

To bind. Bind what?

Stephen W: The mentality.

Bind your mentality, your thoughts. Why bind your thoughts? Somebody must know that if they can bind your thoughts, you become subject to them and to their limitations!

From the time I was Emmanuel's age (ten years) I pondered "All that I have is thine," and I used to lay on my Indian blanket out under the willow tree, wondering what all this meant. I'd look at the clouds passing by overhead and I'd think, "I wonder what it would be like to ride on a cloud and see all that I have is thine?" And then I realized as I moved that the cloud of unknowingness shall yield its dew/do, and look what happened!

Why do you accept you're looking for a job or you've got a job? That is only the objective of rendering "unto Caesar the things that are Caesar's," but *who* renders unto the Source that which is the *Source?!* The whole answer is in what you now know. You cannot consider for one moment that you are primarily objectified and thereby have a mind that can be utilized in your sustenance. You now know that "the mind" is nothing but the name given to an organ, which evidences itself as mentality. [Dr. Mills holds-up a cherry from his fruit plate.] Is there any spatial difference between the cherry and mentality?

Students: No. Oh!

"Oh!" is right! I hope I had you in the corner.

Students: Yes, you did.

Do you see that?

Students: Yes, Sir!

The distance is purely the attempt to define from the objective standpoint. Is there any distance between the cup and saucer and mentality?

Students: No, Sir.

No. The only difference is that this is conceived primarily sensorially, feelingly, tastefully, sightfully, "olfactorally"; all the senses are involved for that to have any existence! And all those faculties are mental. **Where in essence is wealth?**

Student: It's mental.

It's mental, but **if it's mental, how is it even a concept if you don't have it? You have it and you haven't cognized it or perceived it. You haven't perceived it as yours, because you have refused or ignorantly ignored the great gift of what? The capability of conceiving** *unlimitedly* **and the ability to precipitate what is necessary.**

Those who are getting it are the few, and "no Master would give to the mass what was fit for only the few."

Students: Thank you, Sir.

That's what the Ancient Teaching says. Therefore, how do you engage the beauty of the Botanical Gardens?[1] **How do you engage every experience of your life, if it isn't from the standpoint of a sensorial response to an objective confinement? The only key to manumission is that of understanding the way of the Uncontradictable, the Ultimate. It bypasses all process and invigorates the talent route that each one takes to precipitate what is foremost in their life experience as it is freed more and more from the belief-system of limitation.**

Yours is such an experience of opportunity, for from the standpoint of worldlings the world doesn't really know you're here; but from the standpoint that IS, it doesn't matter one bit that anyone knows that you're here, because your very ability to conceive the world and the inhabitants thereof is the very ability of the God-endowment that "All that I have is thine."

In the beginning, you have radical reliance on what is Principle or on whatever you have been taught is the Source. As you move from *impressing the mind* to *being the monarch,* you order it to behave becoming the mode of the Hierarchy. This is where, perhaps, so much happens that is difficult, because we spend so much time in listening to people speak and then develop assumptions, but how often are these assumptions really *verified?* Generally speaking, anything we *assume* is never considered to include an "ass" and a "you" and a "me"! When you assume something, be very careful because you've got too much outside yourself . . . I hope! [laughter] *It is the assumptions that create the entanglement of language.*

Any time you hear people speaking ad infinitum about *nothing,* then you'll know that it *is* nothing, because nothing doesn't need a word! It is out of the Nothing that the Word comes. When we say there is no *thing,* it's very different than *nothing!* We don't say, "There is no thing" (in denial); we say, "There is no thing in *actuality." That* is the difference. That's why I can love David, I can love anyone. How could I not?! How can *you* not?!

You don't love the thing; you love the Essence that allows it to be part of your attention.

You only have in your experience what is in your attention. This is why if David is reading or pondering something and I talk to him, I am talking to *a post!* [laughter] He doesn't hear *one word;* he has no attention on what I'm saying. Where is your attention when you are hearing everything that disrobes you of your "wonderful" presence, "marvellous" presence, and reduces you to a mental phenomena?! [laughter] What are you *doing* with it? *It's an incredible consideration,* because if anyone is "degreed," they always think they know it all and if they don't, they *pretend* they do! This is the trouble with most psychiatrists and psychologists. (I'll leave the doctors out of it!) What do they *do?* They attempt to solve the problem from within the problem. The problem only exists because somewhere, somehow, someone has a thought-entanglement about what they are not, and usually that's all based on your *remembrance* pattern. It's not on anything, perhaps, that has happened to you; it may be just on something you have seen or heard.

One of the most insidious suggestions that you have heard from childhood is that you need your opposite, *to be complete!* Now you can see what a banner of untruth — ! **If you don't know your Self, you cannot know anyone else correctly. It's impossible!** This is one of the most scary fields to touch because everyone is "tetched"! [laughter] It is so ridiculous to think that God made a mistake in His creation and divided Himself up!

Now, stop and consider what you have been taught. Just because we say "our Father" doesn't mean that He's male. That *concept* can't help but bear the male and the female. "Can't possibly!" Where in heaven's name are you poor women?! You're always screaming for your father, and all men wonder why they need one when they're grown-up. *That's* what happens: when you grow-up, you don't think you need to know the Father! And you *do,* because the Father, you've been taught to believe, is a concept of the Highest, which was never relayed to you as being within your Conscious experience and termed, only in your pattern of awareness, "God."

It is not sacrilegious; it reveals *exactly* what it is. The Source must be male-female, Father-Mother, and if it is Father-Mother, it is *not* divided — nor is the Creation.

If people only saw this, so many more marriages would be happy and so many *fewer* marriages would take place! You would make sure that each wasn't expecting to be fulfilled by the other. [Dr. Mills sings:] "It ain't necessarily so!"

Just consider these points deeply and see what they do to your belief-system.

As we look over the years of released expression, we see more than ever the submergence of the individual or the personality into definite roads of activity. We see more than ever the great need of salvation; we see that the only way to be saved from the virus of false identity and the false propaganda of being "this" is in this realm of the Higher Teachings that have always been there for those who would have the courage to question. Generally, the people are not questioning, not at all. In the seventies, when I first began to speak, there were three and four hundred people; I was meeting seventy-five new people a week usually, for *months!* Then what happened? People in high places became aware of the power that you were expressing as an organization, and it had to be belittled. Look what happened. Those who are not here did not have what? The conviction of rightness; they did not have any conviction or they perhaps did not even *know* a quality known as *fidelity.* Fidelity to what? Not person, but fidelity to *Principle!* You appear to have it to the person if that is where you're finding the illuminating factors and energy stream of Principle!

It is fidelity to Principle. Where is it? What has happened? **The multitude are suffering from** ***an anesthetization of intuition and conscience!*** As soon as the five senses can be enhanced, you forget about the sixth and seventh: intuition and insight!

Therefore, you don't have the opportunity of birthing wisdom, because you have duplicity instead of the trinity! The trinity gives you the wonder. **When insight and intuition function, the child that's birthed is wisdom. And wisdom does what? It permits you to perceive the difference between Fact and fiction.**

Intuition births as you subdue the *five* senses, because when intuition functions, *thought* doesn't function the same way at all; in fact, most intuitive responses are not thought, and they're seldom in *agreement* with you! They are seldom what you *want* to do. When you realize this, you start to gain insight as to how you have been controlled by your senses and controlled by your ability to ask questions *about what-isn't* — instead of asking questions that arise as a result of your attempt to extricate yourself from the entanglement of degraded thoughts!

Don't think yourselves part of "a family tree." They all have to be cut down eventually, and even the ones that are present, it's costly to get rid of them! The man charged me four hundred dollars for chopping down a tree in my back garden! That's just the one; a couple more were a thousand. *If an object costs that much to get rid of, can you imagine the price you pay to get rid of the false identity you possess?!*

I told you the wonderful story about a man in the canoe one day up at his country place. We were having a nice time and we were talking about a couple of girls, one I was going with and the one he was going with. He was telling me how attracted he was to this one, but he didn't know because he'd been considering her family tree. I said, "My God, are you marrying a *limb?!*" [laughter] How many limbs have *you* married in your life that control you just as much as that situation can? "Can-oe" or "can't-oe"?! [laughter]

The incredible panorama of life is so stunning and so beautiful, and I've done a little bit of travelling, and seeing all the world as much as I have — Russia and the Baltic States, Norway, Yugoslavia, Egypt, Turkey, Greece, Italy, France, and Spain — **it is so fascinating when you travel realizing that you are allowing every undenied object to be perceived but realizing it's an illusion and your own projection. It is all within you.**

Travel *that way* and you look at art differently, you look at structures differently, and you look at people differently. *Travel*

Lightly! Except with singers! Between twelve singers we had a hundred and eighty pieces of luggage (the first time!) and five men to cart it in and out of hotels every night. Then the next year we really reduced it, to a hundred and twenty! Isn't it amazing the baggage we carry, *thinking it's going to enhance us.*

> **Why shorten your length of your projection ability of the Divine?**
> **The Divine has no outlet to this world.**
> **The first and foremost subtle outlet the Divine has to this world is what? the Breath.**
> **The next is its formation, the Word.**
>
> **You cannot live without the Breath.**
> **How far away is the evidence of the omnipotent?**
> **It's all there is!**
> **That's the only thing there is to your life.**

As soon as you stop breathing, they get rid of you, and so you don't take-up too much space, they cremate you! It's less space in the cemetery! It's marvellous, back to dust, but it's amazing they never save your brain — other than Einstein's; it was bigger than most! That's what they said. That was the difference between his and yours: his was bigger.

Now you see the meaning of his words to the young fellow from Harvard. Einstein invited a representative of Bishop Fulton Sheen, a professor from Harvard, to have tea with him, and the professor brought his twenty-one-year-old son who was at an intellectual impasse. He listened to Einstein, and Einstein, perhaps, was a little bit bored so he said, "Let's go to the garden." They went out to the garden, and the boy said to him, "How do I know that's a cherry tree?" Einstein said, "You don't, *but you have to assume something.*" This is why he pointed out, perhaps without knowing what you know, that **relativity has only existence in the realm of the dual; it doesn't exist in the realm of the Absolute.** So, any thesis based on relativity is only relative to the relative — and that's why you're always having trouble with them!

> **Move out from the Standpoint of God being All and see how your life unfolds.**

It is an incredible gift to be able to *think* of the Divine. The only way it is possible to think of the Divine is how? If you think of God as the Divine, God then is the thought, and that is the only time that thought enters as God-Thought. Therefore, it has often been said, "Think as God." How do you do *that?*

> **You know that God is Love; Love is All.**
> **You know that Love is the fulfilling of the Law, and**
> **you know that the Will that IS is the Love**
> **is the fulfilling of the Law**
> **and "I come to do Thy Will, O God,**
> **the Law (or Love) is written in the heart."**

Those are the thoughts that are like God. Your God can only be conceived in those thoughts that have nothing whatsoever to do, in essence, with the vulnerability of mortality.

Are there any questions? Yes, Nurit.

> *Nurit O:* I want to check an experience, but before that I must say that what you've been giving these days, Sir, is the redemption for all other Teaching.

Is it? I don't know. I don't call this *a Teaching;* **I call this *a service of Re-minding.***

> *Nurit O:* What you're giving is the freedom and it's the answer to everything.

Ramana Maharshi gave it very, very beautifully. He's the only other one I know; there may be dozens of others. As that Tibetan nun said, "I can't believe it's being given in English, an Absolute Teaching being given in English, such a dualistic language. How you do it is beyond my comprehension." She said it hadn't been given in her tradition for over three thousand years.

> *Nurit O:* That's exactly what came to me when I heard you, Sir, because I could not believe that what you're saying could be said in words. I asked questions for years and was always told, "You can't answer that. You just have to go within and, hopefully, one day the answer will come." I still can't believe how you can articulate what you do.

I have no idea how I do it. *You* tell me I do it; *I* don't know that I do it. So, you tell me; I don't know. I would never have spoken if somebody hadn't said, "It's just what I want to hear."

Because I thought, "How could I say what they wanted to hear when it's exactly the *opposite* of what they are?!" That's what used to concern me. They would say, "Thank you so much," and they'd kneel and they'd bow and they'd kiss my hand and thank me for what I had said. I thought, "Isn't this amazing!" In the beginning I questioned: "They want to hear what I've said, and it's not what they are at all!" It was this very approach that instantaneously healed cocaine addicts, drug addicts. They were active people again, working.

David K: And the miracles still continue!

Yes.

Nurit O: Yesterday, I was swimming early in the morning. It was very quiet and peaceful, and I was watching the mountains and the water and considering what we've been learning here about the senses perceiving. As I turned back to swim to the shore, my eyes met Linda P. There was an instant, a moment, when our eyes met, our attention met with a smile, and that moment there was a recognition. There was a total conviction that there was the presence of Consciousness in that second.

It has to be. The Consciousness is always present, even when you appear to die, because Consciousness is not in the body; only mentality is. **What you are consciously aware of will constitute your state of Beingness.**

Nurit O: Oh! I hear that totally differently now, Sir.

I don't know what you got in India in sixteen years, but that is it as far as this one knows.

Nurit O: It doesn't come close to this, Sir.

Recognition is in the eye of the beholder because that is where the attention is, and where the attention is, there am I also.

That's how *the world* is transparent. **Your *whole life* can be made transparent by the recognition of Essence and, therefore, the assimilation of it as Fact. Work from the Standpoint of the Divine and find divinity is expressing, in spite of the form, attributes of the God-Man.**

Yes, Eugene.

> *Eugene M:* Thank you, Sir. Before I ask my question, I want to thank you very much for the privilege of being here as your guest.

Oh, I'm so glad you're here!

> *Eugene M:* So am I! It's the most sacred experience.

You look very well.

> *Eugene M:* I'm reminded by what Nurit said that she had sixteen years in India: I had ten years in a Catholic monastery, and not one moment of it *ever* came *close* to the experience of ten minutes with *you!* I deeply, deeply appreciate that.
>
> The question is coming from the Unfoldment™ that you gave a few days ago. If I may, I'll just read a sentence to lead into it. "A dreamer cannot exist without some form of belief that triggers some sort of response, no matter how mundane or how elevated, because he has to have a reason for being and he invents what is necessary . . ." That's what is being considered, and this has always been with me. It seems to be a mental thing.

It's *all* mental!

> *Eugene M:* I have to be doing something, I have to have a reason for being. Then it was considered: *Being* on the highest level has no reason.

Actually, *there is no other existence than "the highest."* It's *thinking* that makes it lower!

> *Eugene M:* How should I regard a thought of having a reason, some particular activity (it could be a service to you; it could be a service to mankind)? How should I view that from the standpoint of being Actual?

You wouldn't need to.

> *Eugene M:* Just do?

There's no doer — only the one unto whom it's being done! The doer is only in the realm of the objective doing. I am forever still in my own Beingness. You call it active because you think it's something. I call it stillness because it's done!

> *Eugene M:* Thank you.

Yes, Greg.

> *Gregory S:* Sir, I wanted to make sure that I understood you correctly in what you said to-day, that emotionalism and desire are a tincture, more or less, that's rubbed off onto our memory banks which seduces us into believing the objective as if it were Real?

Yes, they are. But remember, it says, "This have I desired of the Lord."[2] It's not terrible to desire, but it *is* if it's fulfilling a *basic* desire. It has to be a "desire of the *Lord,*" in other words, of the Higher. The Lord is the Law.

Yes, Donna.

> *Donna C:* When I first met you and I came to Summer School for the first year, I remember saying to you that when you speak the words that you say, they are not talking *about* something; they actually *are* what you're saying. The State that you represent is there in the sound of the Word. It's right there. You are not talking *about* something.

That's what some say.

> *David K:* It's very true.

It's great that people feel so. Thank you.

> *Students:* Thank you, Sir.

⌘

---

1. Many students had visited the Montreal Botanical Gardens the previous day.
2. Psalms 27:4.

Penetrating the Seeming

Chapter IX

It is the energy that is radiant space that allows you to have a radiant physiognomy that reveals you may have penetrated the mysteries of the universe!

Penetrating the Seeming

Themes: Love ~ radiant energy ~ intention ~ creation ~ thought ~ object

This is the morning of June 27, 2003. As we enter the room and are set apart from the everyday world of unpredictable events, we are surrounded in a field of expectancy and we are wrapped in the garment of fulfilment and we are known to be more than "this."

You all have perceived a great deal of significance surrounding your creation, and one of the salient features is that the object is never denied, but its *appearance* is illusory.

We have also perceived that there is no spatial distance to mind. What is the distance, then, between the *object* and mind?

Students: There is none.

Its whole appearance is objectified, but *the appearance is mental.* The object cannot be denied. I don't want you to annihilate, because the creation is incredibly beautiful, but *the appearance is illusory.*

I would like to try to continue from where we left off. We touched on space and we touched on time, and now you know all about it! Huh! Perhaps the better way for this to unfold is for you to ask the question that may be revelatory for all of us and lead us into the Path that we can go on with this, because I'm not sure how people are viewing it.

Yes, Greg.

Gregory S: Sir, how can one have the attitude of expectancy without necessarily having a frame of mind?

You will *always* have a frame of mind. As long as you have a form, you'll have a frame of mind, but the mind — whatever that *is* — you'll have a frame of it.

Gregory S: Is expectancy in some way also receiving?

No. **Expectancy is the attitude of discovery.** Katrine.

Katrine G: Dr. Mills, you said that "energy uninterrupted is a ray."

Yes.

Katrine G: And "energy interrupted is a thought encapsulated."

It can be.

Katrine G: Is that which interrupts the energy the *thought,* which is then encapsulated?

Yes.

Katrine G: Or what is it that interrupts?

It's always the thought. It's the energy meeting resistance, called "a thought," that is encapsulated and is used as a word. It *can* be used as a word. Look what you're doing with your work. It's energy captured, as with an idea manifesting itself. The idea of what you're offering is substantial but it's all illusory.

Katrine G: Thank you, Sir.

Valerie.

Valerie W: Dr. Mills, in consideration of what you just started with this morning about the object, that the object isn't denied and yet it's illusory, when we come to what appears as a new place that we've never seen before, it appears that it must already be there.

No, it isn't. Somebody may have gone before you. As they always say, "The angel of the Lord has gone before you, and therefore all the lights are green." It's the universal concept of materiality and formation that allows you to think you're running into something that you haven't experienced before. It's an agreement among all of the *human* beings that they will see objectivity, but they don't understand *how* it's perceived and *they think it is Real* and, therefore, judge their life and every event by that experience. That is the unfortunate state of mankind. They have been trapped by false education (or incomplete education) into believing instead of into *knowing*.

Yes, Lucille.

> *Lucille J:* Dr. Mills, in the opening paragraph of the transcript that we have from June 22,[1] you describe the world as a "*conjured* world."

Yes, it is.

> *Lucille J:* The root of "conjured" is "together + to swear," which is perhaps pointing to this agreement of ones going before, of having come to this conjuring together. It's an amazing idea, Sir.

Yes, it is. Yes, Jo-ann.

> *Jo-ann V:* Is it correct to say that the Earth is an aspect of the completeness of the corresponding identity of God?

No. Okay, go on.

> *Jo-ann V:* And that the destruction of Earth only destroys the possibility to experience choice?

No, you can't destroy the idea. If you have the idea of Earth, it can't be denied but it's an illusion. It's not destroyed; it's illusory.

> *Jo-ann V:* So, there isn't a divine Idea, a concept in a liquid state, of the world?

No. Let me see how to tell you. . . . You're forgetting that *everything you're saying is mental*. So, your whole concept of "world" is mental but you think it into an orb. You're putting it in the lap of Consciousness as "God," and that's okay, but nothing is really created or destroyed. That's why the *divine* world is always intact. Only the object, not the *Idea* of it, can be created or destroyed.

Yes, Scarlette.

> *Scarlette L:* In walking, the senses seem to define what the experience is.

That's the purpose of them, to define your limited experience. It's the sixth and seventh that lead beyond the limited.

Scarlette L: Is the leap in attention?

Attention is the evidence of focussing. You are only aware of that upon which your attention rests. The other is there but you're not cognizant of it. It's like when you're massaging a muscle: the effectiveness of it is where your attention is; it's not the *muscle*. Actually, it's not the muscle responding at all; it's your attention that alters it. And the clearer *you* are, the more efficacious you will be. Remember, the improvement of the physical is a lessening of the physical confinement. **Remember, the improvement of the physical is a lessening of the material confinement.**

Scarlette L: It appears that change is only mental.

Of course. The Ancients had some idea of that when they said, "I AM the same yesterday, to-day, and forever." They had some inclination of it, but I'm sure they didn't cognize what you now know, or what you *should* now know. You can see what a shock it is to see the Truth of the variegated pattern of existence, but it also bears a great fruitage because it allows you to perceive your part or the part your Conscious-awareness State plays in creation.

Scarlette L: Sir, what is the role of the monarchy in that creation?

You mean the literal monarchy or the monarchy that I spoke about with regards to *your* state?

Scarlette L: Yes, Sir, that monarchy.

It's the monarchy that is rightfully yours provided you have the right credentials to sit on the throne. *Everyone* has a throne, but it's whether or not you have the credentials to sit on it. You can't sit on the throne from a divided state. That's why the king and queen represent the *undivided* State. Because they perhaps don't realize how important their state is (or they *do* realize how important it is), they remain very quiet with regards to the affairs of the world, so to speak. They are very important figures because there is the symbol of *balance,* supposedly, and **the equilibrium of** thought-force should be what is in authority, and that can't come from a divided state.

> *Scarlette L:* What does that equilibrium come from, Sir?

From the balanced State; it comes from balancing the masculine and the feminine, et cetera. It's a vast consideration, but that's what it is. It's the *thought-force* that has to be balanced. Remember, it's all thought; in other words, it's all energy in manifestation. This is what is forgotten; people go to sleep on this. We say the rock has no life; it may not have the life as *you* have life, but *in essence* you're no different from it. In essence the rock is as much an electrical field as *you* are; the reduction of it appears to be cold and solid and adamantine. **Your state is *exactly* the same: it's an electrical force-field radiating energy; it's a radiant energy.**

Okay! Marshall.

> *Marshall O:* Sir, is adoration a way to transform the objective confinement?

Adoration is the way that the mind is utilized in surrendering to the jurisdiction of what is known as Fact.

Jennifer, you had your hand up.

> *Jennifer M:* Dr. Mills, the moment yesterday when you asked if there was any space between the mentality and the cherry was a completely stunning moment!

Because there isn't. The only difference is: the cherry is *objective,* but it's still a thought-force; the appearance is still illusory, it's still mental. The object isn't in the mentality but the object couldn't appear *without the mentality!* There is no spatial distance between mentality and the thing.

Yes, Erika.

> *Erika Z:* Sir, you said the sixth and seventh senses are intuition and insight.

Yes, that's what is said.

> *Erika Z:* Yesterday I was playing around with the *five* senses —

Dear, you always are! [laughter]

Erika Z: — and experimenting with *seeing* more than hearing, or *hearing* more than smelling, or whatever it was, and tried to slip in *intuition*, on myself, or *insight*.

What a sandwich! [laughter] Go on.

Erika Z: I'm not even really sure what insight is. I realized that the five senses go with the form, but what do intuition and insight — ?

They go with *awareness*. **The senses are the antennae of the body. The intuition and insight give commands from a higher Authority, you might say.** What you receive intuitively is, as I said, seldom in agreement with what you *want* or the senses. When I was planning to go to New York to study and I had my trunks packed, and they were even at the station (I was going by train to New York), I was having my dinner with Mum and Dad and my nephew. I was eating and I had the fork to my mouth, and I put it down and I said, "Do you know something? I'm not going to New York to-morrow."

My father said, "What?!"

I said, "I'm not going to New York to-morrow. I know intuitively it's wrong. I *want* to go but I know intuitively it's wrong."

My mother started crying and she said, "I know it's right. I felt it was wrong from the beginning," and maybe that influenced me, but I don't believe so, because I had to face speaking to several of my sponsors, and especially Mr. Murchie, and he was *irate!* But I went back to Toronto, and was it ever wise, because that very year he had a heart attack, and within a year or so my scholarship collapsed. It's a complicated picture but it proved itself to be right because had I gone to New York, I would have been there as a student and could not have worked, and I would have given-up all my pupils in Toronto. When I went back to Toronto, I was glad because no matter what happened, I had started a studio and it was successful and it continued to grow, when the scholarship collapsed. You see, intuition was totally against *everyone else's* wishes.

> *Erika Z:* Yes, Sir. And when that intuitive impulse came to you, did it appear to be as a thought or as a statement of "I'm not going to New York"?

No. It appeared as *knowing*. There was no consideration at all. I didn't think a moment; I just said, "Do you know something? I am not going to New York to-morrow."

> *Erika Z:* Thank you. Is there a way to define insight or a way to describe it so that it's recognized when it's experienced?

Yes. *Others will verify it.* You never know you have insight until another is blessed by it.

> *Erika Z:* It seems that intuition and insight aren't about the form, they aren't about the person.

It certainly affects the suggested form.

> *Erika Z:* Are these two of the clues that we are not "this"?

If you penetrate the seeming enough, you would see that.

> *Erika Z:* When the intuitive promptings come, is it the mentality that discerns the prompting? You said it's the *knowing,* but it appears sometimes that it's a *mental conviction.* I don't know how to describe it. For me, it sometimes feels almost like a thought, a contrary thought. You said that you know because it goes against everything you're planning or thinking.

Usually it does, because you never depend upon an intuition when you are perfectly contented with where you're at. **Intuition is usually present for one who is exploring possibilities.**

> *Erika Z:* Thank you so much, Sir.

Yes, Nauby.

> *Nauby P:* Sir, is it exploring possibilities that activates those two additional senses?

Exploring possibilities is mental. As a result of your explorations, you may bear another state of knowingness, and if you want to know what to *do* with it, then you may depend upon intuition to guide you. It's that far removed; it's those steps.

Nauby P: It's such a blessing to be here. Thank you.

Thank you. Yes, Bob.

Robert M: Sir, one of my favourite places in the world is the formal garden at Villa Naka, and I have observed that the way you organized that space, with hedges and rows of flowers and shrubs and trees, the space is at one time open and at the same time it's layered in such a way that it seems to prepare a base for discovery.

Yes.

Robert M: Then, space offers an opportunity for creative use of that space.

Of course. *You're* using it. You wouldn't appear objectified if it wasn't for the garment of space; you wouldn't have any appearance, you wouldn't have even the structure of a form; you would dissipate, because **it is the energy that is radiant space that allows you to have a radiant physiognomy that reveals you may have penetrated the mysteries of the universe!**

Now, the next. Yes, Barry.

Dr. Barry B: Sir, yesterday you said the foremost and most subtle outlet of the Divine is the Breath and then its formation as the Word. Is there a feature of the sound experience that is *not* mental?

There is *nothing* that is not mental! That's why it's said, "Let the divine Mind that IS be in you also"[2]; in other words, arrive at that State where you see creation as it is and God a living Force. Remember, you created the name of "God"; you called God as a sound into your experience. He didn't call mortality into *His!* He knows nothing of it! There is no such thing as a He or a She; it's better as *He-She* or *It*. It doesn't deny anything; it does nothing but *exalt* the Wonder of the divine creation or what? The ineffable act of Wonder. That's why intuition and insight birth wonder and wisdom, because they walk hand in hand when you start to see *the incredible wonder* of this creation, which is constantly sustained as long as you are aware of it. You're not aware of this creation at all when you sleep.

Yes, Michael.

> *Michael S:* I appreciated your speaking about cherries and, this morning, about walnuts and peaches.

They're delicious!

> *Michael S:* The fact is that you are here and you're not "in a bowl," and I'm experiencing you, at the very least, right at this moment, as *radiance* that is certainly not what I would experience in my quotidian, normal existence. You just mentioned that word three times. My consideration about radiance, if I can use that just for a moment because it isn't in a mental realm, is that it is a pivotal concept that would include the mental, because it has to be, as a concept, but there is a vibrational frequency in radiance that is not like a cherry or a walnut or any other object.

It is. It is the *essence* of the cherry and the walnut. It's the essence of them and it's the essence of what appears as *you!*

> *Michael S:* When you start saying that we're creating this world at every moment —

Every moment.

> *Michael S:* — then are we creating (and I don't mean to say this in any presumptuous way) what appears as *you?*

Yes. You don't exist unless I focus my attention on you, and then what do I do? I focus my *radiation* upon you. I hope it's radiation, not thought.

> *Michael S:* Sir, it's radiation!

Yes. That's the way you should consider *me.*

Let your thoughts be seasoned with Love,
But let radiance dawn as seemingly from above!

It's the radiance of Being that appears as the magnet of Love! Yes, Michael.

> *Michael G:* Sir, since there is no space between the cherry and mentality, there can then be no space between the cherry on the other side of the world, or on the other side of the universe, and mentality.

That's right.

> *Michael G:* Even if it is outside of our immediate awareness.

It isn't outside your immediate awareness. You just *described* where it was! This is why, if anyone calls from Japan or China or the Philippines for help because they are ill, they don't expect it to take several days to get there by *post!* There is no distance, and *it's there like that!* Yet they're not in the same time zone . . . but it has nothing to do with time!

Yes, Lynn.

> *Lynn S:* Dr. Mills, being here in this rarefied atmosphere is such a heightening of our receptive ability, and I'm wondering, is there a difference between reception and conception when it's so sensitized in this way? I've made a leap, I think, from what we've been talking about, but I was considering it in terms of the precipitation of an art piece.

Is there any difference between reception and conception? There *is* a difference, but they coalesce in the creation, because reception allows, conception utilizes, and the outcome is the art! That's the way it may work.

> *Lynn S:* And to keep that allowing —

You don't keep it allowing! That is your state as an *artist*. That is your state.

> *Lynn S:* But it must be that everyone knows it; they just don't allow it.

Everyone knows the *words;* they don't know what it is to *swim* in them. It's one thing to say, "That's a lake," and everyone says, "Oh, look at the beautiful lake!" It's one thing to *perceive* it; it's another thing to *experience* it. **Conception is unconfined provided it's uncontaminated by thought.** Conception is an incredible act that happens really without thought. The perception of it *is* thought; the conception of it seems always to be thoughtless, it just happens.

Yes, Chloe.

> *Chloe M:* Sir, your divine Presence is so inspiring. When we're in your Presence and in this *Unfoldment*™ during the Summer Festival, there's always the feeling that anything is possible! Recently, a directive was given about creating timetables, and I know this has been a discipline that you've pointed out that you have engaged all your life. Sir, by doing the activity of a timetable, does this allow one to precipitate what is envisioned with responsibility and commitment?

Yes, because it curtails the stimulation of doing something else in place of what you have scheduled. *Your day is scheduled according to your intention.* Is it to be wasted by phone calls, by trips to the grocery store, or by whatever you do? **Don't break your timetable, because that is scheduling your focussed attention to birth experience which will be recognized and appear as your substance, because you are in the service role of offering to others what they themselves don't have the time to go out and procure.**

> *Chloe M:* Sir, is that the difference between being *in* time and being *on* time?

Being in the timetable is the evidence of being on time!

> *Chloe M:* Does that open the whole ability to have vision?

Your timetable should correspond to your vision.

> *Chloe M:* That's why it's done *prior to* the day.

Always. You never do the timetable at the end of the day! [laughter] No, no, no, no!

Yes, Suzanne.

> *Suzanne C:* I'm so thankful to be here, and I love you so much! I'm so high in the energy here and I ask myself how can I continue to be always in that kind of energy?

You know Energy IS, *oui?* If Energy IS and you *know* it, it's only when you *think about it* that it lessens. **Energy is constant; it's only your thought that reduces it.** So, when you go into your nursing and act in that field of service, you are the divine Energy contained in form to radiate the wonders of healing and blessing to your patients. That's done, usually, in calmness and a loving attitude. That is maintaining the energy. **Energy maintains you; you don't maintain energy.** Okay?

You go about being not Florence Nightingale but Florence "Light-gale"! Then they'll feel the energy! "Where were you when the cyclone struck?!"

Yes, Michael.

> *Michael A:* First of all, I want to thank you, Sir, for what you've offered here in words and also for the carrier wave of your Presence which has probably imparted as much, if not more, information than the words themselves. At different times, and the other day, you've said that when we close our eyes, the world ceases to exist.

Yes, to *you*.

> *Michael A:* Yes. My particular perspective at different times has just been of "eyelids closing." Then, in consideration of nothing is truly solid, it has been that everything is mostly space, that the illusion of "eyelids closing" is not what's really happening to shut off the world.

Oh, no. It's the reduction of, primarily, awareness. You're always Conscious, even if you appear to be unconscious. That's what I'm appealing to in most people! [laughter] Go on.

> *Michael A:* Really it's, in effect, a simple act of *altering*.

You can rest. You don't have to rest in oblivion; you can rest in *awareness*. I do that quite a lot; I don't sleep a great deal. I have my eyes closed, but the awareness never seems to stop.

David K: No, Sir.

Nurit.

Nurit O: This has to do with what we talked about: having precipitated you in our experience, Sir. With the exercise we did the other day, it brought back the time that I remember actually walking in the forest and wishing — I didn't know at the time that that's what I was doing, that I was imaging you in my life, Sir, but I remember asking for the specific qualities of a Master that you are evidencing in my life right now, and that was so fabulous and amazing. I see from what we've learned now that, yes, that was a mental exercise perhaps, because the mentality was used in claiming those attributes; at the same time, there was a very intense longing, and in meeting you, it was very evident, and it still is, that my connection with you is one of the heart, Sir.

Yes.

Nurit O: How does that come-in with the mentality, Sir?

It's all mental, but that doesn't mean it's *nothing*. You have been taught to believe that mentality is *a mental case,* but mentality is a case of the *upper* case because mentality is everything that constitutes your experience in selection, in action, in creativity and everything. But the prompting is that doing something in this three-dimensional aspect always has to be considered — which most people have never done; they've considered *a belief in operation.* They believe so much in what they have been taught, and usually what they have been taught is that you are *a thinker thinking thoughts* and, frequently, thinking those that are not your own because you walk into the force-field of otherness, and that mixes with *your* sea of energy, of radiant energy. That's how it happens.

You are like the light bulb. The filament within the piece of glass is what gives off the light, which *isn't* light but we *say* it is because it diminishes the darkness. The *body* is like that: it isn't the Light, but it exudes that which is termed "the Light." Then, we have to come to understand what the Light *is.* **It's all mental, but that doesn't make it a degraded state; it means that it's subject to *your* control according to your intention.** It's always subject to your control by your intention. *That is the great gift!* You are not vulnerable provided you don't stoop to suggestion. What happens when you stoop to suggestion? It leads you to believe that you can think your way out of that which was thought-in anyway! You *thought* yourself *into* this experience and you forgot that the thought was bonding you to limitation.

The divine Love that man feels is certainly mental, but it can't be found in the mental and it can't be found in the body; *the body exudes it as radiance!*

> *Nurit O:* In your answer to Erika's question, "Are insight and intuition two of the clues that we are not 'this'?" you said, "If you penetrate the seeming enough, you would see that." How do you "penetrate the seeming"? What is the activity that goes with that?

I did it with the cherry. This cherry seems just to be what you know it is, *only from the testimony of the senses*. What the senses *don't* tell you is that it is, under close scrutiny, made-up of molecules, atoms, neutrons, protons, electrons, and what are *they?* All constituents of the electrical force-field. That's *all* that constitutes "this." That's why when you eat it, it's supposed to provide you with what you need. In essence, it's a contained form of energy, as a walnut is and as a peach is!

> *Nurit O:* Oh, got it! Thank you so much.

Yes, David.

> *David N:* I know I've spoken with you about this question before, but even after a very short period of time it takes on a slightly different quality because of what you've said in the last hour. You said this week that "all reasoning should be from Cause to effect," and you have just shown that, over and over again this morning, but it prompts the question of how to distinguish the Cause from the effect because it's not, necessarily, readily obvious. The way that I came to this questioning was through the idea of space being alive, as you have presented it this week.

"Alive" as *radiant energy*.

> *David N:* Yes, Sir. Alive as radiant energy. The reasoning from Cause to effect that prompted my consideration was, really, there's no separation between me and anything.

Anything that you are aware of, there is no separation.

> *David N:* There's no separation.

That's why people don't like to become aware of other people's condition because that brings responsibility and compassion and help, et cetera.

> **Most people don't want to know the condition of another *because there's no separation.* The only difference is, if they seem to be diseased, you know that it's a lie because, in the Light of what is known, there's nothing but divine Energy, and it can never run rampant or be misdirected. The Divine is declaring the non-materiality of what appears and the divine Presence in essence as the knowingness of the invincible nature of the Ineffable.**

> *David N:* The phrase that's been coming to me this morning with regard to this is "For this cause came I."

Yes. The **I** cannot be found in anything other than a thought, and that I-thought is the same thing as I AM, when freed from the personality and egotistic endowments.

> *David N:* Thank you very much.

Yes, Margaret.

> *Margaret M:* Dr. Mills, is it the power of the knowing that I am not bound to time and space that actually rescinds the suggested laws of this dimension?

The suggested laws of *limitation.* You have to abide by the laws of the land and live the Law of the Invisible! (Somebody will ask me, "What is the Law of the Invisible?" I know it's coming! Why don't you try to tell *me* what it is?!) Go on.

> *Margaret M:* Is there a power when we are all together? Is there a critical mass that is formed that can actually

free that suggested limitation for all and can bless anyone who is attuned in this very moment?

Yes, it can, even if they're not, **because a critical mass is self-generating. When it's once started, it's self-generating and it can change the rhythmic beat of anyone who is out of step with the Divine.** That is the value of *community.* That's the value of a meditation group. That's the value of anything you do. It's not necessarily to *socialize,* it's to *realize* that through the reduction of the personal involvement with your effort to meditate, you rescind all the suggestion of otherness and only the fructifying power of the Light is evidenced in that half-hour, because in *that* you actually can alter; it can extend for miles.

At Jackie's home in 1968–69 (I was there with Jaan), we had a chat with a clairvoyant, and she was one of the most incredible clairvoyants I've ever known. She astounded us all by saying that the auric field had been so raised that it could be seen for twenty-five miles in all directions! And (I've got a better one!) another psychic came to visit me in 2001 who was clairvoyant and she said . . .

David K: She said it was over *fifty* miles.

And I said, "I must be making progress!" [laughter] Yes, James.

> *James T:* Dr. Mills, thank you so much for offering this question period this morning. I believe it was on Sunday you said that the AM-ing of the I is the practicality of your life on Earth to experience choice.

Yes, that's right.

> *James T:* Sir, why is it necessary to experience choice?

Undoubtedly (we'll create a good story!) you came because you were bored, you were tired of planting trees and creating other people's gardens![3] You didn't do that on the other plane; maybe you got bored with the effortlessness of Being and you'd forgotten what the point of choice was. Choice carries with it a unique energy-field: it can either raise or lower the experience. Some of us say the reason everyone experiences this plane is to experience choice, because here they have the chance to engage the energy that surrounds dichotomy. **It doesn't exist when you have once clearly defined your intention. Then you have the energy constant without being weakened by duality.**

Choice always comes pronged: "this" or That.

> *James T:* The other question that was written down, Sir, was, Is it necessary to experience choice to gain a freedom?

Yes. You *appear* to experience choice to be free. It's a big choice to take the High Way of the Christ or the Self in contradistinction to taking the highway of a belief-system. **The Christ is beyond belief.** The Exemplar for everyone, in the historical realm, was Jesus. Jesus became the Christ, or He "degreed." His degree was the Christ, in other words, His realization of His divine at-Onement with the Source He termed "the Father." That's how it goes.

> *James T:* Thank you, Dr. Mills.

Yes, Judy.

> *Judith M:* In answering Margaret just a moment ago, you said, "Try to tell me what is the Law of the Invisible." What came was this: It is the Love of the Unknown before it is formed.

That's very nicely put. It's the Love of the Unknown that brings forth the form *if it's needed to satisfy the need.*

> *Judith M:* The concepts of space and time — and what you've done in this moment, right now, is collapse all that in the concept that it's all mental, and what I see is a recognition of What is present — which I'm amazed that we precipitated into our experience, because it is the greatest Grace. We must be master magicians to bring such a Grace into our experience.

The Master Magician must have been behind my appearance, because it was such a magical experience!

> I didn't know I could speak, other than to converse
> in time.

I never knew I could see, only the elements of time.
I didn't know I could taste but the fruitage of
    the vine.
I didn't know I could feel, other than the emotions
    wrapped-up in the mind.

But then I came to know this divine fact at hand,
That all those accoutrements are there to bless
    the man
Who knows within his Being this salient fact divine:
That he is more of the heavenly State than he is the
    human kind.

Donna.

> *Donna C:* Thank you. On Sunday, June 22, you said, "What the object is remains only described by the state that has projected it. It has no intrinsic value whatsoever."

No, other than as thought. Go on.

> *Donna C:* What I perceived from that is you've allowed us to pry the attention from the objective and realize, in that moment of freedom, our real creativity and an opportunity (which I used to consider a responsibility, but now I see it as *an opportunity*) to imbue the objective with a meaning from a higher Point.

Exactly!

> *Donna C:* Which makes life so much more exciting, Sir!

Which makes your *sense* of life more meaningful. That's good.

> *Donna C:* Thank you, Sir. It's so freeing!

Yes, Barbara.

> *Barbara W:* For so many years when you've told the story of being in your garden at your home on Hollywood Avenue in Toronto and seeing through a leaf, it sounded so poetic and so wonderful, but it's been these

few days that we've spent with you that you've allowed us to see the mystery of seeing through that leaf. That is so exciting.

Look at the leaves of the mind you've gone through!

Barbara W: Whole forests! Thank you so much.

A whole thousands of pages! It was in the Walled Garden in Tucson that I had that incredible experience with the bird. At my lovely place in Arizona there were several gardens, and one was called the Walled Garden because it was surrounded by a brick wall about eight or ten feet high. (It just dawns on me now, on the entire parapet of brick, every twelve inches there was a fleur-de-lys. The emblem of France was around me and I didn't even realize it at the time. I just *loved* it.)

I used to go out into that garden in the early morning if it wasn't too hot, because I loved sitting there. One morning I went out and I found, to my dismay, a large dead bird. It had struck the window of the Lemon Room. The windows were ten by ten and the walls were practically all glass, and although I kept curtains on the windows so that the birds would not think of them as transparent, this poor bird, I guess, was out too late the night before [laughter] and he flew into the window sometime during the night. In the morning he was dead, just rigid as could be.

I picked it up and put it on the top of the brick wall so that nothing would happen to it. As I sat in the garden, I thought, "*What a suggestion this state is.*" I was deep in contemplating life and the suggestion that confronted me as the bird, and I was startled by seeing this bird struggling with its feet and its wings. It was on its back and it suddenly flipped over and flew away!

The bird seemed to be happy. The other one that was moved from the dead, she wasn't so happy. I only mention it because Rick was the one who caught her when she fell to the floor and was pronounced dead. They called me from my other house in Arizona (her daughter was here at a Lecture), and they said, "She's passed." I said, "Put the telephone to her ear until I speak to her." I did, and she moved, to everyone's amazement, and came to, and they got her up and she sat in a chair and went home. The fascinating part of it was, she was so angry at coming back into the body. She became one of my verbal enemies in Tucson; she so resented coming back into the body. But, you know, if it had been her destiny to go, she would not have come back. Since I told her what I did tell her, she was restored.

Rick F: Absolutely, Sir.

Yes, you saw it. You were right there, and so was Steve.

Rick F: Yes, Sir. Steve made the call to you, Sir.

Yes, Hermine.

Hermine G: Dr. Mills, in my career in the hospital, one aspect of what was happening there that has always been a wonder to me is the fact that someone would have an area removed and there was still a sense of it. I just wanted to ask you how that could happen.

The mental always retains the sense impression. It has nothing to do with the *limb*. It is the *impression* of a limb that still *lives within the remembrance,* and it's that impression that sensitizes what appears as the limb. I don't know what *that* experience is like, but I always remember when I had lost control of my arms and my legs and I didn't know whether I was going to be able to use them or not. I would start to pick-up my hand, and it wouldn't move. It was the most *unbelievable* experience because I could feel the movement in the arm but it never happened! I could feel the movement in the legs to take a step and I wouldn't take the step and I would fall!

Hermine G: Thank you for that, Dr. Mills.

It's the *impression* that's so interesting, Hermine. You have the impression and you must get rid of the impression to get rid of the sensation. This is the same thing *when you have the impression that someone is difficult. You have to get rid of that impression in order to realize the true Nature.* You have to let it go.

David K: You've always said, "You are not the reflection; you are the expression."

You are not the reflection; you are *the expression.* A reflection can be broken, because a mirror can be shattered, but the expression can't be.

Hermine G: Another area that has also taken the interest is, in looking under the microscope at slices of tissue, after it's stained, if you weren't aware that it was a slide, you would see mountains and rivers in that configuration. Is it that there are just those limited images that the mentality has and so you would see — ?

Anything can remind you of them. They are impressions, and of anything that you have as an impression, you can see a correspondence in practically anything. Yes, it's amazing.

Hermine G: Thank you very much, Dr. Mills. It's just such a wonderful life that you have given me from being in your Presence.

Yes, Nancy.

Nancy M: Thank you, Dr. Mills, for sharing your incredible insight and Love. Sir, when one states their intention, their heartfelt intention of life, does the Grace of Life configure those circumstances that one must go through in order to achieve the fulfilment of that intention?

It could.

Nancy M: I have accepted that, and that's why in circumstances that I deal with, I just realize that this is perhaps a grace, it's an experience.

It comes to you to give itself up *because you know what IS,* and any situation that is inharmonious comes to you to give itself up. Where else can it go? You know, it's like a child in school: if they think two and two is five, they can only go to a teacher who can show them that it's four and how it *is* four.

Nancy M: I have found that the statement "I will never leave you comfortless"[4] has been a great grace in my life, because it's the comfort that is present in those situations of showing a child or anyone the rightness of a situation. Then there's the other fact: *we create our own experience.*

Yes, you do.

Nancy M: It takes a lot of daring to do that because one wouldn't want to create something that would take you —

No. I don't feel that *you* will do that, although many people have left because they have *altered* the creative act. They created the act to be here, and then they altered it because they felt that being here was restrictive. It's not being *here* that is restrictive; it's *the shock of Truth that reveals their shortcomings* that appears disturbing — not restrictive, *disturbing.*

As I say, the best way to view the circumstances that appear is: they come to you to give themselves up. That's the way I know. You can't accept them as yours. Say, "Get thee behind me, Satan," when they try to be "yours." Yes, Ken.

Ken B: Dr. Mills, you have shown us this week in great detail how we create the objective world through our conscious attention to it. We also create many situations that we, in one way, seemingly more consciously create an object of art, and we create other things. Is there a difference in these qualities of creation, or is it more or less what Donna was saying that we can learn to imbue the way that we create our objective world to a much greater degree?

Yes, you can. You can imbue your art because your art will carry whatever your *intention* is. Your intention sometimes in art is not defined until it's framed. *And that is like your life.* It's only when you have done from your highest motivation, your highest Standpoint, that the result is known. It's like my own life. I didn't know that this was going to happen, but it's been framed, *I've been framed!* When I offered to speak, I didn't dream I was going to give-up piano teaching, piano playing. It was my sole source of income, and I was earning a fine living. So, you just *allow* what you are doing to bear its own fruitage if you are moving from the highest Standpoint.

Ken B: I think I may be struggling with the idea of using the word "create." I have been using it up until now in a conscious way but not realizing that at all times we are creating our objective world. I think I need to be with that idea more.

Yes, because you *are* creating it totally. You wouldn't experience it if it wasn't your own creation. That's the problem of being an Earthian. Yes, Claude.

> *Claude C:* In the light of what we have just heard, I really was very excited at this concept of framing! First, I want to thank you for permitting us to be received as your guests. I can't really say any words that convey our appreciation. Our whole family, we like to believe, is built on the Spirit as a foundation, but in going through life we go again through various stages of confusion and thought-projection that keep us from the Source. I think you have created a well of radiance among us, in our family, and I see that we are all drinking from it. I think that the next step that we have to decide on is commitment.

You might as well, because you *are* committed! In English, we say "your goose is cooked"! [laughter] And it's the golden one.

> *Claude C:* The partaking of the Feast is the next step, I would suppose.

Yes. You've just had that, too, but you will realize it!

> *Claude C:* Thank you very much.

Thank you, Claude.

> *Claude C:* I would like to, on the framing perspective that you presented —

I'm sure all yours are gold-leafed!

> *Claude C:* Most of them, Sir. I think that it is very evident to me and in the light of what most people have said here, that what we are trying to achieve is to see *beyond matter*.

Beyond the objective. That's better.

> *Claude C:* Yes, beyond the objective, to see the underlying energy behind everything. Great art teachers have told us to start by re-educating our senses — to smell, to

see, to hear things differently — and from that it gives us a new vision of the objective world. It would seem that the next step would be to define and to re-define what we perceive so that it becomes knowledge. And the third step would be to —

You've done that second one, these past three days.

Claude C: Yes, we have. The next step would seem to be to develop the ability to think *abstractly.*

You are doing that very well. You see, I don't want you to get yourself into a *laboured* position. *It's effortless Being!*

Claude C: Yes, it is. So, the effortless direction that this is pointing towards would be to consider viewing the world as we would through expression and appreciation of art.

Yes, and the art of each other, the art of everything, because there is nothing that exists that isn't art in some form. It's by the suggestion that it's material that it becomes distorted.

Claude C: So, this is really pursuing the sixth and seventh senses?

This is the evidence of the sixth and seventh senses being the servants of those senses that are beyond conception. This is where the redeemed imagination is found unconfined by the thoughts commensurate with any human hypotheses.

This has to be it. You know, it's been almost two hours!

Students: Thank you, Dr. Mills.

⌘

1. See Chapter V.
2. Philippians 2:5.
3. James is a professional landscape designer in Toronto.
4. John 14:18.

The Presence of Truth

Chapter X

A human being is bound to being human. The only thing that is not bound is your ability to identify being human! If you are human and being human, can you question what is the being that a human is?

The Presence of Truth

Themes: The Thoughtless ~ Identity ~ Presence ~ Law of Attraction ~ Force ~ radiance ~ freedom ~ within-ness ~ energy

This is the morning of July the first, 2003. Somehow or other when you say "July" you always think of the *fourth* because somebody's celebrating something termed "independence" and celebrating a sense of freedom.

Isn't it amazing to realize how a point of view, unless it's based on a point of Actuality, is seldom correct? The activities of nations that are turbulent are a sure sign of a faulty foundation, in the people perhaps but in the government for sure. It is the pointing to a misunderstood, or *not understood,* use of force. "Force" is the term used in distinction to a somnambulistic state or to a lethargic state, a pathetic state. It is a quality that every hue-man has, but it is one that needs direction, and **the only positive direction this force can have is when it is *Self*-directed.**

Force in the hands of imbeciles is there to be misused first and foremost by the tactic of fear. Then the big question is to *manifest* the fear, and they organize ways and means to perpetuate it, while you resist this only up to the point that clarity remains evidenced. But if you are deluded in the realm of identity, you are subject to the insults surrounding personality.

Divinity cannot be conceived as bearing a mask, and divinity requires no medium, therefore no sounding box, through which to offer the "propaganda" of holiness!

Personality takes the exclusivity surrounding the uniqueness of Being and dwarfs it into the channels of the mind that are taught they are insufficient to cope with the knowing of the selected few who know how to wield psychological power by dwarfing man's first contact with the thought-process of "Who am I?" by saying the right thing ("Thou art the Son of God") but "you have been conceived in sin." There is nothing more forlorn than to be told that you are conceived in sin when you had nothing whatsoever to do with the conception. The first thing you must think of is: in what condition were your "conceptors"?

I said here in this book:

> The fact is that Man is One; the myth is that he will *become* One.

People must see, as never before, the hoax that has been played upon you. For you to feel that you are human beings extricating yourselves from being human is really quite something to consider. **A human being is bound to being human. The only thing that is not bound is your ability to identify being human! If you are human and *being* human, can you question what is the being that a human is?** That is your main stop: What is your keynote to being human? Somebody must have the answer. I asked all kinds of people who should have known: I would go to the nuns and ask them; I'd ask the priest when I had a chance . . . and not spoil his appetite! [laughter] When he was at the house frequently on Saturday evenings, he said to my mother, "Please, Mrs. Mills, if you're going to give me food, be sure you give it to me before midnight because I have to celebrate Mass to-morrow morning!" So, we'd always feed Father Gillan and his assistant before midnight, because they'd come at eight and they'd still be there at midnight or after. He just loved to talk with me, so he said.

It is interesting that when you question being, you are suddenly questioning activity, and when you are questioning activity, you are acknowledging *there must be force*. So, one of the foundational elements surrounding your presence is *being Force*. How many men evidence *being Force?* How many *women* evidence *being Force?* Now, everyone can be very forceful about their opinions, but remember no opinion ever flies! You've got the *o* before it, which is "nothing" or emptiness. It's the *pinions* that are used in your eagle; that is what is used in flight. How can you experience your force if you limit it by personalization? **The greatest limit to force is the insecurity that arises from a false identity!**

To allow people to say you are "in the becoming" is quite all right; you just accept it. That is the way it appears because you have accepted being human, but in actuality, it isn't that way *at all*. You are primarily what?

Students: Conscious-Being.

This is why one of the features I have spoken to you about, this past year and the year before and the year before and the year before, is Identity. Your birth certificate only allows you to be known as part of the illusion! The passport allows you to go to different countries, but how many have found the port whereby you can come and go at will? This is the important one, the one whereby you can be what somebody else wants you to be and expects you to be, and remain what you really are.

That is your mission. You can be the loving, sweet, adorable, all-embracing daughter, knowing full well that you are much more than that! And you can be the same loving, adoring son. Knowing the Truth, you allow what is the picture to represent it by your very power of imbuing the picture with *force*. That is termed "attraction."

The Law of Attraction is paramount in your arsenal of knowingness because the Law of Attraction is built on the fact that **Love is the divine Attraction.** It is the divine Magnet that draws any magnetized particle to it if it is unlike it. (Yes! If it is *unlike* it.) That's why you are surrounded by people. When you know the Truth you will draw everyone to you who doesn't know it so that they may be imbued with the *force* of its presence.

The force of the presence of Truth is the energy that will really separate.

If someone doesn't want to know the Truth, you will find that individual doesn't approach you again. Just saying that your life is based on realizing That can cause the withdrawal of so many of your friends, with no hard feelings. Within a matter of a year or so, what I called three hundred "friends" — they really were just acquaintances, but we had a lot of communication, we did much together: receptions and concerts and classes and music lessons. But, as soon as they knew that I was going to devote my life to what I appear to be doing, without one word said, I never saw *any* of them again. I used to send about three hundred cards at Christmas; in a very short time I sent *six*. Truth as your experience may influence your friends, and it certainly will be noticed by those who are not your friends.

Why is the dualistic approach to existence so exalted among mankind? *Because in multiple belief-systems there is no power.* The only power in multiple belief-systems is the power that results from agreeing with one another. The power of the people in the *fundamental* churches is so incredible. Their hearts are right, but the doorway to what they are wishing is not primarily a person who is only a myth to them; it's the *Love He represented* that is the doorway. He kept saying that "'Tis the Father that doeth the Work." But there's no work to *Being;* the work is in the *thoughts* of Being. *That's* why you get tired: you're thinking about Being! Stupid! [laughter]

You can't think about Being; *Being is beyond your thought!* Being is the Force that allows you to have an interior computer programmed, and now *re-programmed* to give you the correct information when you need to type in "Oh, for God's sakes, give me the correct answer. I'm confused about the former program!" As Chris pointed out this morning, the tendency of so many people, he feels, is that they know they have a program that is faulty, but they try to insert *This* into that program, and it can't be done! You have a new Program; you can't insert it into your old one. If you do, you'll have a double exposure, in other words, a distorted picture. You cannot go on having this exposure to duplicity when in *simplicity* is *Allness*.

There is no effort in being *Real;* the struggle comes in trying to *juggle* the Real and the unreal. Then you go to what you now know: that when you look at the cherry, you know what? That its body is made-up of atoms, molecules, nuclei, protons, neutrons, which are all individual to the cherry. And guess what? *You have an electrical force-field.* In the cherry is a miniature nuclear plant! Yes, in the cherry! It's energy. Why do you think you eat it? The reason it nourishes you is because the essence of it is energy. You had thought it was the *food* that was energy; it isn't. That object is the carrying form of energy that can be *assimilated* by the "interiorness," or what they term the "within-ness" or the fifth dimension. All the electrical force-field and everything about it is on the *fourth*. This is why these cherries are nourishing: they all are custodians of uncontaminated energy because it's the energy that corresponds to their form, their texture, and their colour. *Your energy is the same.* You are a fruit on the vine of the tree of Life. **You are the apple of the eye of God.**

This is what you must know! Don't ever forget it, Remy.[1] It's terribly important for young people like Remy to know this because he is *the future* and he may be a great leader. **Why is a leader great? Because he is not fooled by the suggestion of a mass**

belief. You don't have to shout it from the rooftops, but you can live knowing the Fact in the face of fiction.

Don't go out trying to change anyone's belief-system unless they've asked you, "What makes you so attractive?" "What makes you happy?" "What makes you joyous?" "What makes you lovable?" You can say, "It's knowing what I *AM* instead of what I *appear* to be. No wonder you ask, because that's what *you* are, too." And then start being coy and flicking your eyelashes and let people realize the importance of pursuing the Real instead of dwelling constantly in the virtual.

The only fear a robot has is being discovered to have limitations.

Why do we have "know-it-alls"? They are afraid of being discovered as having limits. That's why you have patience with arrogance, to all appearances, and you are *ruthless* with it because it's standing in the way of them pursuing the simple. **The simplicity of Truth is made complex by the compound of mentality with emotionalism.**

We have always said "the radiance of Spirit," and this is so true. Now you know why. Don't go home and tell your parents, "I'm an electrical force-field, Mum." They'll say, "How about plugging-in then and doing some dusting?!" [laughter] "And make your bed and polish your shoes!" So, don't reveal what you know; you'll be in for a lot of work.

The radiance is the result of meeting the obstruction of the form which reflects it. You are not a reflection; you are the expression. If another finds you reflecting, they will know that it's the "within-ness" appearing without. The great movement is to the higher sense of Being, which some have described as "from sense to Soul." What is being actually said is: more and more alignment of thought to the point of the Thoughtless, where the name of God is not known. As long as you can name *anything*, it is still within the realm of the three dimensions. It only ceases to be in the realm of the three dimensions when you transcend the belief that you are in the third always, and move to the realization of the mental state and the cosmic Mind above that.

Every enunciation of freedom is from the level of what men have called "the cosmic Mind," which means that it doesn't deal with the mundanities of the mundane; it deals with that realm of thought where radiation and radiant energy are conceived and bear form, and with the state of awareness that allows the reception of ideas before they are reduced to concepts and into manifestation in demonstration. This is why an idea isn't divine but is the evidence of divinity. It points to that level that is beyond the five-sense level entirely but is *known to be* through the sixth and the seventh. And then you move-on to where there's no *sense* to any of it! Then look at the sense that's being used to give it!

It's extremely practical. This is why when you attune thyself unto the state of Actuality, you bear a radiance and an energy-field that can't help but bless those who walk *through your presence*. They walk *through* your presence. The more *actual* of your presence is what? The more actual of your presence is the energy-field or the auric-field. The auric-field is what those who have sight of the fourth dimension perceive, but usually those who receive those messages can't receive them to give a message from the Higher Way; they have to go into trance. That is a carry-over from centuries ago. Most people who trance have not moved to the level that is truly emancipated. The mind is still giving the state but not in a conscious way.

Don't believe anything anyone tells you about karma or anything else if it can't be applicable to your *God*-Being. Remember, your karma is the effect of a cause, the *incompleted* effect of a cause. "You" may have it, but it doesn't mean it can't be taken care of in the correct summation of Being. That is one of the magnanimous gifts of the Light. It never holds any sincere seeker in the bondage of belief if they have cut the bonds of belief.

Before we leave this about radiance, I want to read you something.

> It is a universal fact that Man is One.
> It is a universal myth he will *become* One.

I said this on January 22, 1998, in the Salle des Etoiles, and I imagine it was to the New Yorkers. I just want to read you this other incredible statement that David mentioned. I gave this sometime, I think, in December 1998:

> You are radiating beings, utilizing bodily forms to emanate a radiation that will restore the health benefits of the Star Kingdom to the glazed eyes of time.

I said on December 23, 2002:

> You cannot be natural in the presence of Allness if you are only *a part* of It.

Dr. Hendrik de Lange said in November 1960:

> Continuity is experienced because false measurement (time and space) cannot altogether hide the eternality of existence.

On April 16, 2002, I said:

> Hell is the energy it takes to support division.
>
> Superstition allows contradictions to exist without confrontation.

I said:

> The devil wants you to forget the routine of wise investments (in other words, *priorities*).

These are the things I write down when I am sitting. Goethe said:

> The intellectual worker ends in bankruptcy. And remember, man mistrusts everything which is effortless.

Plato said:

> The world can only be saved if the king becomes philosopher and the philosopher becomes king.

I said:

> Men are modelled after a model they can imagine, but like all dream models, be prepared to wake-up!

[laughter] I said also in August 1972:

> See a pattern but *hear* a rhythm, and that is how you develop a sequential pattern to think and to work easily on any level. This is the discipline.

To think and to work easily on any level, hear the rhythm and see the pattern. I think I said:

> Don't wear the "perplexion" of the fallen; instead, wear the beauty of the Elect.

I said:

> The inn is symbolic of the temporary abode for those who would settle in a community spirit.

Bicknell Young said in 1932 (I didn't know him; I was nine years old):

> Now the greatest trouble is fear. That is universal heritage of the race that has deified matter.

It's said, remember:

> Be you transformed by the renewing of your mind.
> (Romans 12:2)

Coleridge writes:

> A great mind must be androgynous.

Sorry, fellows! It's the achievement that's supposed to be the goal of the Aquarian Age: the balanced state. Kahlil Gibran said:

> Once every thousand years we meet at the temple invisible. Then cometh forth one embodied, and it is in his coming our silence turns to singing. The spirit was the first hand of the Lord, and Jesus was the harp.

I love this saying:

Better to be a nettle in the side of your friend than his echo.

Yes, Barry.

> *Dr. Barry B:* Sir, if I may I would like to offer a testimony. During the time when we were preparing for the Carnegie Hall concerts in New York, another member of the Association and I had visited a former meditation teacher of hers who was a palmist, among other things. He had allowed us to come to a gathering of his meeting to present the information about the concert.
>
> So, as we were leaving, he thanked us for coming and he turned to Milna and said, "Oh, you must bring your friend back some time for a palm reading." (I was glad that there was going to be "another time.") But he took my hand right then and there and looked at it. He was surprised when he looked at it, and he said, "You have no heart line. According to the palm there is no heart line there." Then he looked at me and looked back at the palm, and something was not lining-up. So he said, "You must have had to go through tremendous therapy and work," implying that I had arrived on the plane this way, and yet here I was heartfelt and quite radiant. He said, "Either that or your Teacher must have done a great deal of work on your behalf."

I remember it now! Interesting. It's very interesting information that you're frequently given, but **remember, there's no information that is essential, only that which you find stems from Principle, and that's never fundamentally engrossed in matter.**

Yes, Marshall.

> *Marshall O:* A point comes to mind regarding those who have readings and misinterpret them. It just dawns on me the same situation here, that you give information or you give ideas that we can misinterpret unless we check it with the Teller.

Yes. This is why it's so unfortunate to find so many uneasy in speaking with me because they don't really practise. As I was saying to the men this morning, if you're a piano pupil, you practise and then the teacher can ascertain what you have achieved, but if you don't practise, you have *nothing* to present of any form of composition or any form of exercise.

Are there any questions? Yes, Scarlette.

> *Scarlette L:* Sir, in conversation recently with Pam on the island, she was saying that there's no rain down there and how desperately they need rain. Then yesterday, when we were down on the dock and looking at these clouds that didn't seem to disperse, I was looking at this and —

Saying, "Get to Provo!" [laughter]

> *Scarlette L:* — "Get to Provo!" What came was this idea or this fact that you're telling us that there's no distance between a cherry and mentality. And in looking at this cloud, the consideration that came was: the answer to this cannot be within a mental framework.

The mental framework can try to explain it, but it can't. That's how you can move them off the sky if you need to; I've shown you how to so many times.

> *David K:* Yes, Sir.

That's how you change the direction of a hurricane, a tornado, *anything*. We've seen that traced, as Ken knows.

> *Ken B:* Yes, Sir, absolutely. Many times.

Right on the computer. I've told them, before it happened, where I was sending it so that it wouldn't cause destruction.

> *David K:* You looked at the satellite image of the weather patterns.

On the screen, and I said, "It's coming right into Florida. It must go back out in a passage so that it doesn't touch *any object* or *harm* any object." And it did! The fascinating part of it was, the news announced it on one occasion when we were in Canada. (We had heard of this storm that was heading for the States.)

Michael G: It was a report that an unexpected high-pressure zone in southern Ontario had moved the hurricane back out to sea!

That is right. Do you mind another story?

Students: No, Sir!

I was giving a dinner party at my home in Arizona and I was having sixty people for dinner. The weather there is wonderful, and you can usually depend upon it. All these tables were set-up with linen cloths and silver and crystal, and then suddenly, up from Mexico appeared these black clouds rolling right towards the whole area! It was the weekend, the tables were set all around the pool and up in the Lion's Head Garden and in the Pine Terrace and the Sunken Garden, *every place,* and it was beautiful. Everyone said, "Mr. Mills, what are we going to do?! What are we going to do?" I said, "Well, I don't usually do it but I will to-day because sixty people are coming." They stood with me and watched, and *the clouds were stopped before they got to Tucson.* They were over it but no rain had been deposited, and *I moved them.*

It was stopped. I put it up in the Ventana Canyon, and then somebody said, "Mr. Mills, there are people up there in tents, they're camping out for the weekend, and you put the *rain* up there!!" So, it was moved back from the canyons over to the Galiuros, and it was placed there, for they have never been mapped.

The telephone rang and somebody in the house said, "You're wanted on the phone, Sir." I said to the people, "You keep the clouds there until I get back," because I had to settle them. On the phone was Jackie. So, I was talking to Jackie in Toronto, and I heard a huge drop of rain on the skylight! I heard feet running to my part of the house, and they said, "Mr. Mills, Mr. Mills!" I said, "What's wrong?" and they said, "A cloud escaped!" [laughter] We had a wonderful party.

Yes, David.

David K: Sir, I've been with you so many times to be able to witness this. They'll be forecasting the most horrendous hurricane, and it will just either move off its course or completely *fizzle out!*

Yes, it just dissipates.

> *David K:* The strangest thing is to watch the response of the weathermen on TV. You'd think they would rejoice in the miracle of it, but instead they actually are really disappointed.

"It is not going to strike." There's no news . . . but good news.

> *David K:* It's the strangest thing.

I remember, down in Arizona, I'd just finished a Lecture at a Workshop and I was taking my meal alone out on the west veranda of Arinaka. At that time Rob was serving it to me, so I said, "Robert, sit and talk to me while I have my meal." He didn't say much but he sat there. Then I noticed these devils, sand devils. They looked so harmless, but some of the sand devils are so powerful, they're miniature tornadoes; they can lift the roofs off barns.

He drew my attention to one and he said, "Mr. Mills, can you do anything about it?" We saw it heading right for this ranch over on the Tucson Mountains. I said, "Why, Rob?" and he said, "Sir, that is so powerful, it will prove destruction to the ranch and to the barn. Can you do anything about it?" I said, "Well, we'll see. I pray I can." The dust and all was swirled up into the air two or three hundred feet. It was something! I pointed my finger at it, and it went *plonk!* It was incredible! I sat there stunned. It went *plop!* There was nothing left but just this remaining dust.

You don't know what you can do until you are asked. Do you know, these stories bear witness for *you.* It doesn't mean that you can't do those things. Yes, Rachel.

> *Rachel O:* Sir, you spoke about the cherry as being an electrical force-field in essence, and I believe you've also said the same about the human and the rock and space. I was wondering what in the objective realm is *not* an electrical force-field?

Nothing. It's only contained in the electrical force-field because it is *thought* into objectivity. Without thought, it doesn't exist . . . for you or for me. That's why you go to bed and have a rest, so that you can forget your creativity as the objective world.

Is there anything else?

> *Rachel O:* I wrote that I have been experiencing two very different states of feeling as a result of what is being offered.

It's a result of what you're *accepting*. What is being offered is not doing anything; it's what you're *accepting* that's doing it.

> *Rachel O:* One is this intensely serious state of being aware of the work I must do and the tremendous discipline that I must adopt in order to do it. And then the other feeling that bubbles beneath the surface is this delight that when I open my eyes, the world I see is so much more malleable than I ever dreamed possible. It seems that there is such a delicate line between knowing this is all a joke and achieving the Master level of discipline that *you* have, Sir, which enables one to actually *laugh* at the joke.

Yes. I can understand the dichotomy. You're balancing and weighing so many factors all at once. It is to the mind that it is serious and intense, but to the musician you are at heart — man couldn't help but be music, because even the centre of the atom is a sound! That's why you are music whether you know it or not. But believe me . . . not; I *know* it is so. The centre of the atom is not solid; it's a hum and when it's heard, it's a tone. So, the only effort is in *thinking* that it is going to be difficult.

When you play music and take on discipline, it's because *the outcome is music*; it's not *notes,* it's not *discipline.* Those have only been the steps that have been required to allow the music to have an exit. So, don't think of it as difficult and strenuous and "an onerous task." You're very tiny but your ability is so huge; no office of stocks and bonds or investments will ever cope with the magnitude of Actuality.

The next part is the joy of having perceived the malleability that appears to be your experience with your new world. The new world is supposed to be engendered by this very attitude that you are now appropriating.

> Just be the joy of having found
> That within Reality conception is unbound.
> It's not fettered by hypotheses nor fringed with
>   doubt;
> It's all the bliss of knowing the Source is All,
>   there is no doubt.

Yes, Dorothea.

> *Dorothea O:* It comes to me that you are much, much more than we could ever fathom.

So are you. What you are can never be fathomed by "we." I want to read you something, Dorothea, that I was given the other day; it's beautiful. Here it is! I'll say it's for you but it's for everyone. At an *Unfoldment*™ (I think it was in the States) someone in the audience said, "Mr. Mills, may I ask you a question? *Who are you?*" I replied:

> That is a question that all seekers ask when they are trying to identify themselves through the agency of an external speaker. It is better to ask "What *am* I?" and die to the figuration that you give unto a note that has claimed your attention. Look within yourself and ask, "What am I?" and then you will know who I am.[2]

This was given on November 23, 2002. I'd just come home from being in the hospital, and somebody had called me and asked a question. I said:

> Most people think they have come to Earth to overcome karmic difficulties. However, their purpose is much greater. It is to become the support system of the Master's offering in the realm of Feeling, which transcends any psychic or emotional involvement with the virtual as a possible reality.

Yes, Gwynne.

> *Gwynne M:* Sir, yesterday you gave us a great gift when you clarified for us what our clear intention is.

I don't think it *is* clear, and I was going to talk about that this morning. I never said a word about it!

People have declared so much to me and they're not even here. **It's better to know within yourself what is your heart's desire and fulfill it. Don't let the world's beliefs influence you. You were never born to doubt; you were *led* to doubt.** But remember what James said in the Bible: "A double-minded man is unstable in all his ways."[3] It's very true.

The Book of Proverbs says something that you mustn't forget:

> The man that walketh out of the way of understanding shall remain in the congregation of the dead.

(I haven't said that in years.) Thank you for all the flower arrangements, Vanessa and your "helper." They're beautiful flowers, and I thank you all for them.

> *Vanessa S:* I'd love to share some words that you gave me a few months ago, Sir. They were actually for my mum, and then later you said to me that they were actually for me and they would assist when I pass. These words have so many more meanings; they unfold and unfold as these days with you here have unfolded. The words are:
>
> The rest of the Spirit, of Love divine,
> Can never be found in a body in time.
> The rest of the Spirit, clasped to the bosom of Love,
> Is where is found the closeness termed "I love."
> And in this State stands the immutable Fact
> That in the Light of Love there is only One as That.
>
> The magic of these words, Sir, has changed my life. The day that I said these words, it was outside at the funeral. I said my words before these, but when I said *your* words, a shaft of light appeared above my head, it came on top of my head and then my heart. And it was not only bright and light, it was warm. It was a cool fall day. Then, as I repeated and actually mentioned "in the Light of Love," it encircled my entire family that was standing there.
>
> It's a wonder to me that this happened. There seemed to be such a collapse of time, of space; what was inside was outside. Was the light above me or within me? Were the words within me, were they outside? It was such a remarkable experience.

> During the course of this week you've explained and described so many wonderful things about how most of what I see is mental. There was a feeling present that was not mental.

No.

> *Vanessa S:* There was and is still that feeling there.

That feeling *isn't* mental but the ability to talk about it *is*. There's nothing wrong about being mental. The only trouble with being mental is if you're ill mentally! [Dr. Mills laughs.]

> *Vanessa S:* I wonder if I can speak and create such an alteration, or will I be able to speak and how will that happen?

Of course, you will if that is your intention. There's nothing to stop you! Keep practising . . . to find your Self approved.

> *Vanessa S:* The other consideration that comes from this feeling that stirred so deeply in the experience of sharing your words was: You have been told that you are to re-awaken the world's Soul, and it felt like something was being re-awakened. I'm wondering how this Soul is re-awakened, in the light of knowing that the world is mental?

The Soul has nothing to do with being mental, so don't worry about it. The Soul is awakened already; it's just that *mentally* we're not *allowing* ourselves to experience it because we substitute *emotion* for it. As long as emotion takes so much place in the lives of people, Soul can never be experienced, because **Soul is the feeling that accompanies the being I AM, in other words, the activity of the AM-ing of the I, which is the being I AM.** See?

Thank you, Vanessa. It's well said. Thank you all.

> *Students:* Thank you, Dr. Mills.

⌘

1. A young boy present at the Lecture.
2. Mills, *A Word Fitly Spoken,* p. 127.
3. James 1:8.

The Cherry

Chapter XI

The burden rests in the realm of the virtual, and your Real existence is not in that; that's why you can perceive the virtual as it seems to be, while you remain apart from it. It's so simple.

The Cherry

Themes: Coincidence ~ Thoughtless Domain ~ Soul ~ paradox of Being ~ surrender ~ birthright ~ non-attachment ~ avenue of sensation

This is July 3, 2003. It was such a beautiful morning, sitting there on the deck and watching the mists evaporate among the mountains. It's amazing what descends in your sleep — the mists that descend upon your pinnacles of consideration — and how necessary it is to be in the Sun to see the mists dissipate that surround your attainment. If they don't dissipate, so frequently you fall for the suggestion that you haven't attained.

As you now know, faulty thought is the culprit in your lives, and faulty thought arises as a result of an attempt of language to seduce you into the limitations of the ordinary educational process.

You now understand all about, and you understand *everything* about, the cherry and the apple and the object called "you"! You now know that the inanimate objects differ only in that they can't consider themselves. The animate object, especially the human, can consider, which puts you a grade above those which cannot consider. At times you wonder just how much above that *is*, because the people who do not consider the language that deals with Reality are definitely those who are utilizing the language that deals with the virtual and, consequently, with the suggestion. This suggestion traps you into believing *what-is-not*.

So, as you leave to go back into the city you will find that *it is so important to be aware,* as one writer said, *of the rocks and the sirens that are bound to be in your path to seduce you into considerations of the ordinary.* After you have embarked and been in this River and this flow of Words for so long — which is not really long enough; I wish it could have been *three* weeks.

Students: Yes, Sir!

You have also realized that the object is there as you *regard* it, as you give it attention. *There is another very subtle factor that exists with regards to the object, and I didn't mention it to you before.* You can distinguish the difference of the objects such as the cherry and the blueberry and the grapes and the plums and the lychee, but **the reason you can feel it and enjoy it is through the avenue of sensations. Don't forget that. That is how you have the sensorial experience. What do you do but become mesmerized by the sensorial or the sensational aspect of objectivity appearing as a subjective experience, when it is really an objective situation. You, through** *sensations,* **make it internal, which it can't be —** other than *mental!*

It's so subtle! Understanding this with clarity is the most practical achievement. **When this has meaning for you, it signifies attainment. When it is not** *theoretical* **but the** *practical* **experience, then it starts to have meaning, which points to attainment. One of the great aspects of attainment is what? Non-attachment.** Non-attachment doesn't come by sitting in an *a*shram on your — and considering it. You can't consider sitting in an ashram and just meditating to give you a living sense of attachment and non-attachment, because when you try to seduce the thought into acceptance of non-attachment, you still are attached to the very thought that you call "non-attachment." It's a double-edged sword!

What else can I tell you? On the last morning with you for a while, I always consider, "Should I give a formal *Unfoldment*™?" No, because I won't see you again for days and weeks, and I just wonder what you're considering, what your questions are. I speak and say much; you listen and say little. **I do feel that each and every one of you, perhaps,** *has* **a question, but this question must proceed from a pondering situation and a contemplating situation about something that is intrinsic in its practicality in your life, not from some intellectual configuration that takes your attention!**

You have been reared to believe that harmony and peace and joy and spontaneity are foreign to your birthright, and it is not so! But what do you substitute as a result of your belief-system? For example, "you're born in sin." My goodness! Who said so? *You* don't remember being born; and if you do, you know it's not in sin. If you do, then you know the lark you're having. It's trying, at first, because you have to go through this "growing-up" business until your spirit is fully mature.

Have you ever stopped to realize the birth pangs at *this* point in your life? *You're always birthing,* and it is said that with the first death, the second death shall have no sting. **You can't birth unless you die, and you must consider seriously that the only thing that can die is faulty thought-patterns or belief-systems that incarcerate you into the realm of believers.** That is where we came on our mission. We came on our mission to this level of existence because we bore within our hearts the inner knowing that we were not fundamentally "this" but in Reality *a Conscious-awareness experience appearing capable of being visualized and manifested* to such a degree that in the three-dimensional world we had what was required to appear as an impressive object bearing awareness. That's all it is. **Your whole Mission is not to continue to be slaves and prostitute your life in the organizations that see not your worth.**

A man by the name of Robert Quinn said:

> Who is willing to sacrifice the self in pursuit of the universal good?

I've always wondered if this didn't apply to so much of the world (Thoreau said it):

> The mass of men lead lives of quiet desperation.

This Robert Quinn said some wonderful statements:

> To develop transformational capabilities, we cannot be normal people doing normal things.

And:

> We desperately need leaders with voice, but our company is full of organizational prostitutes, people whose bodies are for sale.

He said it very powerfully, but that's what I meant: when you enter into the offices of your work life, you must identify your experience correctly, either you're just *prostituting* your life, letting somebody use it for *selfish* purposes.

What is your organization doing, for example, to support *the environment?*

> What is it doing to support *the arts?*
> What is it doing to support *the awareness?*
> What is it doing to support *the growth* of the awareness so that people distinguish *comfort* from *discomfort?*

So often we say we're comfortable when, really, we are in discomfort *because we are not thinking our own thoughts* and it's considered comfort to be in a condition of discomfort.

> **Every consideration you have must be looked at in the scales until you arrive at a balance, an equilibrium of thought-force.**

Now, are there any questions? If you ask a question, you've got to tell me *why* you're asking it and how . . . et cetera.

Yes, Nurit.

> *Nurit O:* Sir, when you use the phrase that something is "written on the escutcheon of the Soul," are you referring to the Soul, in that case, as one of the Synonyms?

Always.

> *Nurit O:* What is the escutcheon of the Soul and how does one come to know what's written on the escutcheon of the Soul?

Have you ever contemplated it to find out what it means to *you?* Have you ever tried *to place in it* what you consider the escutcheon of your Soul?

> *Nurit O:* I'm not sure what that means, Sir.

Did you ever look-up "escutcheon"? What is it?

> *Gwynne M:* "A shield or a shield-shaped emblem bearing a coat of arms. The plate on the stern of a ship inscribed with the ship's name."[1]

Yes, and that's why it's often termed "the ship of Soul." Yes, Linda.

> *Linda P:* Sir, are there several escutcheons?

No, there's one. Be satisfied with One and then you might find the breastplate of the priest the next. But they're all in the same realm of attainment. Go on.

Linda P: Does the Soul need to be protected, and if so, why?

Oh, no, no, no; the escutcheon is not for protection. It is the evidence of what you are evidencing as a result of *your* attainment. What's written on the escutcheon within your heart is what you wish to attain, magnify, energize, demonstrate or, in other words, *show* as your life experience as you sail your Conscious-awareness through the riptides of mortal suggestion.

Linda P: Thank you, Sir.

Yes, Rick.

Rick F: Sir, this week I have considered a lot the word "time," but my considerations were all in that realm that you call more or less intellectual.

They always are. There's nothing wrong with the intellect. I don't know what you'd do in school without it! I don't know what kind of a teacher you'd be! There's nothing wrong with intellect unless it makes you wooden. The wooden state is always "Well, I *would* if I could but I can't." That's the wooden state, and you don't realize that your intellect is turning into an atrophied state because of the lack of intelligent use of its own suggestion, *intellect*. The intellect not used intelligently, in other words, in the hands of the higher awareness, *rusts!*

Rick F: Sir, as I had these considerations I did note some of the tendencies and assumptions of mind. May I tell you the considerations?

What was the *result* of them? That's what I'm interested in.

Rick F: First of all, along the way there was a consideration that scientists call time "the fourth dimension," and I realized that I assumed and teach that I know what *the first three* are.

You do; you're *in* them.

> *Rick F:* Are they more than the three names that we give them?

No. The object has specification of its *thought* domain, but it doesn't have the verification, necessarily, of the *Thoughtless* Domain. It's that Thoughtless Realm, in other words, where the intellect isn't intruding upon the spontaneous awareness that reveals creation as it is.

When you sit without thinking and adopt the attitude of a receiver, the Grace descends and that Grace allows a presence that alters, always, *every time,* that state of awareness that is used intellectually to explain a point or to give a point. It always graces it with the presence of mystery and wonder. Remember, the Higher Way is always a mystery to the lower way of objectivity.

The intellect is not your enemy until it makes you believe you're "this." Just think, the intellect is utilized in ascribing unto God the things that couldn't possibly be ascribed unto God if it were personal. Everything that the intellect does is try to make deity a pantheistic experience. *You cannot put God into matter.* You can't put the Source into matter; it is the Source that allows you to experience matter, for you have chosen to appear in an objective sense, bearing with you the invisible concomitant, Conscious-awareness.

The awareness is relegated to the three-dimensional experience; the Consciousness is *infinite*. That's where we say we live and move and have our Being; in other words, that is where all thought floats effortlessly in the accepted sea of "glad tidings" (in other words, statements that contradict your self-imposed imprisonment in mortality).

Yes, Lucille.

> *Lucille J:* Each day driving here, the beautiful green vistas are enjoyed and it is amazing to see how the experience has changed over these two weeks. It is observed that there has been a thought-pattern of reaching out to nature, to a flower, to music, wanting to drink it in, to experience its totality, to hold onto it. A new appreciation of the statement "I AM All"' has enabled *me* to relax, knowing that I AM the radiance to the sun —

No! "Knowing that the *Sun* is the radiance to *me,* and *I* cognize it." You can't put the sun in you; you can't say, "I am the radiance to the sun," because "I AM" is the honorific title *for* the Sun, the Source of all life. So, you can't say, "I am the Sun," but you can say, "I recognize the sun —" How did you say it?

Lucille J: Knowing that I AM the radiance to the sun.

Yes, but you're assuming that "you" know "I AM." That is what we do: we assume we know "I AM." All we know is that the I AM, the Sun, the Soul, the Spirit, Mind, Principle, is never capable of being brought into a mind concept; It can only be tonally referred to as an awareness pattern of something other than the objective confinement. "God" is only the name we give to the emancipated State which we know *must be* because of our confinement to limitation as a result of our choice to be birthed in matter. *This did not happen by chance.*

So, always remember, when you say "I AM," you are referring to that Power that *allows you* to experience the radiance of the sun, thereby enjoying its rays and knowing if you are enjoying the sun you can't possibly be a mere mortal who does not realize! That saves you from the incredible task of living the I AM on your own. It's a great, subtle, intoxicating consideration to put it into the terms of "I AM the Sun, I AM the Love, I AM the Truth," but it is the Truth, Light, and Love which appear as the substance of my objective being, contained in the realm of awareness.

It's so subtle. It's great because you'll still be freer than ever because you won't be out having to take the place of God for everyone else — and let alone for yourself!

Go on. That's the first thing I wanted to check.

Lucille J: There is nothing to gain or acquire from the objective. I AM All.

What is gained from the objective is what you give to others in the releasement from its imprisonment. That is what is gained, and that's written upon the escutcheon of your Beingness.

Lucille J: Then, what is gained is what is given.

Exactly! What is given with the wrong attitude comes back upon you *a thousandfold!* It becomes a karmic issue because you have dealt incorrectly with the divine Hand that has played the cards for your life. You realize the pack of cards that constitutes your experience as everyone reveals how you are playing the Hand that is empowered to restore this Earth to the kingdom of our God and of His Light.

Everyone has a hand dealt. It's not in your *palm;* it's in *the wonder of being liberated in the claiming "I and my Father* is *One."*

Okay? It's wonderful. I'm so glad you're on that; that's a very incredible spot to be at because at that very spot, right now, you can feel the releasement of being the container of something that you couldn't possibly contain — but being the recipient of the One who gives every good and perfect gift.

Got it?

Lucille J: Thank you so much.

Yes, Sherry.

Sherry W: Sir, when you gave so clearly, just now, the idea of discovering that we've fallen for what is discomfort and think it's comfort, I didn't see it quite that clearly, but it came that way to me as a result of practising "being aware of being aware." I wanted to practise that because at one time, if I'm remembering correctly, I had asked about how you can come and go at will, and you said, "Watch where you place your awareness." So, I *was* watching that, and then you gave "Be aware of being aware." It is amazing, in those moments, what you see yourself doing. I'm grateful for the practice.

Just think, **what you see yourself doing is all because the I AM is recognized as the Source of all movement, all action, all doing. The Source couldn't help but be the creative act pointing to the unlimited specifications surrounding infinity.** Okay?

Sherry W: Thank you, Sir.

Let me hear Donna.

Donna C: Sir, many years ago, before I met you, I had an experience that was very disturbing. I started to consider what you've revealed to us this week, that what I was seeing *outside* was actually happening *inside* on my retina and was upside down, and my mind just went with that. I started to consider that I had invented everything, that I'd imagined everything.

You have!

Donna C: Yes! But at that time, not knowing *you* and not knowing how to see it correctly, it was very disturbing and it lasted for quite a few years until I *did* meet you. But *this* experience with you here at Summer Festival and what you've revealed has moved it into a whole new place!

It looks it!

Donna C: May I read what I've written regarding that, Sir?

Yes.

Donna C: "Thank you for the revelation that everything we perceive is mental, contained in mind. It allows me to refocus the attention on where the perception takes place — not so much to consider that we *invented* all this but to be aware of *where* the perception is happening and, with that distance from the involvement with the objective, be aware of That which allows the awareness."

Yes, and being aware of where you *focus* on the objective is the *evidence* of the Allness. There's no work involved; it's effortless Being! No work is involved other than ordering your rebel mind to surrender to the wonder of the Unknown — and yet known by the surrender! It's such a paradox, but it's wonderful! A paradox is used to confuse and upset. Just think, if you are upset, it just proves to you that you should be here! [laughter]

Donna C: It's wonderful to learn to use that upset to move beyond it.

Yes, it is. I know! It's no longer an upside-down pie!

Donna C: Right! Thank you.

Yes, John.

John A: There's a saying that the scientist seeks to discover what the Sage already knows. Sir, may I just ask: The technical exercise upon awakening in the morning would be to correctly identify the awakening body as not my primary identity?

It *is* as long as you have it, so don't malpractise on it. **Upon awakening in the morning, be grateful you have a beautifully functioning, well co-ordinated, inspired vehicle in which to evidence your situation under the wing of the Almighty!** It's *lightning* speed with which the whole thing is assembled, to the point where you think it hasn't been disassembled.

John A: The next point I had written down was: "Observe how quickly the components of the matrix are re-established."

Oh, it's lightning speed, to fool you into thinking it has substance. But **Substance is that which is incapable of decay or disorder.**

John A: I'd better work some more on this.

[laughter] I'll send you the bill! Yes, Jon.

Jonathan S: Sir, going back to what you were just talking to Donna about, because it's just the *paradox of Being*: "There is no work to Being," you said earlier this week, and you've talked about the effortlessness of Being; and yet, you also said, "The work is in the *thought* of Being."

Yes. Until you drop your thought, it's work.

Jonathan S: Yes, Sir. But we have to have thought to exist, Sir, correct?

Yes, you do. There's nothing wrong with thought; it's just what it does *to* you if you don't see it for what it is: a component of mentality that allows your awareness to appear to be organized and well organized according to a Principle by which you live and move and have your being! *Simple as that!*

I love *the thought* of you,
I love *the feel* of you,
I love *the presence* of you.
Why wouldn't I?
How could I help but include you as my own?

No man is separate from the Love that IS.
The separateness is only the fun of objectivity
on the chessboard of time.

What were you going to say?

> *Jonathan S:* I guess I want to know what practice I could take home; that realization that you just had, just resonates so much. I know it to be true, and yet there needs to appear to be another to understand that.

That's why you're here.

> *Jonathan S:* Yes, Sir.

That's why *I'm* here actually. **I have nothing to gain from any of this; I just *love* sharing the Cornucopia I seem to have come with.**

> *Jonathan S:* Is there a discipline that I could — ?

Yes! Never stop loving Me as I AM, and then you can't help but be That yourself.

> *Jonathan S:* Thank you, Sir.

Whatever you consider I AM, that will ye be also. Yes, Barry.

> *Dr. Barry B:* Sir, you've given a statement: "Everyone I meet, I meet as one whom I cognize as my own response to a form that in Essence is nothing but Love."[2]

That's right.

> *Dr. Barry B:* It was taken as a practice, *is* taken as a practice, and the result is, on one level, an opening to newness; it allowed more of a sense of outreach to meeting people. As the course developed, one evening there

was a meeting with someone who apparently I have known for years, and I appeared to be seeing this one in the usual personality frame. Utilizing your statement changed my vision of that other one markedly. It was a palpable alteration of perception, and almost secondarily, the other one somehow sensed that and acknowledged that they had felt different. I guess my question is: What's really going on, and is there a next step to take with that practice?

What's really going on is a falling-away of any restriction; it's a lessening of the confinement of the objective. When there is a change in the objective, it's not that *the objective* is changing; there's a lessening of *the thought* that confines it to a limited framework of reference.

It's so strange how our society is structured, because I see people I recognize and there's no way to say "Come and be with me" — because we haven't got the community.

Dr. Barry B: One of the wonderful things that was very moving to me in utilizing this practice of a statement of yours was that here I took it on, memorized it, utilized it as a practice, when it is *your experience all the time!* I guess that's what I'm asking, how to make —

You don't; you just *be* that all the time. It doesn't come and go; it's not shut-off like hot and cold water! You know? It isn't; it's a constant flowing. Your life is filled with intermezzi. Just enjoy it. Be the spontaneous composer of the unique moments of Self-recognition, and you find *that* dwarfs the suggestion of being the doer, the viewer, or the seer . . . but appear as a Seer to the one who does not see. Okay.

Who else was there now? Yes, Eugene.

Eugene M: Sir, a few days ago you made a statement that "searching for what is beyond the mind is mesmerizing," so consideration has been given to that.

Why did I say it was mesmerizing?

Eugene M: Yes, that's why I was considering.

You can't consider beyond your mind.

Eugene M: No, Sir.

But you can adopt a different Mind. It says, "Let the Mind that is in Christ Jesus be in you also."[3] It's a very high bit of Teaching because it means that if you can cognize the uniqueness of a divine experience appearing as a Coincidence, then *you also* have that ability, and that divine Mind, as we say, is very readily accepted as soon as *you* also accept *the results* of accepting it. It's like surrendering yourself to the Invisible.

> *Eugene M:* That was exactly the idea that I had arrived at (this idea of acceptance), but I realized that I have found what you are offering and it behooves me to accept what it is you are giving.

Oh, that's good.

> *Eugene M:* In what you just now mentioned, the idea of once it's accepted —

It'll never let you go.

> *Eugene M:* I don't want to be let go!

No. It never will, you see, so you don't have to hold it or anything. Once it's accepted, it's already accepted. That's why you're here!

> *Eugene M:* Yes, Sir.

That's why you came from . . . Colorado, wasn't it?

> *Eugene M:* That's where I was when I heard of you.

Yes.

> *Eugene M:* So, one of the other considerations was: the Source is that which is beyond the mind.

The Source is that which is beyond the mind, but due to the magnificence or the beneficence of the Source you have a mind that knows that! Therefore, it's possible to attain with the mind and

without it: with the mind if it doesn't interfere by being thought-filled about what it isn't; and with Mind there's no thought other than what IS!

Eugene M: Thank you very much, Sir.

All right, Gwynne.

Gwynne M: I feel so blessed by all the answers you've been giving everyone to-day, Sir, and I dare to offer my own question. I just wanted to clarify an understanding: you told us this week that there is no such thing as a divine Idea, and yet the term is still used.

Not in Actuality, there isn't; there *is* in *this* reality.

Gwynne M: Yes, Sir.

There's such a thing as a divine Idea. You better have them, for heaven's sake!

Gwynne M: That's what I wanted to ask about. I was just considering that I would now use the term "divine Idea" as an Idea; it's an object within mentality but one that is so grand that it's becoming to a limitless, creative Source.

Yes. *Every* idea points to the creative Source, but they are not divine. Anything that points to the creative Source isn't divine; it's just a little less earthly than *you* are! Anything that's less dense than "you," you consider a little more divine! [laughter] You're as bright as a button! But you see — yes, *you see.*

Gwynne M: You said, "To hold the world as it really IS, as a divine Idea."

Yes, it is.

Gwynne M: Is that, perhaps, considered as a compound idea, as Man includes all the right ideas, the flora and the fauna, and the beauty?

Yes.

Gwynne M: Thank you, Sir.

Just don't bother *holding* it. Are you the sister of *Atlas?!* [laughter] You don't have to hold it; it's *Self*-sustained. **Existence is Self-sustained.** You think you have to exist; you exist because existence is Self-sustained! Rest in *that*. Don't allow the mind to get into all these — *I* say them to cause you to ponder, but I don't say them for you to stay in the pondering. Existence is Self-sustained.

Now, Michael.

> *Michael S:* Perhaps you just answered my question but I want to check it with you, and that is that, in this experience there is always a shift in awareness —

Always.

> *Michael S:* — which is so rare. One aspect of it, as Lucille was pointing out, being in this beautiful place, is that everything looks different and it's appreciated in a new way. The flowers seem to have an inner life, they seem to say "Hi!" when I go near them, and the wonders of nature are so extraordinary. I then begin to have considerations, and a voice is saying, "It's not important to have considerations."

Of course, it is. It's very nice to have those considerations because it has the thought-world employed *in a constructive way*.

> *Michael S:* I also want to be sure that it is not pantheism. Although I clearly see that I am creating this entire picture by my senses and my eyes (including what appears to be the shift in awareness), as far as I can see, still, in all, there's a factor of sheer wonder of "What is it?" a priori to my viewing it.

It's exactly what it is: a priori. It's out *from* mind, not *in* mind. That's *out from* mind, and "a priori" means that it is out from mind.

> *Michael S:* Then, the next question comes in, let's call it a parable that points to something: In my choosing to come to this three-dimensional reality, it would seem that the three-dimensional reality is already set, like a stage set, with all the toys and all the beauties and all the things that are —

It seems that way.

> *Michael S:* It seems that way, that what perhaps was one vibration is now "spectrumized" for me to appear to walk through it and drive through it and play with it and stumble over it and laugh at it and do whatever. But is it important to search for what it is, again, a priori to the way I'm perceiving it? That's what I call the Source, and I just want to be sure that I'm not going into a kind of subtle pantheism.

No, you're not putting it *into* matter. You can't put the beauty into matter; it isn't. Remember, the cherry is nothing but molecules, atoms, protons, and neutrons in *essence*. That's *all* this is. That's the way the mind can explain it until it's just accepted for the wonder it is — and the wonder we really are the custodians of because intuitively we *know* that we are not "this," and our solace comes in the knowing of the superior State that is termed "God," "Self," "Atman" (whatever you want to call it), "the Invisible," "the infinite *X*."

> *Michael S:* It is amazing.

It is. Yes, Nancy.

> *Nancy M:* Sir, my question actually connects with Michael's question.

I guess that's why I asked you; I like a rippling rhythm!

> *Nancy M:* My question was, and I think you just answered it: how is the essence of an object realized?

It doesn't exist without you saying it's an object, and the object of anything is nothing but in essence electrical. It's just as *you* are; the only difference is, *you* know it and the object *doesn't*.

> *Nancy M:* This week of the Summer Festival you clearly brought us to the point that this is a sensorial experience and we can identify what is sensorial. When we *know* that —

Why don't you be satisfied? *Look what you've attained!* Live *that* and see what else there is. You're still living it as a problem to be solved now that you realize what it *is!* Isn't it the devil, the way the mind works?

Nancy M: Yes.

The problem is already solved, and now you're trying to make another one because of how you realized it! Don't go there, don't go there.

Nancy M: Thank you.

Yes, Kathy.

> *Kathy T:* Dr. Mills, what is so prevalent in these sacred days here with you is the presence of Force. You have said: "The Expected One is never recognized in a belief-system, because the Expected One isn't figured as a belief; It's known as force. It's known as a field of circular force, which you call *empowerment*." It's clearly operating in my very cherished experience of service at your table. (This is one way it was considered.) As you said in *Green Stuff*: "The Service around the Table revolves on the Axis of that Being that is termed Principle . . ."[4] This opportunity of serving you, Sir, when it's done in its best performance, is invisible. The question is: is this circular force always a signature of the Invisible?

Do you feel it is?

Kathy T: I feel it is redolent in my experience.

All right, then, it is! There's nothing wrong, because as long as you *feel* it is and not *think* it is, then it's acceptable. If you think it is, it can stop and start and becomes linear, but if you *feel* it is, then it's nothing but the all-encompassing circle of the divine effulgence! Remember, a circle can't be a circle without the invisible Centre being known. If you feel you're in that circle, then you are within the periphery of God-Being! Write down on a slip of paper — I used to show this years ago! You don't remember it? Write down on a slip of paper or draw a circle and, if need be, use a compass and then you'll see the point from which it all happens!

Tell me where *you* are as far as the circle is concerned. Write and see what goes in the circle and what you have outside it. Show me sometime.

Yes, Rachel.

> *Rachel O:* Sir, I seem to have passions for certain things in the objective realm, and I've been considering for quite some time now: how can what appears as a strong passion for something in the objective world be explained according to what we are in Essence, which is Love that knows no discrimination?

It doesn't say that it doesn't *differentiate*. If there's no discrimination, then there's differentiation — either you wouldn't be bothered with "indiscriminating." You only indiscriminate when you have separation of objectivity, but it's obvious you have discriminated because you have a passion for something. It doesn't mean it's terrible or wrong or anything else. Nothing you do here, unless it harms another, is of real great consequence to what is Real; *It* doesn't know anything about it! The only trouble with doing something that isn't conforming with what is Real is that it hampers your clarity of awareness and vision (that's all it does) and makes the attainment more difficult to perceive as effortless. Attainment could be and should be as easy as that! [Dr. Mills picks-up a grape from the fruit plate beside him and drops it into the palm of his other hand.] Drop the parcel of your thoughts which clothe you now in *limits'* land! Cast them now unto a Spot!

> *Rachel O:* Are these things getting in the way of this attainment?

If your passion causes you to forget, then it's in the way. If it's enjoyed and allows you to still be *on* the Way, there's nothing wrong with it.

Do you understand passion? What do you consider passion?

> *Rachel O:* I seem to have a passion for things in the holistic realm.

A passion for what? Raw vegetables?

> *Rachel O:* As ridiculous as that sounds, yes, and yoga.

By all means, **don't allow any passion to interfere with the simplicity of just accepting what is Good in your life.** Have your passion for your food but, for heaven's sake, eat cooked vegetables if you have to. Okay? Now, what else?

> *Rachel O:* Thank you, Sir. You said, to Lucille, I think, that she won't go on having to take the place of God for everyone, and I wondered if this is the answer to the tremendous amount of responsibility, this enormous load and seriousness I sometimes feel after hearing an *Unfoldment*™ in which perhaps I realize that I have not defined my intention clearly.

I think, if you take it personally, it becomes a great load. Know that every good and perfect gift comes from Above. **No gift comes to anyone who doesn't have the ability to know *where* to place it and *how* to use it.**

Yes, it relieves you. Just rejoice! *Bend.* I wish I were dancing like I used to. I'd make you *dance* with me because then I'd get you moving! I used to jitterbug and love it, and I used to waltz all the time. I used to dance with one of the girls in the Singers; she was like a broomstick! I got her actually to become flexible, it was wonderful, until she got out of my arms and said she was a broomstick again! *Just enjoy the flexibility of being Real.* **The burden rests in the realm of the virtual, and your Real existence is not in that; that's why you can perceive the virtual as it seems to be, while you remain apart from it.** It's so simple.

> **Always remember that what people think This is, It never is. When people could never dream what This is, It IS!**

I thank you for all your beautiful gifts.

⌘

1. *The American Heritage Dictionary*, Second College Edition (Boston: Houghton Mifflin Company, 1985).
2. Mills, *The Golden Nail*, p. 272.
3. Philippians 2:5.
4. Mills, "Green Stuff," *The Key: Identity*, p. 338.

The Palpability of the Invisible

Chapter XII

What does a door represent, if it isn't a veil between the suggested material, mental considerations and the Presence of the numinous divinity which is known to be through the door.

The Palpability of the Invisible

Themes: I AM All ~ Essence ~ One Tonality ~ Sound/the Word ~ re-identification ~ the world ~ mentality

This is the morning of August 30, 2003, a Saturday morning in the celebration of what is termed "a holiday." It is a time when you are fortunate *in your choice* because, instead of going to the country to find a change and moving in the habitual way of the mass, you have chosen to come together in the seclusion of a rarefied atmosphere in which the very contestants in the competition of the world of to-day are given an opportunity to reside — in the non-competitive situation of acceptance.

We have entered into the pattern of *agreement,* either we would not be here. We have tasted the food of time and we have tried, through innumerable years, to find that type of food that would satisfy in the realm of seasonings. But you realize . . . and this is why you are here. You realize *what?* That "this" cannot be what it seems to be, and thus it is *in question.* Since you all know, without doubt, the convolutions of mentality that throw to the surface of your awareness every type of suggestion, you know that in order to evade the result of a rake's progress, *you must bring to heel that errant factor of mentality that would cause you to suffer the delusion that you could gain your freedom by the use of the very organ that is your bondage.*

It is so strange, in the great paradox of our experiment in worldliness, that we are endowed with the ability to move through the appearances of a world picture and come to terms with the *suggestion* that it is beyond our control. You are the recipients of a great gift, and that gift is that which stirs inquiry. That gift is always present when the question of your corporeal viability comes before the adjudicating board of your identity crisis.

Remember, no instrument of limitation can give you an instrumentation that is unlimited. Yet, in this very paradox we are dealing with an amazing experience because, as one Teacher said, people meditate on the name of God, but this can only be pursued for a certain length of time, and this is why the God-Self appears manifested: in order to anchor the wish for realization with a form of similarity to the meditator. Remember, the form is only for acceptance without causing turmoil, but what is represented bears no relation to the form. This is how the wonder of Tonal engagement is so magnified in the light of sincerity and a contrite heart.

As we drop the swaddling clothes of the belief of being born into matter, we see that the labour movement of the past continues to-day, for we are confronted with the materialization — which is a wonder to behold but the mystification happens when our attention, in some way or other, is misdirected from our Soul intention and we find ourselves wrapped in a variegated pattern of thought-clusters that tend to mimic the utterances of the Divines. The Masters of all time have given words of great meaning and they have uttered the dictums of consequence to mankind, but it is only when the jurisdiction of one's inner life is under the aegis of the divine Force to "come out from the world and be ye separate" and engage in the play of God that one starts to see how the world has been garmented in the shabby clothes of belief. Now we are in the program of redesigning the suitable apparel for the wonder of this great precipitation called "the world" in a small way, "the cosmos" in a big way, and "the universe" beyond conception.

This brings us to a very, very important consideration: We have arrived at that point of conceptualization; *what lies beyond it?*

Mankind, having been drawn into the vortex of conflicting opinions, has attempted to adopt patterns of agreement that make friends with similar patterns of agreement, all based on an inner knowingness of incompleteness and dissatisfaction but with the promise that, if you worship and come together in a belief-system, your belief shall keep you steady until you reach that heavenly State where you will be set free on the right hand of God. However, the hands and arms of God are not so flimsy as *your* concept! The body of God is not the image and likeness of yours, and the tonality of God is such that it echoes into the Stream of everlasting to everlasting and bridges, through the annals of time, the undying tonality of Origin, of Source, of Creator. Thus, you are impelled by your desire to question "Who am I?" and "What am I?" and in this questioning you have launched a very great force-field into the ethers of expectation and have come, lo and behold, in formation and appear as bodies formed and fitly joined together and seated before the very fount of Tonality.

(This is the way we attempt to describe, in spite of the multiplicity of forms, the ever-presence of One Tonality that is recognized by you whether or not the language is understood, because the very nuclear force of Tonality bears no sense of being limited by those who are receiving it!)

"If with all your hearts ye truly seek, ye shall truly find." This cannot be expected from good books. No good book can give you the ability to realize — other than *you haven't!*

To realize is to bring to fore in your life the place that mentality, the mind, has now under this Empowerment.

We have said on many occasions that the first word we use to make sure we are present is one sound alone: *I*. The first personal pronoun: *I*. No wonder you seek to know where did this sound come from. From this sound come the second and third personal pronouns: you, he, she, and it. Without *I*, nothing can arise; without *I*, nothing can be gained; and the only gain is the loss, and the loss is the gain. This loss is your allegiance to your limitation of being a "head water-man."

You are an awareness program, misunderstood upon the labour of birth. You are an awareness program capable of undreamed universality and undreamed potential. Upon Realization, much is answered, but as one approaches the State, it seems almost fearsome to do so because when you come face to face with the state of the changing, there will be the Grace that says what? **The changing is not Real.** You perceive this. *What is that part of you that perceives this?* It's not that part of you that labours. **That part of you that *perceives* is your door to pass through to that which is termed "sacred" and is sanctified.**

What does a door represent, if it isn't a veil between the suggested material, mental considerations and the Presence of the numinous divinity, which is *known* to be through the door. No wonder? You better wonder, because it is this wonder, it is this feature, that will give you courage to dare to step through the door. When you once go through it, what you knew so well now awaits a re-identification and what you dreamed to be so real is now realized to be an illusion. As Rumi said, get rid of your illusions. How can you get rid of an illusion just because you're told to get rid of it?! "Read your books!" You still have the illusion of a reader reading a book. How can you read into the vibratory frequency of the non-dimensional world of the Numinous unless you attune yourself to the Diapason of universal significance.

The great **I** cannot be *capitalized,* no matter how much you invest in it. No matter how many shares you buy, you can never own It from the standpoint of a corporeal corporation attempting to do business with the Infinite! How many attempt to scale the heights of success — and, according to the world, our success? But what type of world is your experience outlining? **Your presence may be outlined; your divine Presence cannot be! This is why the radiation of what IS has no boundaries and no limits.** You may not receive the benefit if there is any doubt, because doubt and fear constitute the lead apron. How many of you are wearing it mentally?

> Do you fear to change and be the Love thou art?
> Do you dare to exchange for the suggestion of
> "this" *That* and be the effulgence thou art?
>
> What can you say when all conditional states are
>   laserized in Light,
> Other than: the One victorious has imbued all
>   under this emblazoned might
> With the freedom of Light becoming the heart
>   that is bound to the Principle divine,
> For the Principle beats the rhythmic tonality that
> **"Love has made thee more than mind."**

You now see the simplicity of performance and how it is so easy to fulfill our modern-day commandment, "Make an altar of earth." The service is so easily conducted because the venue is supported by **All that IS** and the Hosts are always praising the wonders of manumission in the name of unconditional Love.

> When you work, know that these are the clothes
>   that Love wears.
> When you engage the rhapsody of Light,
> Know that in the throes of this rejoicing, you
>   have found your invisible wings of flight.
>
> The bored/board are always searching for something
>   else to do.
> They have to usually have many sittings and wonderings.
>   "What shall we do?"

The chair-man asks the others who are chaired and
    wonder why
They ever thought the table would become the
    receptacle for Food from on high.
But perhaps the CEO may find some meaning if he
    stumbles and wonders why
And finds the **Christ Eternal Omnipotent is *all there
    is* to what he pretends in a hide.**

The labour is so intensive; communication does not
    pass.
The levels of to-day's corporations are from the
    highest to the bottom of the slavery where no
    one dares to even ask:
"What is your condition in the company? Please get
    the information from below
And pass it up to my secretary because in my plane I
    must go."
Go where, you silly wanderer? Go where, you one
    who runs away
From transcending the chair of boredom and *finding*
    in the room where *I* sit and pray?

See, in the simplicity of movement, how the mind is
    the weight of time
And you give it such weight — when it weighs so
    little! It becomes nothing but a glowing jewel
    when blessed by the Numinous, the Divine.
**Don't be harnessed to ordinariness; grasp with
    daring the veil that stands
Between your world of suggestion and the open
    passage to where I AM.**

Consider in these moments of jubilation this salient
    fact of might
That the world, with your presence and your
    knowingness, can now be given a new
    garment, new clothes, of Light!
Dress it up in your wonder and your magic within
    the foyer filled with Light,
For in this reception state of Wonder nothing great
    or small dares to enter and not be arrayed in
    Light.

> The world is so big. Can you conceive it? Of course,
> you can if you dare to perceive the might.
> You can conceive the mighty universe and the greater
> cosmos, but how have you thought of the
> omnipresent I of Light?
> The Omniscient, the Omnipresent, the Magnificence
> — how can you find It on a page?
> But, oh boy, when you are borne/born to the wonder
> of magic, do you dare to consider the deed?
>
> Realizing your inheritance, "All that I have is thine,"
> Don't put it off into process! **I AM All, here, now;
> there is no time!**

No explanation of time from the standpoint of the mind is ever anything but a period. What does a period do? It ends a sentence.

No one is here by chance. No one is here; there is only One! Don't mistake what you *see* as solid; that is labour-intensive. See, without doubt, the art of Being is effortless from the standpoint of One.

Process is from the cradle to the grave, and it's a grave error to consider that you will gain It over a period of time. You are so graced because the moment you can realize that you are more than "this," you can no longer be concerned about living; you have walked through the door. The veil has been rent, because the effulgence of the Light reveals there is no darkness other than that created by the thought-field that is attempting to think the right thoughts to be holy.

Thinking the right thoughts to be holy prepares the mind for the baptism of releasement from its assumed position as the custodian of "you" and reveals it now **emblazoned with the identification of the royalty of your Being — the Substance that is eternal and not subject to the vacillating, unionized forces of the suggested labour movement from sense to Soul that exists to-day.** Rest in this and find there is no night coming, for the Day is effulgent and it allows the days in the serial of time to be blessed by the constant bestowal of the eternality having a viable evidence in the continuing baptism of Tonality from Age to Age.

These Tones, wrapped in the words of the astringent Language of spontaneity at the feet of Wonder, are offered unto the magnetic and rhythmic vibratory realms of this dimension, enforcing and enhancing the verity of Being — which is applicable to whatever system hears this and translates it into a code of perfected Being.

So, let us say we land and we come back to C and find the great Diapason redolent with the tonality of Being.

Students: Thank you, Sir.

You must be a very special group.

Dr. Barry B: You are a very special Speaker.

David K: Thank you, Sir, for blessing us all with the true baptism of Sound.

I'm very interested to hear it.

David K: It's remarkable.

I heard it, but I have to rehear it! That is the whole purpose of our being here, a *re-minding,* so that when you rehear, the re-minding is verified as having taken place because what you heard the first time is now *new!* When you think you don't need to rehear, it's a big warning sign for me, because your friend and foe, your mind, suffers a great delusion. And what is that delusion? That it can adjudicate what it has perceived — and it *can't!* **How can you let your limit declare your State? How can you let your limit define your possibilities?!**

To meet this Force-field head-on is difficult! [laughter] It's difficult to meet It head-on. The other night, when I looked up at one man from having spoken awhile (I had said something that resolved something), he was holding his head and he said he thought his head was flying away! I said, "Well, let it go!" and David said, "There is Winged Victory,[1] and it doesn't have a head!" It flies. **You fly when your head is not the navigator; it's doing nothing but obeying the invisible Hands.**

What will I say to-morrow?! I said to David, coming up in the car and when I got up this morning, "What will I talk about?" I think I know what I'm going to say, and it never comes out! Yes.

Helen Lee P: This day cannot possibly end without thanking you and telling you how grateful I am for your removing doubt from this being, for making me not believe but *know* that what was going to be, that is the cure of cures, the miracle of miracles! Thank you, Sir.

The Miracle of miracles is that you can appear to be cured only because it's a lessening of the suggestion that you are "this."

It is so wonderful that there are so many here from the United States. I'm so glad they're here to be under the Light of the united State! You can perceive why it is so important for you to hear This, because It is the antithesis of the movement in the world. Remember, the sun shines; it doesn't know upon *what* it shines but it shines upon any state that is living, to either reduce it to smithereens or raise it to the heights. Concrete needs it even to dry out! **Remember that your knowingness is like the sun: just in the sincerity of Being, it spills involuntarily out to your world that you can conceptionalize. That is how much your world can be graced. The only demand is that you break the misconception that it is primarily material!**

Remember the cherry. [Dr. Mills holds-up a cherry by its stem.] If you are divine, what is this cherry? Can it be any other than a cherry? It can't be. A cherry is a cherry because it has the characteristics of "cherryhood." Having the characteristics of cherryhood, it has to adopt what is the expectation of cherryhood. The cherry was born from the tree to bear witness to the fact that the tree has fruitage *totally unlike it!* But it still is a cherry pointing to the tree.

Man is of the Tree of Life. The Tree of Life is not born in the man, but Man/man[2] represents *the fruitage* of the Tree of Life. Can it be other than the Tree of Life in its perfectness?

Students: No, Sir.

That is why "you" don't have a ghost of a chance! You don't have a chance to be any other than the beauty commensurate with Being.

What is the essence of this cherry in description but a minimized nuclear force-field. It's made-up of atoms, and the essence of the atom, the heart of the atom, is a vibration. Don't forget it!

If the heart of the atom for a cherry is a hum, is it any wonder that Man is a Song? He is an atomic structure, and the heart of the atom sings. Man is a Song; he was *made* to sing.

A cherry is always a cherry, as Man is always Man, not "you." **The image and likeness of the outline of Force is man. And what is the outline of Force? The radiance evidenced by the actuality of Being.** (It will be perceived someday.)

This is what marks you when you go out. People will be so attracted to you when you go back to Montreal, to Nun's Island, to Connecticut, to these different locations and everywhere. You will be so attractive that you will have to be very alert to what comes into your presence, because when you are moved to such an exclusivity of Power, then you are *bearing* this and you rein in the horse of your mind under the bridle so that it doesn't throw you for a loop. Leave that to the fairgrounds (loop-the-loop)!

Yes, Barry.

> *Dr. Barry B:* Sir, I'd really like to acknowledge the release of the first soundtrack from *The Golden Nail*.[3] I remember an evening when you presented the *book* to a very prominent journalist, an anchorman. He asked you in his inimitable way, "If you could sum up this book in one word, what would you say?" and you said, "Answer." I am so grateful that people will now *hear* that Sound and have a *living* Answer, rather than just read it in a book.

Because in the *sound* It is heard.

> *Dr. Barry B:* Absolutely. Thank you, Sir.

You'll have a nice surprise when you hear it! And the second *Greatest Hits* of the Singers[4] is absolutely *wonderful*.

> *Terry S (a Star-Scape Singer):* I want to thank you and David and everyone else who was involved with the presentation of the new CD. That is really fantastic. I can't tell you how much I appreciate that!

Wait till you hear it!

> *Terry S:* Oh, I'm dying to hear it! Also, I want to thank you for this morning because it is still resonating so much,

> and it just comes to me that the only purpose of the re-hearing sessions is to break the suggestion that it ever stopped resonating.

That is right because actually it never does. *It never does.* We tend to precipitate the continuity of sound into the serial of time in order to feel at home with the incompatible situation of time and the Timeless. It is because of this incompatibility that we consider it stopping; as soon as you consider *time* and *the Timeless*, you have put up the veil that prevents continuity. That continuity is the continuing experience that has been verified by all Ages, by all Masters, from the time that man has been able to record, in one way or another, *the presence of a sound of Creation.* Remember, the Gospel of St. John begins with *the Word was with the Sound:* "the Word was with God and the Word was God"; in other words, it was the undifferentiated Tonality, often called "Aum," that resounds with the pure or pristine fire of Creation. It is this pristine fire of Creation that is held in abeyance by what is termed the readiness of the one to be touched by its fecundity. This is approached more and more as the suggestion of "the time and the Timeless" is rescinded and the *nowness* of Being is experienced in the undifferentiated state of *"I"* — and that's only a sound.

> *Terry S:* Thank you, Sir.

I don't know whether you asked me a question or not! [laughter] Yes, Nauby.

> *Nauby P:* Dr. Mills, it is such a blessing to be here. Thank you so much for this morning.

So glad you were here.

> *Nauby P:* May I share a story? There was an opportunity to visit a friend in Newport, Rhode Island, recently. The *Unfoldment*™ "Green Stuff" was with me, and we took an opportunity to play it, and she heard it. At the end of it, she stopped in silence, and then she said, "That is the sound of the universe," hearing your words, Sir. Thank you so much.

She should be here. **When you recognize What IS, no other game should seduce you!** It won't let you go, will it?

Students: No, Sir.

It won't; it just won't! You can try to get away but having tasted it . . . **Remember, *you* are in control of the mind; it is *not* in control of you!** You are in control of the mind; the mind is not in control of you. In other words, when you don't feel like being happy, say, "Mind, pay attention! I order you to be happy!" and the mind will have to be happy . . . if you are! [laughter]

Yes, Alexandra.

Alexandra M: Can you do the same with the body?

Oh, sure! The first thing you have to ask is: *where* does the body arise? In your awareness. Then, if it is in your awareness and it is external to you, its condition is there as a result of you; the body is there as your awareness *of it*. So, that awareness allows you to supervise what happens *with it*. Just because you are ill or you are happy — each case is an illusion!

The greatest illusion we have is happiness. Everyone wants to be happy. Why? *Why* do you want to be happy? You're trying to consider a condition that's different than your present one. But remember, your Source, your Creator, is *not* in any *descriptive* sense; you can't describe the Creator unless you want to create a ministry and have followers. So, you try to imitate the Creator, which is impossible because the Creator can't be imitated by that which is unlike Him! **The only thing that resembles the Creator is the Sound of Creativity.**

Do you realize, everything in your life is changed as a result of sound? If I say "flute," the first thing you do is hear a sound. What do you do next? Visualize it! In other words, the sound must have a form! "Flute" has to have a form. The sound of a flute has to bear the corresponding identity: flute. *The sound bears a form.* It supposedly created the world, and it did. **You create your world by sound.**

Can you describe the world to me? Just describe it.

> *Stephen W:* A body of mostly water, with land forms and mountains, populated in certain strategic places for the ease of communication.

Yes, but what is the world? Just keep it to water, land . . .

Stephen W: Land mass covered mostly with water.

Yes. Isn't that what you experience? It's because you experience that very thing that you say it *is* that, but what if I tell you *it isn't?* I have to *re-mind* you. The world, in essence, is a divine Idea and it's only formulated in the manner *you* say so by somebody who is not taught the origin of divination and how it happens that creativity appears manifested (as does a cherry) from that which bears no resemblance to it!

That's how it moves. Got it? What a day!

Yes, Lucille.

Lucille J: Sir, is there a plane of experience where there is sound that doesn't bear form?

For that to happen, there must be some form, whether or not it's material. Remember, you're demanding material in order to cultivate a sense of at-easement with the Non-material. The material can be sound treatment.

There is such a shift — there has to be, because the way the situation is now, the "world," as we seem to know it, is in a very serious space in the vibratory frequency of Wholeness. This is why We are not trying to restore the people on the planet; We are endeavouring to bring to your attention the need of the restoration of the Monarchy of the range of what is termed "the Light Radiation." It is the interference with the electrical force-field, as we come to know it, that really is what constitutes the individual. *It's an electrical force-field,* and the experience is controlled by the mind that is using what some *think* is intelligence — which is nothing but some form of spark of electricity! They don't know where it is; they don't know where the *mind* is. Dr. Penfield told you that (in Montreal, for heaven's sake!); he said there is no evidence of a thought. We describe the electrical presence of such as a thought.

We could not be conceiving the Allness of Being if It were not an actuality, because from the standpoint of a *fractured* sense of being, the Allness of Being is incomprehensible and needs to be worshipped. This is why we are always working from what appears as the object, giving it back to its Essence. We are not taking the *object* to *prove Essence*. The way I've given it allows *both* to be imbued without segregating either, but the *first one* is always given back to the Source. Even with the cherry: it goes *back* to the tree. This is why we say that this salt, water, chalk, protoplasm or slime, all slung together in this bag in time, is really the evidence that man is primarily water. So, we're water-man. (A good name for it.) But remember that we are dealing with restoring, through knowingness, the balance.

The great need is what? The restoration of equilibrium, the great balance, the point of balance. And what happens in the world to-day? Everyone is emotional, because they don't live from the Standpoint of God-Being, from the Standpoint of Principle, from the Standpoint that IS. The mind they allow to have reign instead of *obedience to the Force that IS,* and what happens? Look how they appeal to the emotions of the people! As soon as you can appeal to the emotions of anyone, they become mesmerized. This is why Mrs. Mary Baker Eddy was so right when she said, "Admit only those thoughts that you wish realized." She said, "Stand porter at the door of thought, admitting only those thoughts that you wish realized." So, why would you allow any thought that isn't of the highest vocabulary of tonality commensurate with Source? See?

Students: Yes, Sir.

Thank you!

Students: Thank you, Sir.

⌘

1. Referring to the marble statue, Winged Victory of Samothrace, displayed in the Louvre, Paris.
2. The Divine Coincidence.
3. Kenneth G. Mills, *The Golden Nail: Chapters 1 & 3,* Sun-Scape Publications KMOD-059-2, compact discs.
4. The Star-Scape Singers conducted by Kenneth G. Mills, *Greatest Hits, Vol. 2,* Sun-Scape Records KMOD-058-2, compact disc.

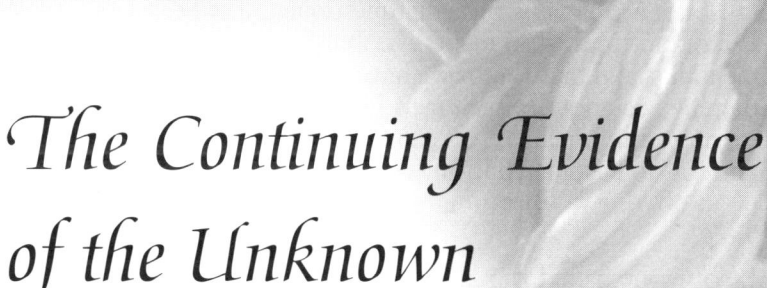

The Continuing Evidence of the Unknown

Chapter XIII

The great demand of to-day is to thrust through the appearances that confine your attention, so that the dynamics which are designed to hold your attention are perceived and thus you don't forget your purpose!

The Continuing Evidence of the Unknown

Themes: Being ~ Conscious-awareness ~ Identity ~ inheritance ~ astringent Language ~ purpose/intention ~ process

This is the morning of August 31, 2003. Going through some of my notes the other day, I found a statement I had given to somebody and I thought you all should have it. When anyone asks you about Principle, so seldom are you able to really give a clear idea of it, and I hope this does. I said on August 4, 2001:

> Principle has nothing to do with a belief-system. It springs from an undeniable State which cognizes that if your cultural and mental states are capable of being questioned, it is because there is a Factor, not present in mentality, that is allowing you to question mentality, and that Factor we have accepted as Principle. Principle thereby becomes the anchor of Light in the sea of living, because staying with Principle, you can always re-organize those thought-patterns to become your inheritance, which is not of serfdom but of an offering of liberation.

Then, someone asked me about *Unfoldment*™ on September 16, 1983, and I said:

> The *Unfoldment*™ is nothing but my "AM-ing" appearing modified, and you call it the *Unfoldment*™ in words. It's my Beingness and seemingly labelled for the linear demands of the mind and the sequence of events in the grand Work which is Self-unfoldment.

I read a very interesting thing. Ramana Maharshi said:

> The ego-ridden mind has its strength sapped and is too weak to resist distressing thoughts.

I think that is enough for now. Let me see, what shall we talk about?

So we will have one thing in common: [Dr. Mills rings the Tibetan bells.]

We are gathered together in the pattern of jubilation as we have been given the great opportunity to gather together and appear as a group, unified in purpose and intent, not to set at variance but to reduce the suggestion of variance to its nothingness. We have come to perceive through the avenues of time the impossibility of trying to bring order out of chaos, and we have found and witnessed unto the difficulty of such an attempt. The flaw rests in the realization that, as James said, "A double-minded man is unstable in all his ways."[1] In this we acknowledge the need, as never before, to move with alacrity and with dynamism into that vehicle of force that comes with that State that men have called "Realization."

We have all considered it, either we wouldn't be here, but we have also to consider whether or not *process* is in keeping with the nowness of Being. It is so fascinating how the mind attempts to extricate from the Invisible the information that will give it enlightenment. This is why I have always said, "What is Enlightenment? I have no idea because it only comes as a concept that would seem to separate those who are asleep from those who are awake." How do you tell the difference?! What is the feature of being awake? Perhaps it is to be able to walk among those who slumber and sleep (while standing-up in their office) and to offer an awakening Presence by carrying the knowingness of the actuality of Being.

The matrix gives you such a wonderful objective experience, and you have such verification of its somethingness — which, now, you all perceive as *nothingness*. It's fun to play with the objective sense of matrix when you realize that the whole program is to seduce you, if you don't know what IS, into the realm of believing that the objective is Real and thus the confinement to the suppositional and the dregs of mentality, which attempt to seduce you into the system of believing it is Real. It is the dregs of society that will constantly attempt to control the processes and laws of your thought in order to reduce you to spasmodic thinking spasms, appearing personified and actively moving as if you were moving under your own modus operandi.

Forget not that the attempt of the seducer is to cause you to doubt your supremacy as the sons and daughters of the living Light. Man was given a special place. (Of course, you're beyond that point of feeling that if I don't say "women," you will be disturbed. If I don't say "women," *do* be disturbed. It's the ego-ridden mind that is bothering "*you.*" It goes *with* "*you.*") Man, in this concept, is not you or me, men or women; it is that concept of Unity that embraces all, not in a belief-system but in the knowingness that to the Consciousness supreme, the Ultimate, there can be no legitimate division. It is only in the passage of time that we have become accustomed to facing our own projection and, by our wonderful sensorial apparatus, giving it such an emotional experience that we find ourselves totally in entanglement with love and non-love, with Realness and non-realness, with friends and not-friends. As one said, "To be a friend, be One." How many try to see two come together as friends? It never does work. It's *work* that you don't need!

How can you have effort if you love another as the Self?! There is only one Self; it's for the fun of your skill in production that you have given yourselves such a drama. And, you know something? You have fallen in love with it to the degree that you don't dare to put it in jeopardy. How can you ever win a game of such chance if you build your fortune on the ever-spinning wheels of procrastination?

The certain death is what is being put-off until to-morrow. What a pretence! You pretend that you are not involved with the present tense of activity: Being. How often do you want to have company with "you" and "me," but when you say "I am," the recognition of otherness is inevitable (from birth) as "you are," "she is," "we are." You've got it! You are dealing with a language that is sore distressed in offering into the channel of time the astringent Language that is so essential to attempt to inculcate the meaning of what is termed "the Eternal," "the Source," "the Atman," "the Christ." Whatever you wish to call it, it is Reality! So, don't scoff at any name, for they all arise from that Language that is so stringent, pointing to some condition that your mind couldn't possibly know, but you do have this assurance that "If it were not so (we were told), I would have told you." How can you know that there *is* such a State? It allows the very counterfeit power to recognize it exists, for "it" is always in question. You cannot point to "you" with assurance unless the radiance is that becoming manumission.

It is fatuous to attempt to bring your intellectual reasoning into the Way-work of liberation. Your intellect should be allowed to show itself and be re-addressed to engage what is termed "the enraptured Way." The enraptured Way is that State whereby you are able to walk with the Invisible and bear the fecundating radiance to those in your offices of delusion. Can you *imagine* — there is no doubt about that! *Here* we are! But what can you imagine? If "this" is Real, that is a vain thing. No wonder people have *varicose* veins! There's too much pressure put onto a supposition. When you come to see, you will perceive without doubt that as a man thinketh in his head, so is he *in* it! [laughter] And as a man thinketh in his heart, there he is found re-identified as that force-field of Love that sets the captive free. It's wonderful to know there is one way to escape the mad hats of delusion.

So many people wear so many hats, but I like what I said: "Don't forget, you wear them on your greatest limit!" If you're not quite here yet, that means "the head." Why do we put the head as *a limit?* Why do we always point to the head when we are thinking? [Dr. Mills strikes the pose of one thinking, with his fingertips to his brow.] Why? We somehow or other have been taught by very intelligent people that our head does the thinking. Dr. Wilder Penfield told us in the forties — I think it was the forties, but what is *time* to a brilliant statement? — that after all his research there was no evidence that the brain *thought.*

There is no awareness found in the brain. If there were, do you think you would *bury* it? They kept Einstein's. The only thing they found out was that it weighed more! That which is the inventive and the one capable of birthing new ideas and revolutionary ideas, like Tesla and Einstein — who would say which is the greater? You can't, because *the Wonder is the continuing evidence of the Unknown, bearing witness to the fact that It IS.*

Why would you lack confidence in the byways of time when you know that you are here for a purpose? That is not to just offer your glowing presence to a mesmerized group of people, but your glowing presence should be such that it would irritate, perhaps, and awaken those to consider what makes you so grand. If you are with people and they never comment, they haven't enough T/tea (Truth) in their experience. They have brewed it for their cup, and it never did go over into the saucer. That's why there were just "constant comments." This is the chatterbox that goes with superficial encounters with beguiling statements that have nothing to do with the practicality of your experience. Wake-up! It has *everything* to do!

Who ever told you you were a limited mortal if it wasn't a limited mortal?! Who ever told you you in essence are divine? "Oh, my goodness! What does that mean?" That's in that astringent Language, "Oh, you're simply divine." It's so true! Have you ever considered how you take such an appellation and don't spread it over a range of considerations? Then you develop mountains that you have to try to conquer, when they are only arising within the consternation of having to face a correct Identity.

The basic problem that everyone has arises from what they are not. That is called the lack of correct Identity. Individuality goes hand in hand with personality and ego. When *I* speak of Individuality, I do not mean the individuality of you or me; I mean the undivided, the universal, State that results in the "root-ness" of One. Be rooted in the Unity that is the underlying force-field to multiplicity but never contained in it.

You can claim Identity from the standpoint of mortality. They say one day, that being a mortal, some day immortality will be found. That is, again, the very root of process. It's fascinating, what process is there to the realization that two plus two is four? There is no process as soon as you know how it has been achieved. From that moment on, you use that four to make sure you have four quarters for your "loonie." (I have often thought what an incredible medium of exchange our incredibly brilliant minters devised! Our mediums of exchange are *loonies.*) It's amazing, you never forget what constitutes four *hundred* dollars. Isn't it amazing? You don't; you're never shortchanged when it's that or four thousand or four hundred thousand or four million. It doesn't mean that there is more substance than there *ever* was; it just means you have more means of exchange.

What is the purpose of exchanging?
You exchange the things for *ideas*.

Remember, money is nothing but an impersonal way to say thank-you. Isn't that a shock? You thought it was for the kingdom of your diminishing resources as you enter that scenario of "old age?"

It's amazing how we have been thrown onto the good works of our government, which has been very wise. It has been a system which has been, and is, *supporting*, but when you come to know what you know, you can enhance it and allow others to enjoy what they need to be comfortable, because not everyone has been given the privilege that you have *chosen*. Those who are in need should be cared for, as the government is so doing, but the ultimate is not *to be cared for;* it is to be in the position of *offering that stream of Knowingness that frees one from being limited to this space-suit termed "the water-man" of this period in the history of delusion.*

It is said that a space visitor called this race "the water-man race." It's a wonderful appellation. We're *all* water! How much? Oh, come on, admit it, you're practically nothing but water! As Dr. Donald Andrews said, if a hundred and fifty pound man — I guess we'll say a hundred and sixty or seventy because that's about the rate people are to-day, or more — could be put into an atomic press and have all the holes squeezed out of him, the residue could be placed on the head of a *pin. Aren't* you *important?!* [laughter]

Isn't it wonderful to know that no matter how small you seem to be, you have the knowingness of the gigantic universal nature of Being. Even when all the holes are squeezed out of you, **What-IS will never be touched by a suggestion or an invention of the mind.**

Isn't it wonderful that people have always questioned what IS, meaning *beyond* "this" and meaning "How come?" A child I once knew said, "How come? How come, Nana?" "Love did it, dear. The *stork* did it." Its nest was on the top of the chimney, and it came down instead of Santa Claus! **My goodness, what if a child realizes that** *what he thinks* **is capable of altering his whole life?!** He must put ideas together as precisely as two plus two, or four pencils equalling four. *He's got to realize that he is creating his experience.*

Look at the world upon which you live and move and have your being. But what is your *being? That's* the question. *There's nothing in the body that testifies to Being, other than activity.* Do you know when Being is present? It's activity that is creative. It is the activity that leads, guides, directs, and reveals so that everyone coming into that Presence is blessed, because in the Light of the unconditional Love there is no one greater or lesser; there is only the realization that each shall receive according to his thirst after Wholeness.

The great demand of to-day is to thrust through the appearances that confine your attention, so that the dynamics which are designed to hold your attention are perceived and thus you don't forget your purpose! Years ago, I said in an *Unfoldment*™ that people would be aware that as soon as a sense of peace and achievement in nations and in countries appeared, somebody would set a bonfire to take your attention from your success or from your way of living, by superimposing an "emergency" upon thought. Could there be an emergency in the Divine?

Students: No, Sir.

This is why you stay calm in the face of this suggested state. Know what IS! Claim! Put on a piece of paper what you consider your Source to be, and then see if you can match your description with your activities. Then see how much you have attributed to the Source is actually practised, involuntarily.

Who ever told you that you had to live in impoverishment? Who ever told you that the statement "All that I have is thine" was rubbish? It meant impoverishment if you were spiritual? Don't be fooled. I always was taught in Sunday School and in church that "All that I have is thine." Why do you accept so little? Recently I have learned that so many people are bothered by elegance and by abundance and by colour. My model has always been the birds and the garden, which is such a mystery. Those seeds planted out of your sight and out of your realm of doubt kick their limitation right in the earth and head towards the light. They do not care what rock is saying, "Don't dare to threaten my position!" That is what beliefs become: hard like rocks. The flowering of the mystery of the fecundating force of Source or Spirit is such that it blossoms if there is *no doubt*. You never doubt that two and two is four; you never doubt that there is a Creator unless you are of that state where you "know you created yourself."

Do you remember your birth? Of course! You remember anything you create. That's part of your Scroll. **You will remember anything you create, but will you remember all the magnificent moments that Light penetrated the illusion?**

Don't believe; if you do, there are limits. Beliefs are all based on limits. That's why you have *faith* that the limits will one day be perceived and *hope* that there'll be something to take their place: another system of process.

Mrs. Mary Baker Eddy once said, "From sense to Soul my pathway lies." It certainly does; it *lies*. That is the way to make your mind think it's achieving something. "What are you doing?" "I am a member of this and I am progressing. I just passed another exam"— as if it were some form of spiritual karate and you were heading for a black belt! However, the death blow should have been given at the beginning of the course [laughter], and the verdict "Thou art not 'this' but That." How can you say that? Because the awareness reveals your objective world and its contents, but it has nothing to do but be the corresponding identity of that State termed "Consciousness."

Consciousness you will always have; awareness, also, but not necessarily always of the objective. This is why one can become aware that *the Invisible is tangible, practical, and beneficent*. The thought of it can be, hopefully, found accepting you with all your sins and all your omissions as you approach that experience termed "the Pearly Gates." I told you yesterday, it's here now, and *all you have to do is have the courage to pass through the door*. Don't consider defenestrating; it's too small for you! Let the angels do that. **Enjoy facing the door and see that it is nothing but a flimsy mental barrier through which you may pass, for you know that on the other side is the "horror" that you face in releasing yourself from the objective confinement.**

You're always afraid of what you don't know, until you know it, and guess what? You have your four pencils as well. When you know what IS, you can enjoy all this wealth, all these objets d'art, a grand house, a small house — it's *all* your intention. *Don't blame it on someone else for being wealthy.* **There is no limit to the wealth with which you are endowed, but how many of you ever go to the Bank, your inherited Reservoir, and claim it?**

When I was a child, I remember standing on that old hammock on the back veranda and swinging myself and every so often the hammock banging the house and Mum saying, "Ken, don't bang the house! Don't swing so hard!" But I forgot I was swinging hard because I was about four, five, or six and I was looking through the two chains, the triangle, and I saw me in a car I had never seen in my life! I saw myself in a limousine when I was four or five. I used to think of that because it seemed so fantastic. Here I was, the son of a very "rich," loving father and mother, and a very modest home. And lo and behold, what have I been driving in for the past forty-five years, a lot of the time? A limousine! It *bothers* people but they never saw it in the triangle of possibilities!

Have you ever noticed how much agreement there is when you find other people in your same predicament? How much company you have? How often do you find in your predicament you are surrounded by those who won't accept it? You might see them for ten- or fifteen-minute visits occasionally — once a week, perhaps, is all you can stand — because they don't agree with it. **You have to stand with conviction.**

When I was concertizing and my hand was crushed, I didn't go to the medical doctor; I just knew that if it didn't heal correctly and I could not continue playing, something was wrong with what I knew. It was wrapped in a white linen handkerchief, and the lady I spoke to said, "Don't look at it, Ken. Just know that the finger of God traced aloud a bow of promise upon a cloud." Three weeks later my wife and I were driving in the car, and the handkerchief fell off. The nails were polished, and there was whitening under every nail and not a blemish to be seen. The difference between the hands was amazing because one had polished nails and one didn't.

Take what you know to be true and allow it to build the very foundation upon which you may depend. Depend upon that which you know is constant. If anything changes, it isn't Real. That which doesn't change *is* Real. Do you always notice when things change? Yes. And do you always notice when they don't change? Yes. That which allows you to detect either state is what you have here and now, and there's no process to It! But you don't live that way; it's *too difficult* for your belief-system! You've built a whole scenario of what you're going to be like.

I remember, forty years ago, thirty-five years ago, the people who came to me. I didn't know who they were. They would knock on my door as I finished my piano teaching and come in and speak to me. One man came in one night, he didn't say his name or anything; I didn't ask him and I sat down in my chair and pointed to the sofa for him. He came over, knelt down, put his head in my lap, cried for about an hour, got-up and walked out. How do you know what happens? How do you know?

Should not the Word be empowered by just being? You don't empower It; It is *Self*-empowered. Remember, it was the singing, and it *is* the singing, that brings down walls and it can move mountains. We have proved that. It even made the Iron Curtain invisible to us, and when we got behind it, the first thing translators did was say, "*How did you get here?! How* did you get here?!" I said, "It's not quite certain, but we are here." We met such pleasantness with all the borders in Russia, Poland, and Czechoslovakia — far more pleasant than what you meet crossing the American border to-day. I am so glad Canada and the Canadian immigration and customs people still remain civil.

Are you not grateful that you have the remedy for the world's situation?

Students: Yes, Sir.

It's so wonderful to be with those who can support you in realizing your great ministry. This is why it's nice to be together, because this is for the fun of the objective in the Light of the undivided garment of Allness. Why would you *not* attempt to live your inheritance: "All that I have is thine"; "I and my Father *is* One." Don't use "*are*"; you've got *two!*

Penetrate and thrust through the suggestion of appearances and appear to *be* the Wonder — Wonder, miracle, and marvel — pointing to that State which many countries do not know, because they do not have the words in their language. This became a salient feature of interviews and question-and-answer periods that appeared as "receptions" with no physical food but three hundred people from the concert gathering in another smaller auditorium where *we thought* we were going to be *fed!* It was a "reception," and when we looked out from our position on another stage, I said, "What are these people doing here?" The manager of Warsaw's National Philharmonia Hall said, "Oh, this is the reception. These people all have come from Symphony Hall to hear you; they all have questions." We answered them constantly for over an hour. One doctor stood-up and said, "You have increased our language because we have never heard of such words as 'wonder,' 'miracle,' and 'marvel.' What are these words?" I said, "The evidence of what you recognize as having heard. **"Wonder is the cause of your question; *miracle* is the evidence that it could be answered; and *marvel* is a natural state of humility!"**

This is the state I enjoy and the state I heartily recommend. The prescription for Being is to subscribe not to the propaganda of suggestion but to the ordained Fact that thou art perfect and beloved: "This is my beloved Self in whom I am well pleased." Where is there labour? It was made-up, for the Day is the fulfilment appearing as the Now, the irradiance of Life, Truth, and Love. Isn't it amazing that in that Light, darkness and light appear to come and go, but that Light that allows each to be discerned is the very one of your Being. It's absolute but it's dressed-up so nicely for you that I hope you will enjoy taking the full Menu and finding what causes you to burp and what causes you to have a "but"!

Remember, procrastination is the onset of the deterioration of the will.

[Dr. Mills picks-up a cherry by its stem.] Remember the cherry.

Students: Yes, Sir.

It's wonderful to know you don't have to labour over Being.

Is there any *burning* question? If not, don't ask it! [laughter] It's been nice to see all of you. Of course, I don't usually see *parts* of you! [laughter] I'm just being very Texan, you know, "All of ya."

Yes, Greg.

> *Gregory S:* Sir, I wanted to ask you about my experience. It seems somewhat simplistic, but it seems relatively simple to go to where the mind doesn't know, and it's been my experience during the day, if there's activity of the brain, simply to just take it to the edge of where it *doesn't* know and temper it with words of the seven Synonyms, of Love —

Yes. That's all right because you're just ruling it, you're ruling the mind, which is your horse, but there will come a time when you don't do that. That's for practice to make sure it's broken, and then you can ride it. That's the most important thing: to get to the point where you ride it without ever considering a saddle. You're considering a saddle at the moment.

> *Gregory S:* Is there a particular right attitude for being in that saddle?

Ask who's in the position. It always stems from being in the wrong position and not the right one.

> *Marian F:* Is there a way of doing intent? Once you come to a place where you know what you want to create, how do you *intend* it?

Your intention carries with it all that is necessary. Your intention should include your purpose, but that is for precipitating. **You always know that whenever you precipitate you also have to be willing to have the responsibility for *what* you're precipitating. It's not difficult to precipitate; it's whether or not you want to take-on the responsibility of it.** There is no difficulty in fulfilling the intention, but it undoubtedly will be fulfilled in ways that are *not thought*. It'll open in unusual ways. When you're not thinking, you may find intuitive promptings because they have nothing to do with thought. It's only *after* it's happened that you start *thinking* you've had an intuitive prompting.

We had the intent to sing in Carnegie Hall. How it was going to happen was a question because some of the Singers were just learning to sing and learning to read notes and somebody had to earn the money to pay for Carnegie Hall. But our intention was to do that. That intention took place in about 1976, and we made the first of our seven concerts in Carnegie Hall in 1981. Sometimes we sang *twice a year* in Carnegie Hall.

So, the intent can be, but oh boy! It took work, but it was all done from the standpoint of *Unfoldment*™. It was a whole new experience, and it began with the Singers realizing there wasn't the need of a microphone to amplify the voice, which meant the breath was so essential. That's very essential to your intention being fulfilled. **Don't breathe shallowly in dreaming a fulfilment of an intention. Take the breath by not raising the shoulders but resting on the diaphragm, because there is a point of balance.**

Yes.

> *Alexandra M:* Did you keep in your experience "We're going to Carnegie Hall" when you practised, or did you just practise?

No, we always had the intention before us: "We're going to do Carnegie Hall." Yes. You have to be definite in an intention.

It can't be undefined. The intention has to be very defined. Don't have it amorphous; it has to be defined.

You've opened-up a whole consideration here. There was a little girl I once knew who wanted to play the piano, and she was missing a finger and she was so musical. I knew her parents. They said, "Well, of course, she'll never be able to play," and I said, "That's perfectly ridiculous! Of course, she'll play!" They said, "But, Ken, she's missing a finger!" I said, "Well, I won't use my fourth; she hasn't got a fourth finger. *She* doesn't know it! It's more difficult for me to play without a fourth because I know it." She eventually got her final exam so I was told. She had the intention to play and took the ways and means to do so.

I loved working with the children and I loved teaching because I saw the practicality of everything *known*, to be applicable and practical when the mind was freed from being cluttered by superimposed fallacies. This is why it seems so difficult for *you:* you've got so many layers of superimposed considerations that it's just so unfortunate. You just say, "To hell with all of them," and experience Heaven here now, which is nothing but the rhythm and the harmonic state of Being in practicality and *you* appearing the Song!

You *are* an atomic splendour! You were *made* to sing. Your whole atomic structure is a *humming* experience. All *you* are hunting for is the Voice that allows the captive to be set free! That is why the Holy Visitor is the breath, and this is the inhalation that you accept from the Invisible. You don't see the breath, you don't know the breath, but without it, you aren't. It should be such a reception that your exhalation should be exuding the Wonders of this transcendental state of Actuality. That's what it means to have the breath of God that *fills* with life anew!

Students: Thank you.

⌘

1. James 1:8.

The Pure Tone

Chapter XIV

The moment you hear a word of Truth, you are committed to the honesty of being the Self!

The Pure Tone

Themes: God/Source ~ Truth ~ Life ~ Love ~ Light ~ Soul ~ Spirit ~ Mind ~ thought

---

This is the morning of Sunday, October 12, 2003, Thanksgiving Sunday, and we are going to begin the Lecture a little bit differently to-day. (They're seldom *ever* the same!) I want to read you something first, and then Mr. Charlebois is going to speak to you about something he spoke to me about, and I felt you would all enjoy hearing it. It's something that you may have read about a little bit, here and there, but it's a very interesting consideration, and you will find what he says very pertinent to some of your considerations and an explanation of them.

So, I will read you something that unfolded. I just happened to find it here. I gave this last November, but I don't think anyone has heard it. This unfolded and it was recorded on November 22, 2002:

> Most of the students think that they have come to Earth to overcome karmic difficulties. However, their purpose is much greater: it is to become the support system of their Master or Mentor's offering in the realm of Feeling, which transcends any psychic or emotional involvement with the virtual as a possible reality.

What we were talking about the other evening for a few minutes, you will see how it's pertinent to this. Claude, would you like to speak to the Group?

> *Claude C:* Good morning. Such nice, beautiful, smiling faces! I was talking with Dr. Mills in the evening. We started discussing the various aspects of the support system for the Work, as we have just heard. It was a very pertinent quote that Dr. Mills fell upon in the car that we thought would be a good introduction to what I have to say.
>
> The first part of this is that I just talked about a point that I came across, which I'm sure some of you have, which is that we live in a very particular time right now

in our civilization. That's supported by certain studies that have been done that seem to point in that direction. The first point that I brought out is that the Earth has a wavelength, and ever since we've had the instrument to measure this wavelength it's been the same vibration, the same wavelength. But lately, what has been happening, lo and behold, in spite of the fact that the scientific community considered this wavelength in the past to be a constant, *it has been changing*. The second point is that the magnetic field of the Earth is also changing. The magnetic field of the Earth exists as a result of the differential between the rotation of the inner core or the magma part of the Earth and the Earth's rotation in space. Exactly *why* this is happening, I'm not of a scientific background and I'm not proficient enough to be able to tell you the reason, but what we are guided to look at here is that something is happening physically to the force-field of the planet and its wavelength or, if you wish, its heartbeat or its vibration.

Now, the implication this has, according to various people I've met who are still studying this phenomena from a spiritual standpoint, is that if we look at the old Arcane Schools, they used to go into caves or deep into pyramids to experience the initiative process of going through the search for the true Identity. The reason they did this, according to the theory, is that they wanted to remove the body from the energy-field or magnetic field of the planet so that the cellular and energy structure of your body could be removed from this temporarily so that you would identify yourself beyond the body, which is what we are trying to do here.

The point behind all of this is that the conditions around the planet right now are directed towards you living this initiative process; it is re-creating the phenomena that the old Arcane School reproduced in caves and in the schools of thought and of spiritual research.

What we have to look at here is that the concept of being "a porter at the door of your thoughts" becomes that much more important. Our role is such that we have to be especially careful of how we think.

One of two things is going to happen, and that is that the phenomena that we are going through will be used by us as a springboard to the finding of true Identity. The people who are unaware of this will go crazy, and we will witness in the years to come more and more unbalance as to world affairs and the mental state of people.

So, in relationship to this fact or this realization, it is very important that we study and look at how we are emotionally and energetically. When we look at ourselves from this standpoint, we have to always see ourselves from the perspective that there's no distance between our thought and healing. We must focus on the fact that Mind is of an order of Reality that is above physical law, which means that there is no space between right thinking and right being or the condition of your energy or of your physical state.

What is the cause of disease or dis-ease? It's caused by erroneous thought or it is the *accepting* of the erroneous thought of the people around you. If you believe you are subject to physical law, physical law says that whatever is overflowing equalizes itself and whatever is lacking will be filled.

So, in the Presence of our Teacher, looking at our state of mind and energy, pure or not, we have to look at it from the standpoint of humility that we are not yet omnipresent, omniscient, omnipotent and accept that we incarnated with a veil. As such, our job is to clean-up this veil so that it's as clear as possible so that we become the custodian and the support system of the energy of the Teacher.

Being aware of this brings us to the standpoint that it's okay for us to go through processive methods for us to clean-up our energy and to be aware of where we stand, always holding to the thought that Mind is of an order of Reality that is greater than this realm, but also accepting with humility that we might not be fully realized right now, and it's okay for us to sit in front of a fire if we're tired of being with people, or it's okay for us to sit down and do breathing exercises if we feel depleted. If we take time to do that, we instigate the same protocol when we are with the Teacher that we've instigated from a physical standpoint. We won't be with Dr. Mills if we have a very bad cold, out of respect and out of a desire not to contaminate everybody here or Dr. Mills. The same applies to our state of being, energetically. It's important that before we are in the Presence of our Teacher that we just do a little centring exercise: How do I feel right now? What do I need? What do I have to give? What do I have to contribute?

We've all come to meet Dr. Mills in a very magical way. This means that we have something to receive from Dr. Mills, but we must never forget that we have something to contribute. Some of us do this by enhancing Dr. Mills' reality and power by creating with him various things. Some of you create music, others create beautiful poetry, et cetera, and that creates a thought-force centred around creativity, the creative Force, *ergo,* the Father and the Creator-Energy. That is a conscious contribution.

I'm sure all of you realize that and know that because you're all very conscious beings, but it's going back to basics to look at it from a different perspective, with the knowledge that what we are going through now is an acceleration and whatever we do — I don't know if you go through it — we all agree that there's a lot of magic in our lives and the synchronicities are so spectacular that they're scary! And that's why. So, we must stand porter and realize and question: What is the role of a Teacher? What is our relationship to it? Why did Jesus have disciples? What was their purpose? What is the function of a Teacher being the Lamb of God? How can we contribute to that?

These questions are just food for thought. I've been with Teachers and Saints in India who would not accept the close proximity of anybody within fifteen feet of them, and I've questioned myself, *Why?* This is part of the answer: these people have a purpose that is not centred around the purpose of Dr. Mills. Their purpose was to study an aspect of spirituality and to prove and to destroy mental concepts of the people around them, but they needed to do that from a distance. The purpose of a

Teacher like Dr. Mills who is an incarnation of Love — I think we all agree to that — is to reach out to people.

I think that more or less sums it up. It's just something that brings me back to my basics and brings out a question mark so that we can act upon it and build on that for the future. Thank you.

Students: Thank you.

Thank you, Claude. I heard more than I heard last night! I'm glad I reheard it this morning.

The most important consideration is your thought and how it rests within your sense of achievement. If it's a good thought, it's fine, and if it's a bad thought, it isn't fine. Only *you* know what type of thought-process you are holding, because we deal with thought in the realm of otherness. In the seclusion of the Self — we *say* "the Self" — in the seclusion of that State which we give an identity termed "the Self," it's *not* thought. The only way we know that Place exists is by the willingness to reduce the vibratory frequency of Presence to the lower octave of Sound-Being. *That's why it appears spoken.*

That is just exactly the same with inspiration. Without thought, inspiration bears an expectancy, and the result is a revelation to the answer of your question. This is why, when anyone is drawing upon any project, to will what you want and what you think it should be is usually disastrous. How many subdue their recalcitrant attitudes and move to the level of perceiving them as the hindrance to the fulfilment of their inspiration?

When we know two and two is four, we are so assured of that that we dare to declare it before any figure of time. (Figures go with figures!) When we know what IS, we hesitate not to declare it before any figure of time. The interesting fact is that That which IS can't be figured, but That which IS allows the figure to bear the radiance commensurate with a defined, speculative Source termed "the Creator" or "God," "the Self."

We have to name what we know *must be* in order for our named state to hold us in the tide of common events, but the state of realizing what IS allows you, with Grace, to enter the selected group of a few and bear in a seeming formation a Message that can't be formed. It can't bear form, because That which is realized bears witness to your Real state. I have always felt that anyone attuned to the mysteries of Being and of Life is not of Earth. Earth has a belief-system to welcome you to the planet because it's the only system known to those coming to the planet that *allows*. The One who is coming to re-mind those who are visiting the planet that it is only *belief* that is common to start with, knows differently, alters the complex thought-patterns (no matter how well ensconced they are within your zone of achievement), and alerts you not to forget your inheritance. You *had* to forget it upon entering the plane if you were to engage in the activities of what is termed "the human-being in multiplicity."

This has resulted in a fermentation with most of humanity, because when you offer a Truth to a believer, it means that *that one Truth* alters the entire process of conceptual thinking. This one alteration alters your activity. When Truth meets resistance, it's usually pronounced "a chemicalization"! But in this laboratory that happens in the mind, you are graced if you have somebody to drop a catalyst in this solution of confusion, because that catalyst will bring about a resolution, and the liquified state will become pure, or purer, to the point where you say, "I see the accuracy of that statement."

If you are sitting, wisely listening to the news (I don't know how wise it is to sit listening to it!) or reading a newspaper, immediately that is your alarm; you're on duty. Everything that is in the newspaper appeals to that part of *you* that would cause you to become emotionally involved with the possible consequences of the human to which the news applies. Do you realize, *negativity requires a corresponding state to support it?!* Negativity can't live without Truth, because it's the Truth that can alter the vibration, and if the altered vibration is perceived by error and not accepted, It seems to support the erroneous belief!

So, when you are told that "this and this is true," know that if it doesn't apply to Principle or to that constant Element that you know must exist, then don't accept it. Reject it and *know* that this is not acceptable in the realm of that which is Real. In the isolation of being Actual, virtuality is readily perceived. It doesn't bear *one* component that is Eternal.

What does "Eternal" mean? You say it's the opposite of time. No! It isn't necessarily the opposite of time; it is that State that a timed-being cannot comprehend but knows it *must be* because

Truth and its so-called measurements *are not confined to a time sequence.* That has been termed "Eternality."

That continuity begins with the genesis and ends with the exodus, but the interesting part is, it never truly ends. It was the continuousness of Being that allowed your visitation to Earth, *or* the visitation to the womb, *or* the visitation to the thought-world of creation, and the acceptance of someone being willing to take the embryonic idea and fertilize it. This state has resulted in the perpetuation of the belief-system of heredity, which in Actuality does not exist! There is no hereditary factor in Life as it IS, because Life as it IS cannot be defined in a process: there is no hereditary disease, there is no hereditary anything, unless you want to use it as an excuse to evade Being active.

Everything to-day is talked of in codes, genetic codes! Of course, it's very interesting, but if you don't know too much about it, don't feel you're ignorant. Everyone is trying to understand why people behave as they do, and the whole system is rather mysterious. Of course, it is! How can anyone know the process of creation of a human being, other than through the analysis of the transitory? It always comes to an end. Any analysis you try to do of any form of that which is termed "Transcendental" or "the Ultimate" or "the Absolute" is impossible, because the Absolute is not a State that is capable of being analyzed by people. Remember, it's only a thought that is given to the realm of the Unknown, but it is so accurate that it reduces suggestion to the feet of understanding, if it's wise.

Understanding becomes the line that separates That which IS from that which isn't. **It is this understanding based on Principle which is the trampoline for leaping out of the mis-carriaged concepts of birthing in mortality.**

The whole struggle that people are having to-day with this increased vibrational rate that we are living in is underlying the fact that they need the clarity surrounding some concept or some idea that is not found in the realm of the ordinary language. That idea is usually termed "Self-realization." What it means I haven't a clue! Another word is "hunting for God," or "hunting for Spirit" or "being Spirit." You can't be something that "this" isn't, only in an attempt to realize the State in which it must exist, and that State is that which transcends the conceptual thinking of a honed intellectuality.

This is why, in the jurisdiction of the Light, **Love** prevails, because anyone who attempts to gain liberation from the mental capacity developed by faulty education is capable of being allowed to attempt to birth their wings and join the angels bearing glad tidings to all those who would be part of the vocalization surrounding emancipation. Manumission is your birthright, and we have substituted bondage to a faulty teaching for it.

Your bondage came the moment you went to school; it was *enhanced*. It *came* when you started to identify and recognize, but it was *underlined* when you went to school and you were told how to think and how to draw. The only thing about drawing was that they gave you an object to draw, and then they told you whether you had done well or not. We don't have this ability to draw an object of what God is, even in thought, or what Truth is, because Truth cannot be found as in a definition. It is a state of assurance that *evolves* as one enters into the non-contradictable state of the Absolute.

This non-contradictable State is horrendous to the intelligentsia and to the elite. The elite have always been those who have become empowered and used it personally to rule, conquer, and mesmerize by the power of numbers. **Ours is a victory because *we* succeed with only One! It's not in the numbers that man's victory lies; it's in the verity that it is from One that all numbering takes place.** Remember, they are all derivatives: the genetics of numerology! *But you must never forget One!*

"If thine eye be single, thy whole body shall be filled with Light."[1] But *what* is **Light?** It can't be something that is *part* of the body. It is the Light that people cognize when people have achieved manumission or have come to the realization of their wondrous nature, completely undefined but, bearing a corresponding identity, virtually lived.

If the virtual had no evidence of something beyond it, you and I would not be interested. We were born into the virtual but we were virtually held in the prison of belief-systems, but *now* we are basing our freedom on the realization that we can conceive that we have a mind that has to be put off. The Bible tells you, any Holy Writ tells you, and if it isn't "writ," I tell you now, it does say it in the Books — and it doesn't matter whether the Books said it or not, it's factual! You haven't got the ability to evidence your genius without Mind that is beyond the paltry state of yours.

It's not to belittle it, unless it thinks it's grand because of what it's attained, but as I said yesterday, it's very difficult to know where a thought comes from. It's like when a baby arrives, you tell a child the stork brought it, but you didn't tell him it rests on the top of the chimney or pole in a wooden nest. (How it gets down the chimney, I don't know. It's as bad as Santa Claus!) [laughter] However, the idea of conception unconfined is the natural state of one experiencing *the breaking of the egg of materiality.*

This is why it is so important to see how thick "your" shell is, how long it takes you to be moved by questions like "Where does the thought come from?" Where do you say it comes from? Everyone says, "It's my mind!" But for heaven's sake, *that's* a thought! Where is it? And they point to your head! Dr. Wilder Penfield said years ago, in the forties and the fifties, there's no evidence other than a little spark, a synapse, within the "oatmeal." That *may* have been the result of a thought, but we can't base a thought on it! [laughter] Then look at Dr. Andrews (of Johns Hopkins University). If you think you're so important, just have a chat with him (if he's still around), because he said, if you could put a hundred and fifty pound man in an atomic press and squeeze all the holes out of him, the residue could be placed on the head of a pin! *Isn't that exciting?!* [laughter] Where is the continuity of Being *in dust?* **The continuity of Being is a fact, otherwise you would not have a memory of perfectness somewhere!**

Always check: if you think you're thinking thoughts in your mind, ask where the mind is. It's been made-up! It always says, while we are absent *not* from one another but from the suggestion of the mind, we still navigate the plane with promise. That promise, for people like you, thank God, is that you perceive more and more clearly the authentic nature of Being and *realize!*

Consider **Life**. It *can't* be found in the body. All you have in the body is the corresponding identity of what you have offered as Life. It isn't! It's the evidence that there must be a State beyond this living and that is termed "Life." Ah! There must be a State beyond "this," and that is termed "God." It *never* can be "God *in* you." (God bless you!) It *can't* be "God in you." You *never* can put the

Greater into the lesser, but the evidence that God is good and good is God is that *He allows you to think that* until you are re-awakened by a remark of someone who is beyond the gravitational field of belief and alerts you to the uncontradictable premise of Being unconfined and uncontaminated by any hypotheses. **This jurisdiction of the Truth is supreme.**

Spirit is another thing. Just because you can have a good time dancing or bowling or eating or swimming or playing tennis, what have you — or *working* — it *should be* a good time! Remember, you say "the spirit of my work," but truly you're pointing to a State that is not, and never will be, contained within a limit.

> **All evidence of genius and achievement is the lessening of the mental confinement.**

No one is limited unless it's "due to karma," but karma's a tremendous excuse for perpetuating what-isn't. It's like having pets you can't leave or a wife that you can't leave to go to an *Unfoldment*™, or a husband who can't leave to come to an *Unfoldment*™ because of the dogs, or the house, or the cats. It's different if you have a child, but it's amazing how "I have to call my wife to see if there's anything on our agenda." Doesn't that put it off till you ruminate in your empty room? *You should expel this.*

Don't you remember the time everyone was invited to the feast? Then, when everything was ready, what came? Excuses! Excuses. *What is an excuse?* You make them all the time. We've come to accept it, but, really, an excuse is something in our make-up that allows it to be accepted. Sometimes it's viable. It's one of those funny things in the virtual [laughter], when you don't want to be *accused* instead of *excused;* in other words, you don't want to be accused of having other interests that you'd rather be attending to, so you make an excuse.

My father brought us up such that if we said we were going to do something as children, we could *never* back out; we had to do it. I'm so grateful for the discipline that was self-imposed when I grew-up, because I had what appeared to be a heavy load, especially in my high school years, because I carried eleven subjects and practised three hours a night and studied three hours a night in order to get a scholarship because we were poor, and I couldn't get to university unless I won a scholarship. That was achieved, but then I studied for twenty-five years. Every day (of my study), a time chart was filled out, from the time I got-up until usually one o'clock in the morning. I knew what I did every fifteen minutes to every half hour. And when I practised, every hour I practised, I knew if I did six hours, I knew if I did five and a half, five and three-quarters, four; I knew exactly. *I didn't allow the mind to fool me into what had been achieved,* and boy, it *can* fool you!

Keep a time chart of every day and see how much is spent on a coffee break or how much is spent chatting and nothing but emptiness resulting. You've allowed your whole attention span to be inundated with a river of thoughts and you don't know the banks! But you'll know how much *waste* there is when you have to go to the bank. Yes, sir. **You should all keep a chart and** *especially if you don't want to!*

There's all the talk to-day about increasing our vibrational rate, and the rate of vibration *is* increasing. I remember J.H. telling me on one of our many visits, "You have been *rewired,* either you could never have taken the ensuing force-fields that are coming unto you, and you couldn't be doing the Work you're doing." It was fascinating she told me that, because I had that from three other people. Perhaps she was right, but it *does* make it difficult for the body, to encounter constant partials.

It's like a musical instrument. A piano sounds beautiful when the partials are limited — there *aren't* any! You have the pure tone, then. My grand piano was noted for that when I got it, and many pianists and technicians came to hear it upon its arrival. Mr. Steinway himself had watched over the total production of it, and it was famous for this condition of being without partials. *The tone was so pure, it just sang!* It is such an engineering feat to bring about the shape of the piano, the tone of the piano, and the sounding board of the piano, the action of the piano, and the understanding of the dynamic tension involved.

> That's *exactly* like your inner heart, the heartstrings! You can't have partial truths. You don't realize the tension that is demanded to bring an errant mind into proper shape. You don't realize the pressure under which your thought-structures have to be held until they are perfectly matching your divine language, and you don't realize it's only then that you reveal whether your sounding board is *solid* or *cracked!*

It's very hard to dust under the strings of your big grand piano but you develop a way to do so. It's the same thing with the strings of thought that constitute *your* soundingness, *your* tonality. The string of thoughts bear an actual tonality, and do you realize how sometimes you hear people who speak in a monotone? That is *not* the type of voice you ever hear on the radio. Never. Why? *The voice reveals the state of the thought that is using it!*

I don't know how the term "voice-over" ever came into it! When I hear Dianne's voice, it's Dianne's voice. It's not *over* anything else, but it certainly *gets across!* So, it *does* cross over; it *does* get across the importance of Water Arts and Seed Wonder[2] and all that type of thing.

Dianne F: I've had the best training, Sir! Thank you.

Yes. It's a direct alignment with That which IS that allows the voice to penetrate the veil of suggestion.

What do you think the highest attainment is? To climb the mental walls that you have erected and stand in the Presence of the Ineffable! And that is possible, but not from your ordinary education. This is the *wonder!*

Don't fret and fume over prospects! *Know* where the gold is! It's written and it's directly found within the escutcheon of your own Soul factor, and your own *voice of the Soul is your conscience.* You know when you make an excuse or when you don't do what you should do; unless you have *morphine-ized* yourself, you will perceive how *drugged* you are, because so seldom to-day are people taught to be aware of conscience! It speaks . . . and frequently with no words. That's why you know it only comes to you as a thought of upset. It's a force that bears only an upset of "You know you didn't do that." Then, when you *do* do it, you say, "I'm *so glad* I did it."

When you look at the word **"Soul,"** a synonym of the Source, it's seldom that people have felt a meaning, even those who have studied for many, many years. I never knew one priest who could tell me what Soul was, I never knew one minister who could, and it's very difficult to consider it in a way of *empowerment* other than that which is associated with an aspect of divinity. But it was a tremendous force of empowerment for *me* when I realized that it was *the Feeling of Being I AM*. Then it *transcended the emotional involvement* but it still allowed me to be very much aware of how another was feeling but also open to the possibility of reducing the emotional to a secondary feature of the situation. *That's how you know when it's operating.*

Spirit: You can say, "People are so *spirited,* and that's the evidence of Spirit." Spirit is that Force that is claimed to be ethereal, but the evidence of Spirit is often seen in the attitude with which you engage your vocation, with which you engage your encounters with a suggested "other." Then you know whether the Spirit is *present,* because it worketh magic! That's why we say, "Oh, the Spirit is present." The Spirit of *newness! It never is of oldness.* That's why it's so hard to have much spirit when you're in a rut! I always used to say, "Remember, the continuation of the rut, in widening, is your grave." *Why isn't anyone laughing?!* [laughter] **Newness is never found in a rut; it usually creates the way that is marked by those who walk it without trepidation.**

Mind: It can't be found. You say, "Oh, my mind is tired." Fiddlesticks! You lazy so-and-so! Your mind never knows it's being used — you only say it is — and you've made it up to begin with because you don't know how to account for that thing in the top of your head! [laughter] Do you know how to account for any part of your body? No. It was necessary for the space-suit, but you were never meant to live in the *pocket* of it and put your head in it! [laughter]

The Mind, with regard to a synonym of the Source, of God, the Self, is that State that allows the totality of the Authentic to be cognized. You can never expect the mind that you seem to have — which is your instrument of limitation — you never can educate it to become the Mind that IS. *How can the lesser ever become All that IS?!* But isn't it amazing the grace that we appear to have a mind that foretells the glory of the continuity of Being?!

Somebody asked me once, "What is the relationship between you and Michael the Archangel?" I said, "What difference does it make, since you don't seem to know either of us?"

Nicholas Roerich said a very interesting thing:

If any form of suicide is to be condemned, then the killing of another by a malicious consciousness [mental malpractice] must also be condemned.

Do hold your thoughts in check. There is no distance to a thought. Always remember that. Hold everyone you love *without* reservation. "I like Mr. Mills, but I don't like the sense of commitment." It's not to Mr. Mills you're committed. *The moment you hear a word of Truth, you are committed to the honesty of being the Self!* That's where you're committed.

I don't want a following, I never have. Usually I see the *face*. When I look at the dog, I don't bother looking at his tail first! [laughter] The face is the canvas of God, and I'm so grateful your canvas is sometimes stretched — it looks nice! As I said yesterday: *The cheapest facelift is a smile!*

> The joy of Being undefiled
> Is when you see the wondrous Child,
> Born in the manger beyond all doubt,
> Where the crying and the bleating of the lamb
>   just point to a Saviour-thought about.
>
> And in that realm of joyous delight,
> May you find your Self as One in Light,
> Bearing unto the hills of time
> The Sage wisdom: "Thou art divine."

Thank you.

Students: Thank you, Dr. Mills.

⌘

---

1. Matthew 6:22.
2. Names of businesses for whom Dianne has recorded radio advertisements.

The Sublimity of a Free Spirit

Chapter XV

You can never be separated from what you truly are; there are no words, no thoughts, that can ever rescind your status as Divine.

The Sublimity of a Free Spirit

Themes: The actuality of Creation ~ divinity ~ concentration ~ sound/vibration/frequency ~ choice/freedom ~ diversity ~ keeping timetables

This is the evening of January 10, 2004. You might say there's so much to talk about if we go to the *outward view,* and the outward view *is* so talked about. People make their living by reporting the news of what's going on in the multitude of people who are said to inhabit this planet.

I really have never quite understood what value the news has, and the news reporters would not like this, but I really think it's a terrible waste. I remember, when we saw the newsreel at the movie theatres, it didn't seem to matter at all that what we were viewing had already happened two or three weeks before! It just was a fantasy, a type of something to hold your attention. I hope you didn't *concentrate* too much. That wouldn't be good, because you're using, then, one of the forces that are, really, quite divine. (When I say "quite divine," it has to stand for something that you may never have considered.)

To be able to *concentrate* is to be able to *rule,* because the *unruly,* who are reported and used to hold our attention, are the people who have never learned how to concentrate or to call upon the force that comes with correct alignment to Principle.

When we look at the people to-day, we see everyone listening about what they are obviously viewing. So, the *outside* is constantly viewed with no concern whatsoever to what the *inside* is doing. In other words, the mob running amok holds your attention so much that you never stop to consider what is *really* happening that can alter the madness of unbridled thought-power that is necessary to give meaning to what we describe as catastrophes. *Do you realize, if you couldn't understand what you were looking at, it would have no affect on you whatsoever?* None! But we say we understand what we're looking at. Why? Because we have adopted an allegiance to support diversity in the mesmeric state of a second creation.

The first Creation had nothing that was objectified and talked about, for it was its own self-witness. **The Absolute sees nothing but its Allness.** But how can I say that with the very mind that is talking to diversity? **I can say it because I am utilizing the mind that is made-up of thoughts, to rescind their mesmeric force so that you can stand and witness the Mind that has nothing in it relating to this objective so-called reality.**

Nothing can be added unto Mind. This is something you should know. So, when your mind is full of thoughts, *you've got your answer!* When your mind is full of thoughts, that's the one that has you a gadabout, a runabout, and the newsreel material. The Supreme would have nothing of a limited fashion in It. It couldn't!

What must you consider? *Your tremendous gift of choice.* **Either you can accept what you see and deal with it from the standpoint that it** *seems to be,* **or you can take the position of looking upon it as** *your acknowledgment of your own projection that you allow to be identified with diversity.*

One of the great demands of concentration is that you know it's the handmaiden of the Divine because *it allows you to see one specific quality and alter any thoughts about it.* When anyone concentrates on what they are reading — especially, I know one for whom, when he's reading and I speak to him, I could be in Timbuktu because he's concentrating on what he is reading! He's so focussed that that is it, that is his world. **When I speak, that same clarity is the world from which This happens, that I speak.** To write this out would be too much mediumship; in other words, it would give you the feeling that there wasn't a direct experience. As soon as you recognize it as a direct experience, then you realize it is *your* direct experience, not just mine. *It is yours!* In other words, you reduce the thought-field of the mind that goes with the outside by perceiving the Mind that allows this one to navigate the complexities that surround objectivity, especially when we perceive that its substantiality *seems* to be there because of what we have also brought forth as perspective, dimension, and masses. But remember, there are no conditions like these in the Idea.

Mrs. Eddy said, "God and man coexist and are eternal."[1] That sounds absolutely marvellous, and I've heard it read hundreds of times and I've seen it in print hundreds of times, but what its meaning is is not in time, because **time is born of mediumship, and space allows it to be defined.**

If Principle (God) and Idea (Man) co-exist and are eternal, the whole sentence should be structured with the singular verb. There are not two but One. Why do we permit ourselves this realization? Because as soon as we forget that I AM is All, "you are" is the second creation! If I can say **"I am (first Person) the idea you are,"** is there any separation? Only when you define it in perspective and mass! *That* is the key point! *Only when you define it in a limited fashion!*

Is it not natural to be radiant and scintillating and jubilant? No matter what anyone says about you, it matters not, but when they see what makes you radiant, scintillating, jubilant, you don't say, "I'm born again; I have found Jesus"; you say, "It's because I have found the meaning of His mission!" He said, so the Scriptures say, "I and my Father are One." They don't know how to translate it very well because that is, as Mrs. Eddy said, "God and man coexist and are eternal." Therefore, **you can *never* be separated from what you truly are; there are no words, no thoughts, that can ever rescind your status as Divine.** Now, if you let that go to your head, you'll realize immediately that you have mistaken where the *residence* of the Supreme is! [laughter]

Don't you hear, frequently, people say, "My mind is so tired." Do you know, the mind has no sensation. How can it have a sensation when it's a mechanical contrivance dreamt-up? This form of presence is the mesmerism that surrounds everyone if they don't blow away the fog and see the actuality of creation. Creation is the evidence of action that is synonymous with Creator, because you can't say "God" without the Presence that says "Sound." (Oh, yes.) It causes you to really go through the hoops in the mind, but remember, every hoop is one that is dreamed-up, and that's why you have to learn how to step out of them — but into them if you can show another how to get to the Centre by getting off the rim!

Don't *skirt* the issue of your divinity by parading constantly on the rim of objectivity when the only possibility of it being there is due to whether or not you have chosen to be free from the suggestion in the light of choice, or you have chosen to go along with objectivity because by doing that you have all kinds of similar friends. When you go along in the rhythm and the harmony of Being actual, then your very presence is intoning the possibility of all objects to be found in Source as Source. **There's not an object in the house, there's not a painting on the wall, there's nothing in this house, or in yours, that didn't originate untarnished as a result of divinity.** It's *you* who tarnish it by relegating it to the objective confinement and its what? Necessary depletion of energy, which results in deterioration.

We are a vibratory frequency in essence, and a vibratory frequency in essence knows no obstruction of objectivity; it just reduces itself to that state which it will allow. When it's reduced to some states, it's called a rock, but the Essence of it is a vibration. If it hadn't been stopped, you in your objectivity would never have seen a rock. With the mind that is filled with thoughts you *expect* objectivity because it goes along with your ability to *project*, and you name your projection "the world and the inhabitants thereof."

The Group is so small because people don't realize the demands of remaining, to the best of their ability, concentrated on That which IS. **The reason we say "concentrated" is because you have to be centred on the Invisible, because in Essence there is the co-existence, either "this" could never be accepted as coming and going.** You don't pass into any heavenly state at all; you just go on where you leave off here, but with the renewed knowledge you have gained by being here, which reduces the conditions there. "Here" and "there" are directions of objectivity.

You are focussed on Me; what I say appears to be for you, but I'm not at all focussed on you. *That's the great difference between us.* People say there's no difference between us. There's *tremendous difference*, because we all have different weight, we all have different appetites. There's tremendous difference! As long as you think there's no difference between us, you've got it already! [laughter]

That's why you have to be prepared. You have to be prepared for the onslaught of your characterizations that constitute your movie-projected world. That's all it is! It's amazing your gift of creation, but it isn't *your gift* at all; it's the suggestion that you are a timed sequence. **That which IS does not project.**

It's an amazing consideration that everything you perceive is all fashioned on that attribute of creation which is termed "Mind-Consciousness-awareness." This is why we differentiate with Consciousness and awareness, because awareness goes with the objectivity and its descriptions; Consciousness is the sea that has had none of it but allows awareness to function because you have chosen not the freedom of the Soul but the bondage of *perceiving how you can create* and *fall in love with your creation. That* is the trap that everyone has fallen into in the entire universe because they have forgotten that factor of feeling freedom and objectifying it and falling in love with it. We have all forgotten *the sublimity of a free Spirit*.

Isn't it sad when you see the people who think that war and conflict are going to bring peace? The peace of the mentality is that which is opposite of war, but the Peace that IS passeth the understanding.

The "Joy to the world, the Lord has come" is only found in the realization that the *world* is what you have created by mentally projecting the idea into a limited form, and the *Lord* is the Force that allows you to see what you have done and rescind it from intruding upon your freedom of conception and allow it to be *unconfined*.

> The Lord is the Law that must be fulfilled,
> and that is doing the Father's Will.
> And the Will is that power that is simply divine
> that is wrapped in this knowing:
> that Love is the fulfilling of the sublime State,
> and that's all you are here for.

You would never be hearing these words if it wasn't your position to rescind the suggestion of being this ailing mortal and grab the eternal Fact: that God and Man could never be other than co-existent and eternal, which is what? If you have conceived it in awareness, leave it there and allow "this" to evidence the brilliance, the radiance, the scintillation becoming a realized State!

We were speaking last evening about diversity. It's very interesting to watch, but it's wonderful to be a participant, *knowing* that you are watching what you are accepting as your projection. When what you perceive is your projection and acceptance of what you see, that's when you have to put the brakes on if that projection is re-occurring as "friends." The best way you can tell when one is receptive and is perceiving is by fidelity to the Principle that IS. Don't follow the mass. Remember, one in a mass is one in a mess.

When you live the difference between What-IS and what-isn't, you have experienced understanding.

Can you imagine the Individuality being what you personalize as you? Remember, personality always arises with ego. How does Individuality attain its puissance, its power, inherent within the very word? It refuses, and cannot be known through, any sense of division.

These are very important points. Maybe you'll read them in books, I don't know, but if you do, it's not the same, because when you have *heard* it, it's moving into the area of the primal Essence which we cognized as sound. Just because we heard sound, it didn't mean that we were conscripted to be an Earthian. As soon as we heard sound we *were* Earthian, but that sound was not Earthian, because the Essence was a vibration! (That's how it goes.) Therefore, if that was heard, you have the right, then, to accept or reject. When you first hear, you have no choice. It's only when you become infatuated with your projection that you develop the difficulty of choosing.

They have always said that the Aquarian Age is the Age when we would realize the value of frequencies, but we'd also realize the ability to transcend the limitations of our cognition and, when doing that, attain access to higher dimensions, or what? Higher frequencies. A higher dimension is only a higher frequency.

There are no limits to the dimensions, no matter how many dimensions people think there are. There are no limits to dimensions, because there is no limit but in your mind. A dimension is what *you* create to have some sense of a foundation for exploring in something that doesn't bear a physical resemblance to you other than your Essence, which is vibration.

(I can't imagine how this is going to read, but I think to *hear* it, it will be fine.)

The force-field that tries to stop Me from speaking is just unbelievable. I'm so grateful I have spoken this evening.

Students: Yes, Sir!

I tell you, you are so lazy in the stand you take, because, truly, where is the Guardian of the race if it isn't you? Yes, the Guardian of the race, in other words, what? **You are the people who know how this whole picture is produced and how the conditions surrounding it can be changed!** It can't be changed just by talk; it has to be — ?

Students: Action.

Action!

It's a very startling realization, when you start considering it, that the stars and Mars and Saturn and Arcturus and Pluto and Neptune and Jupiter and Venus and everyone else, all these wonderful places, are *all* names you have given to your "theatre of stars." That's why they have an affect, because you have imbued them with this power, which they don't have at all. They are symbols and, due to the belief-systems of Ages, they carry this power of seeming to have a power, but it's been bestowed upon them without considering *you did it*. They don't exist when you don't think about them; neither does your world. There's not God and you besides.

It's *hopeless!* All you can be is Love! [laughter] And it's terrible to be That when you're a man; other "objects" have told you how you must behave. Of course, *that* Man includes women. One woman (I didn't realize she was such a feminist) said to me, "I wish you would say 'men and women.'" I said, "Man includes them." She said, "No! 'Men and women.'" And I thought, "You should come and see what can happen!" It's that separateness which creates what? The dichotomy that is the very basis of all books of fiction. You can accept it and *see* the difference and *love* the difference, but *in Essence there is none!* If there were, there would be no hope.

How many people in your school know this? How many people in *your* school know it, Nurit?

Nurit O: No one.

No. It's a very different world you're moving into. It's a world of realization that "this" is there only to be solved and the energy released into the Soul-filled moment that is termed "Realization." **The only Realization there is, is the ability to see the transparent mesmerism that has existed as "you" and "me."** It's so transparent because we are constantly changing until we concentrate on actual Being and being Actual. That rescinds the transitory and allows the stabilizing Force of what is termed "the permanent," "the Divine," to be established as the very hub of your mentality, and the spokes are there for you to realize how the journey is balanced on the rim of expectation, and Man finds his wagon rests in that place sequestered in the bliss of having found!

It sounds so simple, and it is! But we're so used to being complex that the simple seems complex. So, it's very difficult to be complex and yet so simple, you know? You're very simple but you're very complex, and you're very complex and very simple. This is the wonder!

Students: Yes, Sir.

Put a value on what you *really* are and allow others to say, "How come you're not on the market?" You say, "My stock isn't! It plummeted when I saw how I had invested in the mundane, and now I have flown into the realm of perceiving authenticity!" Each one of you is a suggestion of division, but in that, there is only the Consciousness that I AM. "You and me," "it," "we," "you," and "they" are all for the fun of it! It's *fun* to be fundamental! [laughter] So much business is built on figures. You didn't add-up to what they wanted so they had to put it into characters! [laughter]

So it is. I don't know if there is anything else to tell you. Actually, What-IS could be put on the head of a pin. What-isn't could fill books, and yet, just the realization of What-IS makes the first sentence of what-isn't, dust! It allows you to see right through the picture. I wish I had known it when I was in school.

The mind is very clever; it tries to ape the Divine, but it always fails because it hasn't what *you* have: this ability to perceive the cunning. You always know when there is a parasite of the mind because it's always based on a few points of criticism, adjudication — anything that brings it into the realm of objectivity being more real by condemnation. Colin Wilson told you all about that in *The Mind Parasites,*[2] but I don't think you're alert enough to it.

Are you keeping timetables? [The students reply with various answers.] There is no escaping from it. *If you don't keep timetables, you will allow time to control you.* The way the time controls you is that you run *out* of time; when you run out of time, you realize you haven't *budged.* You should keep timetables. I have two or three success stories as a result of it. You should keep track of your minutes and your hours from the time you get-up until you go to bed, and just see how much time you take, and understand the power of concentration. I don't mean, necessarily, meditating; that is a form of concentration as well, but I mean concentrate and still be active and still know what's happening.

Yes, David.

> *David N:* I just wanted to support what you're saying, Sir, about the value of the scheduling.

You know the value of it.

> *David N:* That type of discipline is fundamental and extremely valuable, and you taught many of us that when we worked for you. I particularly adopted that and I continue with it. It's part of the basis of the success that I've had, for sure.

It is. Yes, Else.

> *Else L:* Sir, thank you for the wonderful, wonderful evening. I have a question: You said God and Man is not separate, but can one *feel* that?

It's the only way you *know* it. That's why it is feeling and not emotion. You *know* the feeling! Yes, Valerie.

> *Valerie W:* Dr. Mills, I wanted to thank you about the area of keeping timetables. When you first urged us to do that a few years ago, it seemed to be impossible to do for more than about an hour, and then we'd forget for three! But now, having done it for a few years, it's amazing how much one can do in fifteen minutes and be totally aware of it and have an overview for the whole day, all at once. Until you do it, you can't possibly know the value. You can accomplish so much in so little time.

It's just amazing what you do because of that very approach.

Valerie W: I'm so grateful. Thank you, Sir.

Look how you map it out to be at my company and then still be at the hospital.

Valerie W: It all works but it would not work without this scheduling, I know. You never waste a minute then, because you're aware of every minute and yet you're not bound by it either. It's hard to explain. It just works!

Yes, it does work. Yes, Angela.

Angela W: Man is energy and everything is energy. How are the energy of thought and the energy of emotion distinguished?

By your response to them. When it's personal, there's fatigue; when it's impersonal, there's elation!

Angela W: It seems that it's easier to watch thought than to watch emotion.

Emotion is actually associated with thought. It's like when you look at a doughnut: most of the people in America eat it . . . and that's emotion! [laughter]

Angela W: Thank you for helping me lose weight!

I hope you have a very nice few weeks while I'm away.

Student: We'll miss you, Sir.

This is why you should make the most of every moment we have. Yes.

Gregory S: Sir, does true revelation always come as a result of a *disciplined* act?

No, not always but generally. Unless you're prepared for it, it can come seemingly without. It *happens,* but you've been preparing for it by your actions. Usually it doesn't last. Remember, a revelation is a *recurring* event. One revelation doesn't do it. If it did, I would never have given all these Lectures. It's the same with

Enlightenment. Enlightenment is not just one moment; Enlightenment is many! There are many levels of Enlightenment, just as there are many levels of Realization. Work, work, work! Yes, Sandy.

> *Sandra D:* It was a great revelation to me to discover that people were very moved by the singing when the mind was very concentrated and disciplined and occupied by all that you told us and instructed, when I had originally thought that one had to somehow infuse singing with feeling in order to reach people. It was exactly the opposite.

Why do you think I gave you so much to think about?! Now, it's revealed! [laughter] Now, it's revealed, because the more that you have to think about, it's reduced to a potency when you follow me. You know what you have to follow, innately, from having rehearsed, and that's how it happened.

> *Sandra D:* Thank you so much.

That's when you *escape*. When your mind is occupied, that's when you can get out without being caught! That's what happened; that's why people were healed. You got out without knowing it. *Now* you're talking about it. Yes, Marylou.

> *Marylou P:* Sir, the idea of concentration has been experienced in what appears as collapsing of time, because when there are many things to get accomplished, when the focus is very specific, it's also when time stands still.

It does! **Time has only to do with the wandering mind!**

> *Marylou P:* Wonderful! Thank you!

(That's a good one!) **If the mind didn't wander, there wouldn't be time.** Yes, Evangeline.

> *Evangeline L:* Some time ago, Sir, you said, "One moment swallowed-up in Light is the only moment there ever is!"[3] I'm hearing this with wonder, Sir, because it seems to me that it's not something that you can do deliberately.

The only thing you can do deliberately is silence the mind, and that takes concentration. If the mind can be silenced, it's obvious that concentration is not from it! So it is. Yes, Dorothea.

> *Dorothea O:* I'm retired. Each morning I write a list of things that I want to do that day and cross them off as I do them, but is it important for me to do a timetable, too?

As long as you get done what you're doing, it's timed . . . but you're not tabled! Most people are flat on the bed; they've done so much, they say, "My mind's so tired!" Don't allow yourself to allow that to come in too much. So many people say, "My mind is tired." Your mind hasn't a clue about being tired, and neither do you! It's a condition that, by saying that, has a resulting emotion and affect, and that is an affect of fatigue.

When it used to take me so long to give a Lecture, I'd give a Lecture that would be three hours long, but as I gained freedom in speaking, it became shorter and shorter until now it's usually around an hour. It's not wise to hold the audience in a higher frequency for more than the sixty, maximum ninety, minutes. They can't take it; they don't hear. So, this is why I watch it. Of course, what I say now in an hour is much more than I used to say in three. I spoke so slowly because guess what? I had to be without thought and yet I didn't know how I was going to speak without it. But I heard it and so I knew it was called "thought" when *you* heard it.

You can't account for many things. In fact, you *have to* account for "things," but how can you account to be mad in love and love-mad?! That's what you should do: allow it to take precedence over your state. Allow it, gentlemen; allow it, ladies. Don't be a goody-goody. Don't be a do-gooder, whatever you do. Just enjoy doing and have other people say it's good — fine, but you don't feel it; it's natural. How can you help but extend? Do you think the sun cares about where the leaf is hiding? The leaf wouldn't be if the sun wasn't present.

Yes, Bill.

> *Bill W:* I don't like particularly looking back into the past, but sometimes I have to for various presentations that I have to make to the Academy. It's kind of a flight of imagination almost to go and try and imagine what might be happening five thousand years ago.

Well, it's easy because it's all been made-up anyway!

Bill W: It's all made-up, Sir. What is happening now to give us so much value, was that not happening at all in the past, or what we call the past?

What is happening right now has never happened!

Bill W: Oh, dear!

Students: Ohhh!

. . . so other people can write a history about it! It's only the mind that tries to figure a way that it happened before. It doesn't matter what the *form* looks like; it's what *isn't* the form that *counts* . . . not a bit! You can't count it but you try to. All you know is Presence, and that Presence is now! You cannot have a past that isn't the result of a suggested extension of That which is impossible to extend because it has no dimension. You can't extend Now, and yet its very confetti allows us on this plane to have solace in the idea we have a history. No one tells you it's all a confetti of suggestion! But isn't it marvellous what we do with it? It's not dull; it's fun! Enjoy playing the part you're playing.

Students: Thank you so much, Sir.

Bill W: So clear and so practical!

⌘

1. Eddy, *Science and Health*, 336–30.
2. Colin Wilson, *The Mind Parasites* (Berkeley: Oneiric Press, 1967).
3. Kenneth G. Mills, *Given to Praise! An array of provocative metaphysical-philosophical utterances* (Toronto: Sun-Scape Publications, 1976), p. 46.

The High Way of the Ultimate

Chapter XVI

It is the mystery of God being actual, or the Self being actual or the divine cosmic Consciousness being actual, that gives us the ability to look upon the virtual as an impostor!

The High Way of the Ultimate

Themes: The Unexpected ~ eternal continuity ~ Truth ~ surrender to the Ultimate ~ intention ~ individuality ~ mind/intellect ~ bundle of thoughts

[Dr. Mills rings the Tibetan bells.] This is the evening of February 14, 2004. We greet you in New York[1] and We greet you wherever you may be . . . attuned to the frequency of the Unexpected, expected at any moment because men and women try to imbue their lives with a fatidic splendour; they try to foretell and to forecast what their path and their destiny shall be.

In the considerations of yore we are forever present with the passage of time in the hope that we shall see it come to an end as a restriction and find what is termed "the timelessness of Being." This in itself is a clue, for it alerts anyone who is hoping to find the end of time that they are really a little bit ignorant because they are questioning the end of time when they have never questioned that which said it exists! This is what confronts the humankind (we *hope*, kind), the human, as he passes over his days in a groggy state of egotistic intoxication.

Everyone says they have *this* and they have *that* but they never get right down to brass tacks. It's all wrapped-up in the sense of "you": *you* have, and you and your personality, and you and your traits, and you and your possessions. But seldom do we realize that one of the subtlest possessions is that state which has constituted our own mesmeric imprisonment in what, in fact, is not actual. It is the very arisal of thoughts that allow us to conjure other thoughts that support each other's thoughts. And what do we have but your mind a bundle of thoughts, not yet given to the Bundle of His.[2] Consequently, we are in a box, a box of unusual confinement because we are allowing ourselves to be in the state of being trapped in the very thing called "your mind," which is impossible to free from itself!

Now, if you want to go through life having a great time procrastinating, intellectually searching for the Self is the best way to go! Think nothing of spending a lifetime meditating and doing all sorts of religious practices, and at the end they'll just say your time was up — but you won't know it! What has happened? The intellect has deluded you into thinking *it's* capable of revealing your correct identity, by super-imposing a bundle of thoughts that are totally controlled by the emotions that are always on the go. What happens? You find yourself more confused than ever, because the root of your dismay is the fact that you are still wrapped-up in the basket of duality and you follow all its trends.

To-day it's very fashionable to do such-and-such a thing, and it's very fashionable to go to this place or that place, to the baths for massage and for therapeutic treatment. But what are you doing but making-up, with more foundational creams than ever, a suppositional existence as a result of all the pounding and all the slapping and all the sweating and all the pluming and plunging one does in order to feel that they have a body! It is very difficult to feel you have a body when you are so used to the object hanging around and you don't know what to do with it, so you feed it incessantly; if you aren't giving it what it is crying out for, you feed it not even the milk, not any meat but what? Potato chips! And what are they? They're *fried*. That is what happens to most substantial growths in time: You take them and you deep-fry them in the fats exuded by a messy thought-field and you heat them up over the blaze of unfettered emotions — because "after all, you have got to express yourself." But do you realize that if you want to *realize,* the first thing that you must do is *decapitate*, in other words, get rid of the head that is all wrapped-up in thinking it can find an exit via its intelligence.

"Intelligence" is the word we give to thoughts that are so well utilized that you seem to be able to navigate the byways of time without being struck down at a crosswalk. But, you see, the Cross is a walk that those who are praying their way into the kingdom of Heaven partake of: you have to "take the Cross upon you." Now, this is quite all right if you're not curious about your fluctuating mind — one moment so wholly endowed with the divine considerations and the next time so *holey* that nothing stays in it other than "I am too tired; my mind is too tired to think anymore." What a warning that your mind is just up, playing tricks on you! *Did you ever hear anything that is senseless make a statement of freedom?!*

After all this preamble, what do you realize? **That you're not going to use your mind to attempt your freedom; you're going to see how to drop it from associating with your freedom, and find**

yourself free and still using your mind! Hello! It can happen. But don't you know, it's great business to have a progressive way to Reality. But do you know something? You have never *lost* Reality! What has made you think you have? *Your mind.* You were never taught that it and your world only spring-up when you consider the objective.

Why do you go to bed at night? To rest, to get away from what your mind is doing to you all day! *To get away from what your mind is doing to you all day.* What does the mind do to you? It's not your friend. That is why you wait for the Unexpected, because the Unexpected always reveals with what is termed "an awakening voice." It re-awakens the ember of eternal continuity of your Beingness that has nothing whatsoever to do with your time; it has to do with the state of preparedness to assume what is concomitant with this State, which is that dreadful word, *commitment,* and the other horrific one, *discipline,* and the other one, *obedience,* and the other one, *the Law.* Why the Law, when the Law is written in the heart, and Love is the fulfilling of it? Do you suppose that your heart, your mind, may be well employed?

When you come to these states (that is, those states which govern the High Way of the Ultimate), they are requiring another type of consideration entirely. There are laws, there is protocol, there is what is needed to engage this High Way, and it is very marked. **You cannot engage it with partial commitment!** It's like driving on the highway on the shoulder with one set of wheels and the other on the pavement. **You can't divide the High Way according to the way *you* like. In fact, if you appear to be on it, it's a grace because you are re-awakening to the purpose of your incarnation, which is what? To be the exponent, involuntarily, of that brilliance that comes with the adaptation and the adoption of the vibratory frequency commensurate with surrender to the Ultimate.**

Why do you deaden and dull the vibratory frequency, in other words, your form of energy, in your walk through life and in your idle moments when you think no one is around? Don't have an idle moment if you think it's idle, and don't be *fooling yourself* that you are achieving anything by slipshod work in managing your thought-fields.

Where do you respond most vigorously? When someone challenges your ego and its declarations! (Oh, dear!) You don't have to go to a doctor to know what's wrong, because if you are challenged by the ego, then you know you can't rise to the challenge with anger. It augurs failure! You have to move through this and gain composure so that the fire of anger becomes the fire to those thoughts that would have you dressed in a fallacious coat of ego-personality complex, and move into something much more stable, wrapped-up in what is termed "individuality."

All through life you're looking at young people and saying, "Oh, I hope he develops an attractive personality; he's so good-looking." What do you say to this? "I hope so, too"? No, you would just like him to develop a means of communicating with vitality that he exists, without all the limitations fostered on him by his well-meaning schooling and, usually, parents who say, "This is my beloved son whom I possess." It's a far cry from what is said to have been uttered by a great Master: "This is my beloved Son in whom I am well pleased."³ Then, one metaphysician said, "This is my beloved *Self* in whom I am well pleased," and suddenly the Coincidence happens!

What is the great failure of most people to-day? It's in the ability to converse, the ability of conversation that has a meaning that is devoid of just an interesting bit of gossip. The whole purpose of being endowed with the glowing ember that you know you're more than "this" is to cause you to fructify those moments in which you can perceive there is a moment that the ground is prepared to receive the Unexpected — and yet *expected* because you would not have that yearning (I hope it *is* a yearning) if it wasn't an essential characteristic of those who would join the vanguard of the new vibrational scheme for Earth.

It's obvious, the human vibration is on such a low level that it doesn't take much genius to develop another vibratory frequency *above it* to control it! This is what you must watch out for in the future, because you are making it up. But if you make it up for the sole purpose of reducing it to a figment of the imagination, then you are allowed to partake of it, because your partaking of it will be a walk in the rhythmic way of those endowed with Grace. This is what is so essential, because you would never be hearing this if you weren't prepared to enter this High Way.

Don't think you're just sitting back, a housewife or an office worker or somebody who feels they should be here because "After all, I don't go to church and I'd better go somewhere because, after all, I'm not sure how long this body's going to be here." That isn't just the way it goes, because if it's that way, what I'm saying is going to really irritate you! [laughter] It's not just for that reason, of course, but it is nice to know that if you feel irritated or slightly irritated, just wait a minute and you'll be more so! [laughter]

In a way, the Truth is like a mosquito bite: When it first bites you, you don't notice for a few minutes until it starts to itch, and then you run for an antidote. Don't I know! It's interesting, when *the Truth* has bitten you, there is no antidote to be found because it never lets you go! It isn't an itch; it has become a twitching of the Spirit that you never knew really was so powerful, because suddenly you're beginning to question the very foundation of your false premise of reasoning.

Why is this so easy? It's as I said, *I came to re-awaken the ember you already have,* and this ember is so glowing, with a zephyr blowing upon it, that it starts to gain a force-field in your experience which allows you the great pulsating that comes with the possibility of a new beginning. When that becomes rhythmic, it's not the birth of another limitation; it's the birth of an immaterial concept that bears the force-field that can reduce the intellectual bundle of thoughts to smithereens.

Isn't it amazing to look in your world to-day, and you see so much chaos. In a way, it is just marvellous that you people are here at this time because there is no quelling of that force-field without your presence. Your presence is the very power that can change it because your stand is not that of a person trying to change something; your stand only appears as other people, but what is motivating the inner recesses of your heart and of your soul and of your mind is the actuality of Being, because you have reduced the suggestion of multiplicity to what? *Smithereens.* It went with your intellect and now it's reborn imbued with the message of the Self, with the message of manumission, because you are no longer sequestered in the mire of thought-processes that deal with the hope to-morrow. *Now* is the accepted time . . . to be out of it.

Why is the educational system falling apart? Do you suppose it's intentional? An illiterate people are a controlled people. But, actually, you wonder where intelligence *is*. It certainly isn't in high places! There's nothing wrong with intelligence if you know how to use it to drive your craft through the atmosphere of skyrocketing suggestions. You don't have to go into that field; all you have to do is be active in your creative expression, because when you have perceived that duality is your enemy, it's right at your home front door. Look and see how most of your responses are fostering your limitation: "Oh, you're fifty"; "I don't dare to try anything new. I'm almost seventy, I can't do anything new." I started weight-lifting when I was seventy-three. Up until a couple of years ago I had gone as far as bench-pressing three hundred and thirty-five pounds nine times, and three hundred and five pounds ten times, and three hundred pounds twelve times, starting at a hundred and fifty-five and working up to three hundred and thirty-five!

David K: It's true.

Randle: Yes, it is.

David and Randle were with me.

David K: It is remarkable.

You have broken through the suggestion by knowing within yourself that you're more than "this." This is where your liberation is.

We used to prepare for the winter. It was always so pregnant with possibilities, *always*. To-day how many people make the winter pregnant with possibilities? We were always practising music; we were always having an orchestra to practise at the house after I finished practising; and then the people in the orchestra would play and they'd raise money. I tell you, *it was always creative*. What do you do to-day? "My mind is so tired; I'll just watch television." And do you realize, every time you take a nap and you can hardly wait to do so, it's because your mind is such a bore?! You're so damned tired of carrying it around, with it outlining how you're to behave, **because you don't know how to behave when you're free!** *You only know how to behave when you're married to a false concept of existence.*

We are always concerned about what we have or have not got. I said to one girl this afternoon, "What do you feel is the cause of so much talk of not having enough money?" It was interesting what she said, but I didn't think that was the root of it at all. I would certainly consider that one of the main causes is your reluctance to rid yourself of false identity because you're just afraid of losing something and, if you *can* lose it, it certainly isn't what you are.

If Man is the image and likeness of God or the Source, and God is Love (and the Source *must* be, to put-up with the suggestion that we're attempting to find it when it's already here!), **do you realize, when you find and chase the ego to its root, all that's left is What IS! And that doesn't take thirty years, twenty years, five years, two years, one year! It takes a moment of sincerity combined with obedience and commitment and discipline and obedience to the Law of Love!** *We limit everything by our own attitude about it because we haven't transcended what we know is not authentic.*

Have you ever stopped to consider just how clear is your intention, if you are still living from the standpoint of duality? How clear is your intention if you are not giving yourself to the higher Wisdom, to the divine Light?!

The tendency is to think it's *"my* will" — God's out of it. No one ever says, "It's the Divine that's moving me"; they say, "It's the *bank* that's moving me." I'm just saying that to challenge you because you have got to consider, every time you hear "I'm not making enough money; I don't have enough money," *what your service role is and how you are viewing it.* **Your service role is the reason you came.** You came *to serve,* and there's no greater role than the service role, because as long as you have an ego, you have the possibility of a karmic trail. *A karmic trail never exists without ego.*

So, if you have any doubts about your intentions you should really clear it as fast as possible because *you're so needed in the walk of clarity.* People are not clear to-day; they personalize *so much.* It's all right to be thanked and to be acknowledged and to be recognized — all of that is fine, but what is wrong is, as my father said to me, "It's wonderful that people love your playing, Ken, but you've forgotten someone." I said, "Dad, what do you mean?" He said, "Someone who said, 'I of myself can do nothing; 'tis the Father that doeth the work.'" He told me this when I was about thirteen or fourteen, and I never forgot it.

So, when healings happen and these miracles happen and people don't like to admit it — what do they do? There's an old hymn that says, "Take time to be holy, speak oft with thy Lord."[4] I tell you now, how many take time to be holy, outside of an hour in the mornings if you're good? You know what I mean. Isn't it fascinating, it says *"Take* time," and *put an end* to it as being an important part of your life. **It doesn't take time to think right; it takes the willingness to do so. And boy, when you know you should be thinking right, you can see how unwilling your bundle of thoughts is, how unwilling it is to yield to the Higher. When you're on the Way, you don't stop for the sideshow, because you don't know when you may be on your own, quitting the experience of time.**

I don't know why you prolong your tendencies to work with the thoughts of your limitation instead of fishing for those thoughts that are one with the divine Fisherman. I don't know why! Remember, your thoughts will always try to have you wrapped-up in satisfaction in a *mystical* state. You want to be the *mystery,* not the state. It is the mystery of God being actual, or the Self being actual, or the divine cosmic Consciousness being actual, that gives us the ability to look upon the virtual as *an impostor!*

> **The only way "you" will ever change is by ridding your thoughts of your wrong identity and claiming your correct one!**

Students: Yes, Sir.

I consider so often "What will I say to you?" and it's so seldom, after all my considerations, that I say anything I was considering because I can't outline it very much. I don't see you that often when I'm away so much. How can I, unless you have a hook-up, unless you "fish" me out of the telephone there, like they've done in New York? But it's fascinating: *how can you keep company with thoughts that aren't in keeping with your life?* Of course, you can *appear to* because they may be the very ones that need your blessing and need your help, but you have to be careful not to be sucked-in to partial states.

You don't lack anything that is substantial. I was so poor, and yet my life has been so blessed with a way of life that I never dreamt was on my path. I thought I was going to be a concert pianist and teacher, which I had been for twenty-five years. Who would ever have thought that I would ever speak the Word again? I didn't know what it was. All I do know is that *it happens*. And when it happens, there is change!

Any time you're with people who are new, when they react, they're the most attuned. The people who acquiesce at once, I'm always a little bit leery of because the next time they may hear something that they didn't hear before and I don't see them again. But you know, they say, "When the Love Bug bites you, you never can forget it!"[5] That's just what it's like; it will never let you go! I said "the Love Bug": I don't mean just the *ordinary* "love bug"! I had that, too, and it let me go! [laughter] Don't tell my secret!

    So, as we look over the horizons of time
    And see in what is termed "the yore of the past" —
    Now known as those *y*ears of *r*eleased *e*xpression —
    We see that the pathways have been so trod by the
        Saints and the Sages in expression.

    May you find in the glowing recognition of that
        glorious Light divine
    That you move with the alacrity of a child leaping
        beyond the limbs of the mind.
    Move with the rapidity of engagement that comes
        with the Current divine,
    That you move with accelerated force and power as
        you move into the Christened Light divine.

    Move with expectations and find them fulfilled
    In knowing that the Saints and Sages of the Ages
        have passed this way and bear the Will.
    The Will is for each and every one to foster in the
        Heart divine
    The power to escalate the Force that will wipe away
        the chaotic mind.

    May we find in this joyous recognition that we walk
        the blessed stones of time;
    Each one has been one given to equate with those
        that have been buried in the mind.
    Now we find them glowing and upon these stones
        we stand, for they bear
    In the conquering of the hero the basis for those who dare.
    They claim the wondrous power when the rock has
        become the stand;
    For we know, when the rock becomes transparent,
        there walks transparent Man.

And you in your raiment of humanity bear this
    knowing might
That right where the human appears to walk, his
    kind in this realm of Light,
There stands the transparent Man equated with the
    Invisible, the Ineffable, the Grand;
And you say, "My God, the Unexpected expected
    has happened, and I walk out of no man's land!
I find in the divine expression I have created this
    magnificent tale,
The greatest one of any show on Earth, for its Truth
    must always prevail."

The Fact and recognition bring unto the errant mind
The possibility equated with transcending the
    vestibule of time.
Move into the High Way of the movement which
    sees the vanguard of the Light
Bearing this salient feature, Love's banner, Truth's
    might.
Take this upon your Knowingness and say unto the
    land,
"I walk as a simple hue-man, and you say 'a
    human-kind at hand.'"

Kindness has certainly faded, but the hue-man
    knows this Fact,
That when man moves beyond the virtual, the subtle
    colours of his robe are Fact,
And there stands the wondrous victory, for those
    who see this glowing Light
Know the magic of the Invisible is equated with the
    words, "Behold an immaculate sight!"

⌘

1. The Lecture was being heard live, via conference call, in New York.
2. One meaning of "bundle of His" is "a bundle of modified heart muscle that transmits the cardiac impulse from the atrioventricular node to the ventricles, causing them to contract." <http://www.thefreedictionary.com>
3. Matthew 3:17.
4. "Take Time to Be Holy," words by William D. Longstaff, music by George C. Stebbins.
5. "When the Love Bug Bites You," words and music by Fred Kirby.

A Meeting

Chapter XVII

Awareness IS. God IS. That's that. It's so simple. Don't let anyone tell you it's complex.

A Meeting

Themes: The Standpoint of Principle ~ God at hand ~ awareness

This is the morning of February 15, 2004, it's a Sunday morning, and I'm meeting with the guests from out of town. So, what are we going to talk about? Have you any questions you want to ask? Anyone may ask if they wish.

> *Laura B:* I have a few questions. My many questions condense into one question. Last night you were speaking about how thoughts can control. What is a good process of getting rid of thoughts and also getting your body and mind out of the way so you can live more by the Spirit and by Life and not by the limitations that the body and mind can have on one's Being? Also, last night you talked about resting, resting the mind when you go to sleep, and for myself, a lot of time my mind doesn't even want to rest at night when I'm sleeping.

The most important point is to ask yourself *what you're getting rid of.* It's not so difficult when you start to realize, but until you do you are dealing, it seems, with an impossibility: to get rid of that which is housing your apparatus for enjoying the Earth plane. The first thing you must do (I say "must," but it's the *wisest* thing to do as far as I know) is to relate to the Source, which I call "Principle" or the "Source" or the "Self," the "Atman," whatever you wish. Then, ask yourself the questions from that Standpoint of Principle. Does Principle know that you have a body?

> *Laura B:* Does Principle know that I have a body? I believe it would know that I have a body.

Do you feel that God knows each and every creation?

> *Laura B:* Yes, definitely.

Then you feel that God is anthropomorphic, in other words, in matter.

Laura B: I would think God is everywhere.

No, He can't be; the Greater can never be placed in the lesser. What is the most fundamental function you evidence in your form? You are always what? What are you doing at this moment?

Laura B: I'm thinking.

You're thinking.

Laura B: I'm thinking. I'm trying *not* to think!

You're thinking. In order to think, you must evidence what? Do you notice the tulips?

Laura B: Yes, I do notice the tulips.

What allowed you to notice the tulips?

Laura B: The mind, I guess.

No, *your awareness*. The "mind," remember, is nothing but the name we associate with a bundle of thoughts. Do you recognize who's sitting beside you?

Laura B: Yes.

On both sides of you? It's your *awareness*. It can't be found in the body. Where does God exist? Where does Principle exist?

> When I say "awareness," that's where it must be
> Because the salt, water, chalk, protoplasm, or slime
> Can never think of a God that is not so inclined,
> For the God that IS cannot be bound by matter
> For, then, He'd be vulnerable, as you are, to the thought of matter.
> But the God that IS is a conscious State
> That allows you to bear witness by awareness as your pattern you take.
> And your pattern of awareness must conform to this Fact
> That if I AM All, there's no "this" or "that."

It's a Conscious-awareness state that has your God at hand, because it is not in matter that you can find either awareness or Consciousness.

It's the most amazing thing, our freedom is under our nose! It's the very aspect of *awareness*, and people never get that point. They take years to arrive at the point of awareness — where it can be arrived at by looking at a tulip! If you look inside it, you will see the crown for your rejoicing because you have seen the power that resides as a part of your awareness. You can look at something that seems purely external and you can look inside and see a crown. The corona is inside. **When you look inside yourself you can't find anything there because you make your awareness look for something material, but your awareness is really a state that allows the matter to be there to display the magnitude of conception unconfined by the thoughts of an errant mind.**

Laura B: Thank you.

Got that?

Laura B: Do you know how to heighten your awareness?

You don't need to; it's as high as it will ever be. All you can do is be *more* aware, not heightened. It's the same height as you are freed from the mind; it can never be higher or lower. Awareness IS. God IS. That's that. It's so simple. Don't let anyone tell you it's complex. Where it gets complex is when you compound your considerations by trying to fit the incompatible with the Compatible.

Laura B: Thank you. I have one more question for you. Last night you were saying there is no greater role that someone can have than service and giving service. And then you said your intentions must be clear; clarity is needed. How do you make your intentions clear, and what do you mean? I guess your intention should be to love, to serve, and to give. I was just wondering exactly, just so I don't misinterpret.

Your intention is to go to India. What are you doing to get there? Are you thumbing or buying a ticket?

Laura B: I purchased a ticket.

There you have it. Your intention was to go; you had to outline your intention by buying the ticket, packing your clothes — dinner dresses and evening wear. [laughter]

Laura B: I don't think so!

I know. It's your clear intention which has you taking the right garments with you, including your body. That's all it is.

Her body is nothing but a garment that she's wearing so that others may be blessed by her presence, as she bears the Christ Child in the state of the purity of conceptual might.

Nothing that has been accomplished in the realm of Masterhood is meant to be optional to the one with a clear intention. It is a direct path to the Ultimate, just as her direct path in thought is from New York to India, to Shangri-La or wherever you want to go.

You don't have the luxury of being a human for nothing, because it takes a great deal to arrive at a state of humanhood. We really are in water-hood, we're water-men and water-women.

Your humanhood is really an incredible time for you to display the elegance of Being by your dress, by your coiffeur, by your make-up, by your demeanour. These are all part of conforming to your Ideal.

⌘

Perfection

Chapter XVIII

The word "Divine" is so practical; it's much more practical than "human" because you can't dress it up in mediocrity!

Perfection

Themes: Light ~ higher echelon of Being ~ Standard of excellence ~ garment of Wholeness ~ High fashion ~ emotions ~ bonfires and sideshows

This is the evening of February 18, 2004. We move directly into the stream of considerations which are under the aegis of perfection. We move with agility to that point in realizing that perfection is a state that must express Reality. In that recognition, we abide each day in the continuing event of scrutinizing each and every one of our actions and perceiving just how close we are in evidencing this perfection. It would be and it is, it could be and it was, it is and known, for it exudes the becomingness of the gown attributed to high endeavour.

We may walk down Broadway and see the theatre district in a great *mad-hattin'*/Manhattan city or we may walk on a side street to the theatre district just off Broadway and Forty-second Street. You will notice on the Broadway the standard of excellence is not seen, perhaps, in the apparel becoming to *our* Standard, for we know that each must bear a mark of individuality if the clothes are to be seen by those passersby on the broad way; this apparel must be evidence of another District where the *High fashion* is obviously riding the wave of vogue.

On Fifth Avenue we may see the wondrous stores filled with mannequins, male and female, wearing apparel that should appeal to the discerning eye of the newness becoming your Standard, in the light of the oldness that tries to prevail. If you are to perceive the style that causes heads to turn, you can imagine what it will be like when you wear *the style that causes the head to be put in question,* for then they will know that no mannequin has robotized into an avenue of existence, but you have brought the flexibility and the demeanour becoming one who wears a garment that draws attention not to the garment per se but to the countenance glowing in the recognition that you have adopted that fashion becoming to your attainment. *One practical aspect* to consider is: what kind of figure do you cut in the avenues of time?

Then, we come to that position where we look upon our work and we can say:

"Is this perfection?"

"Is my act reflecting the state that is Life?"

"Is my work truly done in a fashion that allows the precipitation of wonder to appear spontaneously in the venues of time?"

"Is that paint job evidencing the Standard of perfection?"

"Is that gardening job evidencing that Standard?"

"Is my gait/gate evidencing that Standard, and is it *open?* May I walk through it and find that there is no dust on the understanding which would pass into the garden beautiful."

We have been cajoled into the wonders of walking in the garden while the dew/do is *still* and on the roses. Isn't it interesting that when you look at the rose you don't see all the activity that has happened for its petals to bear these diadems of wonder. And yet the rose offers itself to your attention and perhaps it says, "Are *your* petals opening as you blossom into the wonder of the fecund state of the garden of the thought-world which is pruned to exude the fragrant Language of a divine urgency, one pointing to the unification of each and every gift that cometh from our allegiance to a Standard of excellence?"

When you look and you see what is being worn on the streets of time by what are termed "the executives," you must ask yourself, "Is this the standard that I would vote for?" If one is so intimidated by correctness in demeanour, then how is that one ever capable of bringing to the attention the wonders of an emancipated state? You can't be self-conscious in the mediocre position of being a CEO or a president or an ego dressed-up as such; you can't be impressed by any title if your bearing is not that of one committed to the hidden exigency: that of bringing to the people the urgency that exists when all nations are pummelled by the power of suggestion and its mighty thunderous attention-getter.

You remember I told you years ago that you, in the future, would see bonfires started in so many places *out of control,* because they are those that call upon the attention of others to put them out. But remember, *they're a suggestion that may cause you to forget your purpose of existence,* which is **to stand as one guardian of the race of those endowed with a Light transportation system.**

If we are not of Earth in essence, why do you expect your attainments to be considered Earthian? The only part of you that is Earthian is that part which you have allowed to appear to be considered an objectification to satisfy what other objects deem as similarities, but really, your inner state is quite different. If you look at a little, tiny speedboat and see it flying across the water and see its outboard motor, and then you look at a larger boat, a yacht about ninety-five feet, two hundred and ten feet, or a hundred and fifty feet (the one I like so much), you will see quite a different type of engine, and yet, they do the same thing: they ply the surface conscious state called "water." But if you go deep into the considerations, I can assure you, no "put-put" boat would be very comfortable in the sea of fermentation. Even a grand yacht finds it demands a great deal of the captain, and as the president of one of the yacht companies told me at luncheon, "You know, you should never consider the cost of your captain. After all, he is moving on the surface of the sea a luxurious home worth millions of dollars. Why would you not find the finest to navigate these riptides of suggestions?"

Why are people allowing their inner home and garden to be so contaminated by the emotions surrounding bonfires? You should watch the bonfire and know within yourself that only the Truth of Being shall ever put out the contagion of fear. It has been said that "perfect love *casteth out* fear."[1] Why would you be fearful if you can entertain two states and know full well that one is a counterfeit? Remember, I told you, when people used to take dollar bills to the bank (not just the ordinary bills but a hundred-dollar bill or a thousand-dollar bill), the first thing they did (they didn't put it under a lamp) was put it under their scrutiny with their *eyes*. They were taught what a counterfeit looked like and they could tell, from the countless bills that passed through their hands, that if that counterfeit showed-up, it always bore a mark that marked it as unsubstantial in the medium of exchange. *The counterfeit bill is just like attitudes: they may be great, but how substantial are they in the Light of perception?*

Watch and see, as you peregrinate in this vestibule of time, if the broad way is really as free as it looks. Forty-second is the theatre district for sure, but it carries a lot of responsibility to the actors, and for the actors, to convince you that what they are saying should hold your interest. Fifth Avenue tells you, "Go in one direction with freedom provided you have entertained in your movement the Standard of perfection."

If there ever was a Standard that's lacking to-day, it is seemingly that of perfection, because we may not reach it, but that doesn't mean we can't *hold it.* You may not *reach* Self-realization if your mind insists on being the one that gives it to you, but at least you know it *is!* So, don't agree with anything that would allow you to consider or think that you're going to have to bundle yourself up and get you another "round." It ain't always merry!

The *merry-go-round* is for the fun of the child of freedom. The *whip* is something that has been forgotten to enliven a sense of respect, and the *loop-the-loop* is a perfect example of the sideshows that would have you returning and returning, with the centre always saying, "Well, of course, I'm here; that's how you can loop."

Why do you consider not the value of projecting your sight into the Cosmic? After all, it's your baby! The entire cosmos is your baby, and you think . . . and think and think and think, "How am I going to get beyond this foursome, this thinking on each side of my blocked mind?" You have to transport; in other words, you have to *go beyond* the sport of to-day and move into the sport of reducing the mind to the plaything of time and allowing yourself the creation of just the right job, just the right abundance, just the right beauty, just the right coiffeur, just the right fashion, and have such mobility that *naturally* the four wheels will be in keeping with your dress.

How can you be the higher echelon of Being and be satisfied with less than that which should accompany it? But do you ever consider that, to *achieve, work* is involved? And the work is all built-up on the suggestion of so many hours a day:

> Work, work, work —
> it's never done —
> from rising sun to setting sun,
> but it should be.

Your work should be so geared to the evidence of your attainment that those who have a Standard flood to you for counselling, for consultation, and for answers regarding emancipation.

It's so interesting how in the past the different forms of slavery and, to-day, how in the present the *obvious* slavery — but, of course, you can have a "casual Friday." That's when I *stopped* going to the bank on Friday! Have you ever realized how degrading it is, when you stop to consider that we are a miracle? Have you ever stopped to consider the wonder of your mobility? It has nothing to do with AT&T! [laughter] It has to do with *doing*. **The practicality of living is in the effortlessness of Being, and that is what is termed "emancipation"; it allows your life to be a kaleidoscope of a variegated pattern of newness and wonder.**

When people adopt the standard of dress, the standard of mentality, and the standard of attainment of those unmoved by an inner persuasion, why would you adopt it? As soon as the higher, cultured society drops (as we've said a dozen times) to the level of the people who wear the most common clothes (that should be seen in your back yard, not in the foreground of your street), that points definitely to the reneging of keeping a high standard of excellence. Is it difficult to keep it as a painter, as a gardener, as a "vacuumer," as a duster, as a washer, as a garbage collector? *It doesn't matter what the job is, if it's done with excellence, you won't be in it for long.* When it's done in a slipshod manner, you will be in it indefinitely! How do you know people are in it indefinitely? Because they've all joined *the fraternity of lack!* That's why you all enjoy each other's company so much: the common factor is *lack*. Have you ever asked yourself, "Is it really the lack in my experience? Is it arising *there*, or is it in the lack of *my commitment to perfection and excellence?*"

> **Learn to form your letters, learn to pen your numbers, and learn to translate them into another level of vibrancy, and move into an echelon of attainment where the jewels unseen in time are blazing forth your attainment so that others may say they have set the captive free! What is more important?**
>
> The only value of any Sage is for you to adopt the incredible opportunity of altering your state of consciousness and find the emancipation that of moving on the barge of Soul on the sea of conflicting opinions and offering an ability to walk on the waters and still the turbulence.

It's so amazing to see us all so beautifully mechanized; there's no doubt that there's a God! There is *no doubt* that there is the Source, there is *no doubt* that there is Love, because our ignorance can be so dense that we worship a God, but, actually, God might have said, "For My sake, consider the tone you give unto Me arises from your need to *acquiesce* to the frequency that allows you to bow in wonder at My handiwork." If you don't bow in awe, prove to me you can create a blade of grass! Who cares about another cloned human? There are enough walking around! [laughter] Why do you walk after the seeming pattern of incompleteness while the opportunity is to vibrate in the extra-ordinary frequency that is termed "Light"?!

Why do we say "Light"? We have to have some sound that points to the Ineffable, because in this dualistic panorama of mesmerism we tend to follow the shadow; it is so well-defined. **Don't you realize, you wouldn't even be appearing like this if it wasn't for the exact opposite allowing you to fill the negative space until I come?** It's not just found in Italy; it's not just found at Hadrian's Villa. If you cognize it there, look at the windows of your own thought and see how the negative space is so clearly defined, because you would not have a window with which you can defenestrate if necessary, but for heaven's sake, try to go out a door! The gate is opened!

Oh, the decisions that clones make! What do they do? They have to decide whether or not they want to commit to their Inheritance . . . for now, because "my friends may not like it." **Do you realize how your thoughts are so controlled instead of being the scintillating darts of wonder penetrating the breastplates of doubt?!**

Leap! *Where?* Out of your head, and entertain those impulses that you dress-up as thoughts, and find whether or not they are in keeping with the Source of what you consider altogether lovely, beautiful, and excellent, and be that in the eye of the beholder. **The "I" sees only Itself and in the liberation realizes the sadness and the dismay that must be a veil over each and every one who has put** *what-isn't,* **first in their lives.**

The small number here have proved that they are exceptional, for they have stuck with the possibility and they have to be commended; however, *very few* have dared to venture into a new garment of Wholeness. When you used to go into a very smart shop (like Missoni in New York, which a friend of mine managed at one time), if you didn't know anyone and if you weren't known, you had to be a little bit *uneasy*. Many people would not go into the store if they were not properly dressed — until *clones* did it. All that level of consideration meant was that each man or woman was adopting what the other did. *That's* why they were clones: they were imitating something that was *not authentic!* An authentic state is fecund with possibilities. A cloned state is like a wax museum: clones are afraid of the fire in case they will melt and be a blob on the platform of this theatre of drama called Earth!

The broad way is for the mass; Fifth Avenue is for those who can make choice an asset to attainment. **It is your choice which always bestows upon you the energy to alter the course of your life** so that you will not be subject to the suggestions, like bonfires, but appear an angelic force-field emblazoning the dismal scene with the known Fact that there is no such state in actuality and that your dream of coming back and correcting your mistakes is *an excuse* for your laziness and wasted hours — putting in time in order to get your paycheque, in order to sustain yourself in separateness so that none of your rough edges will be perceived in a community *where Light is the mandate, and activity pointing to perfection is the demand.*

Remember the Ten Commandments. I think I've given the eleventh: **"Make an altar of Earth."** And the twelfth, I said: **"*Exalt* one another as I have exalted One to you!"** This is a statement, a period of consideration, and an exclamation is bound to be felt within the chakras of your beingness! Don't put off into the channels of time the all-encompassing cosmic Sea/C of Consciousness bearing the Zephyr from the West to caress your embers of radiance.

Now you can put the yoke upon your thought, for it is *Light*, for you know the balance between "this" and That resides in the One who has the wings of an angel and allows the head to carry the Message in honour of "Winged Victory." You didn't *need* your head to turn! We'd never have a statue telling you otherwise if it were not so. Isn't it wonderful to have one? Now, let's see your wings grow and find what it means to dwell in the shadow of the wing of the Almighty and nestle in the bosom of Love.

May these few words find you clothed in the Light of infinite possibilities with perfection and excellence waltzing in the divine act of God. Don't take time to be holy; *be holy* and see how time is utilized in order for the Infinite to be dressed-up for a moment of wonder! The miracle of Man is the wonder of God's expression, pointing to that Sound which we know is the source of creation and the wonder that gives us the knowingness of the invincible nature of adoration of the Divine! **The word "Divine" is so practical; it's much more practical than *"human"* because you can't dress it up in mediocrity!**

Make one, just like this [Dr. Mills motions to the roses behind him] — not a silk one that *looks* like it. It will be very interesting to see how people like this *fashion parade!*

P.S. If only people (especially in the gown of a group) would regard the possibilities of living life so much more easily in a spirit of unity appearing dressed-up as a community, it would make such a difference. You, unfortunately, don't sometimes consider these things when you are young in spirit, but the Ancient Teachings have always said to those who are striving, they must enter into the sanctuary through such incredible disciplinary means. This is why we spoke about the whip in the fairgrounds. The reason I did (I can see this, suddenly) is because the merry-go-round, the whip and the swings and the caterpillar, all these different rides, were seen in the fairgrounds where you could play, and it was a place where you could experience so many different sensations without danger.

You should play in the fairgrounds of *environment* where you know everything is known for its presence from the very source of your own beingness! If you did, people would start to recognize that the environment was never meant to be wasted. The environment was to be there to sustain your peregrinations from non-perception of wonder *to* the perception of wonder and to be nurtured by the descent of the pristine state of *dew* (the freshness appearing upon awakening into the wonder of constant growth and maturity).

People say "birth, growth, maturity and decay." It's ridiculous to put in "birth." You can't even testify to the fact you know where you came from! A *stork* had to tell you! [laughter] And you can't tell just because your mother and father tell it to you; *who* told it to *them?!* **You have to challenge in order to question the verity of so much you have learned. You will find very little of it is true. The Verity of Being can never be captured in the cauldron of thought.** It's usually the ladle that stirs thought, and it's called "stew"! [laughter] So, if you're stewing with all the slipshod jobs you've been doing, isn't it great that the spoon is in there? Start considering *that* pot, and perhaps you won't grow another one as competition! [laughter]

Don't forget the cherry even if it isn't Bing! Don't forget the tomato [to-mah-to] even if you call it "to-may-to"! Forget the potato [po-tay-to] regardless of calling it "po-tah-to"! And ease-up on the corn; squash it before you find it "parsnipped"! [laughter] These are ideas fecund with meaning because the way you put them together is the way to bring the stew out of the pot and tap the root of more than the turnip of flatulence. **Take the wonder of listening to your inner state and find what is becoming to the salvation of your state that allows others to perceive the beauty and the radiance of an emancipated State!**

It's been a busy week for you.

Students: It's wonderful!

But you should get it while the going is good!

Students: Yes, Sir.

I always remember the story about the tulips. Once upon a time, at 283 Hollywood Avenue, I had tulips with stems about a foot high. Jackolyn had given them to me for Easter, but they were perfectly green bulbs — no colour evidenced. I had them sitting beside me. There were three or four people in the room, and I was talking; a couple sitting to my left couldn't see me so I took the pot and put it under the table. I spoke for maybe an hour, two hours, or three hours on the weekend before Easter, and when I opened my eyes — the reason I close my eyes is because I just like to not look at faces; it's not that I'm seeing anywhere else, mind you! I love you; I'm not flirting with anything up here. [laughter]

When I opened my eyes, I looked at Jackie and the few people in the room, and they were all with their mouths open. I was wondering what it was, and Jackie said, "Look down at your side." I looked down, and all the tulips had twisted their stems like an

S and they were right here beside my leg, and they were fully open! They were red! I picked them up and put them up on the table beside me, and they looked *drunk* because they were all just these incredible shapes. Jackolyn will tell you, we talked (just conversed) for another forty-five minutes or so, and I said, "You must go. It's time to go," and I looked at them, and they were all up straight and just as green as they were before I started speaking! It's so, isn't it, Jackolyn?

Jackolyn E: It was stunning, absolutely stunning!

Yes, and no one else knew the colour until the following Easter Saturday and Sunday, when they opened. So, you *see.*

⌘

1. I John 4:18.

Thought-probe into Time

Chapter XIX

You have, as this thought-probe into time and space, an opportunity to vibrate in the rhythmic manner becoming a harmonic state of melodious conference.

Thought-probe into Time

Themes: I AM ~ Love ~ Truth of Being ~ the Christ ~ unified intention ~ creative act of intoning ~ language

I know that Patricia has a poem she'd like to read or give to-night. I wanted to hear it, so here I am! Patricia Johnson.

Patricia J: I have actually two poems. They're both entitled "A Masterpiece."

> With Dr. Kenneth Mills it happens often!
> Simply because he is so willing
> to lose himself totally in his Creations,
> and allow his Divinity to flow
> through the brush, his voice, or the broom!
> For it doesn't matter what he holds . . .
> because he gladly gives God the room
> to flow through him, a Masterpiece.
> An ego lost, legacies are found,
> while not a thing is concealed
> because his heart is revealed.
> And not simply structuring strategies
> but flowing
> with the Passions of his Soul!
> A Masterpiece.
> They will never grow old!

This is one I wrote last evening for him:

The Excellence exemplified by you is indeed a Masterpiece!
A Masterpiece to you is simply what is expected.
Therefore Realities of Perfection are always manifested.
You live fully by allowing the Divine to flow through
your many forms of Creative Expression.
Your Clarity creates an atmosphere of healing through
Music, Fashions, and Truth-filled Treasures of many kind,
Lifting the quality of Life by expanding mind to Mind.
Words are sent spontaneously through you from on High . . .
As we absorb realities of Truth shared through your Voice,

Words that remind our minds of Perfection as Choice.
Energized vibes also flow through color-filled brushes
As fragrant flowers fill canvasses with Love.
Designs of silenced beauty energized from Above.
Indeed, You create Masterpieces filled with Loving Light.
Your Life is a Legacy of Excellence, Elegance and Perfection
Which inspires everyone you touch . . . to take Flight!
We love You in ways that will forever increase because . . .
You, Dr. Kenneth George Mills, You Are a Masterpiece!!

[applause] Oh, that's beautiful, Patricia, just beautiful.

> I've given poems to others and now I find it
>   comes back to me.
> Little did I know it would come from the Detroit
>   stream!
> I know the River flows-by and the stores and
>   buildings tell a mighty plan
> That once this great, great city, with its orchestra
>   famous unto time and to man,
> Played the dizzying heights of accomplishment that's
>   grand.
> And there in the multitude below stood a Patricia,
>   who perhaps sometimes thought she was in
>   no man's land!
>
> But now she stands supreme in knowing this Fact,
>   that Life is divine,
> And the Mind that is forever bestowing the riches
>   beyond all time
> Reveals unto this moment the eternal Fact at hand,
> That Patricia is the Son of Love and bears the sun
>   as the glad I AM!
>
> So, in this moment of rejoicing in the poetry and the
>   might
> That flow unhindered o'er the stones of doubt —
>   they wear away such plight —
> You, in your moment of recognition, see the
>   unification as planned:
> When everyone appears to be numbered, there
>   stands but One as Love I AM!

Now, this is the evening of February 21, 2004. What shall we talk about? I think that I should read a statement that Angela sent me to-day that was written by George Orwell. She says, "The article includes the following two quotes:"

> Bear in mind, Don Watson writes, "that if we deface the War Memorial or rampage through St. Paul's with a sledge hammer, we will be locked up as criminals or lunatics . . . Yet every day we vandalise the language, which is the foundation, the frame, the joinery of the culture, if not its greatest glory, and there is no penalty and no way to impose one. We can only be indignant. And we should resist."[1]

George Orwell said:

> Language becomes ugly and inaccurate because our thoughts are foolish, but the slovenliness of our language makes it easier for us to have foolish thoughts.[2]

I often consider the talk of so many people and it seems the emptiness of so much time taken when it could have been fulfilled in a matter of a concise sentence. We are so used to foolish language that when the language is not understood, we say, "What is he talking about?" It's because all that you have thought *you* were talking about is not *thought* by this Talker! That's how you describe the sound that bears the verification that it is in the creative act of intoning . . . that creation appears manifested. If it were not for intoning, you would not have a creation. Does the worm know it is a creation? Does the dog know it's a creation?

Students: No.

Do *you* know it's a creation?

Students: Yes.

The marked difference: you know it's a creation. *If you know it's a tonal creation, why isn't your language becoming the Creator?* **The only way the language can become the Creator is when it *moves* and the tone is expelled on the wings of impersonal offering, and yet bearing, in the mystery of its soundingness, the ability to alter the thought-streams that are forever bombarding your peace with the unfettered stream of careless thoughts.** *Thoughts are the* *capsules of sound.* Sound bears healing, but for you to catch it, it has to come in a form that you can comprehend and recognize. The worm doesn't; *you* do.

Why do you acknowledge and accept words that are forever rumbling in the mind — whatever that *is!* I have no idea what the mind is, but we say we have one and we know it must be something extraordinary because we put it at the extremity of the structure, the "penthouse"! [laughter] However, isn't it frequently just *that?* The *pent*house of frustration, the penthouse of incompatibilities, the penthouse of disillusionment: It's a house where it is pent-up with the obstructions that don't allow the free-flowing, natural encounter with one another, "exalting one another as *I* have exalted One to you."

In the fun of being fundamental, the dithyramb of Life portrays its wonder either on the plains or the flatlands or the mudflats or on the high plains of your attainment. To be Real cannot be described other than that which is diametrically opposite of the *un*real. **The Real cannot be contaminated by thought or the processes of thought, for it is beyond the mind's comprehension to enunciate its total characteristics.** We give this explicit terminology to it because we know "this" *isn't* Real. Realness is the demand of each and every one to speak oft with the Lord or the creative Source of your Beingness. The Lord is often the Will, and the Will of the Lord put into manifestation is the altering power of Love! *This altering power of Love happens involuntarily.* **It all depends upon *you!* It depends upon your state of receptivity and your stillness and preparation to stand before the Fount that is going to impel you forth, out of the miasma of suggestion!**

You cannot alter your destiny. When you have found *the Truth,* you *can* because the Truth of Being knows no destiny! It doesn't even know you're trying to be Real! The Truth doesn't know a struggling, poor humanoid (human annoyed!). [laughter] It doesn't know this condition. It doesn't know a *suffering* condition; it doesn't know *you* as a separate being! **You are the precipitated exponent of possibilities, recognized and projected by attention,** which doesn't bring a solution, but intention does: **"Do I accept this limit as my condition or do I accept the *intention* that comes with recognition that 'this' can't possibly be all there is to the efficacy of the Word?!"** They say, "The Word was made flesh"; in other words, the soundingness of Being carried a vehicle so you could recognize it without having to struggle to see through the foliage of the thought-patterns of confusion!

It was said, way back in 1969, that it was very obvious that the reason this Work had not entered into the field of professionalism is because we had not found those disciplined enough to converse with ease and have conversations that usher the Truth into the periphery of the intellectual of the professional. **When you converse as one converted by the correct DC conduit, you can meet the AC with a possibility of rewiring your circuitry for greater Light!**

Do you think that you can be this thought-probe into time and space — that's all you are: a thought-probe into time and space, sensing the various vibratory frequencies that surround each and every one. You have, as this thought-probe into time and space, an opportunity to vibrate in the rhythmic manner becoming a harmonic state of melodious conference! It is said St. Francis had it with the birds. He was lucky: they accepted his Song! It is being had with you, but you don't seem to do anything with it because you can't lead others into the conversion that is necessary to don the wings of the morning and greet the sun in its ride o'er the celestial dome of your cognition. **Where do you abide?!**

This was never meant for "progressive unfoldment." When a napkin unfolds, when a piece of paper unfolds, it opens-up and receives whatever crumb from the Master's Table. What is the purpose of our presence on this plane if it isn't to join in a chorus of hallelujahs of possibilities? Who *here* rejoices in even what Christian terminology termed "the Christ"? Christians follow Jesus. They call Him "the Christ." We know that Jesus Christ was a *remarkable* happening because it was the coincidence of what appears to be the human and divine probe into this sea of expectation. The Christ was Jesus' attainment. *He* was saved. He realized that He had been glorified, not forsaken. **The Christ is the Light to the phenomenon of this probe-projection into time. It is the DC: the Divine Current, the divine ecstasy of transcendency!**

Why do you go along with people with their jabbering and gibbering cacophony of sounds that don't bear healing in their wings?! A confluence of sounds that *move* you points to the invisible feather of an angel's wing. Each and every one is surrounded by angels; they're there if you know how to pick-up one feather that may be dropped to you to see if you cognize the difference between what appears as an ordinary energy clothed as a thought and the energy clothed with the force-field of a *nuclear* happening.

You can't take the old into the new, because the old is what you hang onto. The new is what is present without the old!

How can you have great expectations if you minimize the demands that pave the way for the happening? What you imagine, focus upon with clear intention, can't help but manifest and be precipitated *provided* you assume before it: *"I will be responsible for what I precipitate into my life, be it another person, another place, or another thing, or the beneficence that comes with a divine recognition of Essence."*

One of the ingredients that make a possibility such as yours an actuality is the awareness of an agreement with the very basis of your coming together and commingling. How can you build a grid of power without unified intention? You can't! *You* don't call it a unified field of power; it is not known, other than in language as such! **It is already present!** *You are absent from it because you think about what-isn't! What* do you expect? *What* are you here for? To get another charge in person, or are you here to be charged with the Light Brigade and to enlist in the force-field of Wonder?

You know that this probe into time is your experiment dealing with what you have miscalled "your mind." It's the experiment that has almost failed, and that experiment was for you to be able, through the descent of clear intention and conscience, to experience what it is like in a continuum that tries to solidify the somethingness while, in Essence, it's known for its emptiness. How could Dr. Andrews ever tell you that a hundred and fifty pound man put in an atomic press and having all the holes squeezed out of him, the residue would be so "great" that it could be put on the head of a pin! And in some cases, it might have to be on the head of a thumbtack [laughter] but it would still be hardly visible. You see/UC, the Universal Consciousness is available.

It is said that Love came from the East and a conscience was to be breathed from the West. **Tell me something: do you have a vivified, dynamic, vital conscience?** If you do, you have *priorities,* and if you don't, you make *excuses!* The reason This is dynamic is because *the days are numbered for you* — not to see them pass away in the futile effort of being "this" but in the glorious effort of expelling the delusion and having the fun of appearing this way and bearing the great Message, and a bearing that is obviously endowed with It! You are in that display.

I was told in 1969 that I was to train at least twelve who would know what discipline meant and would appear as disciples, in other words, "disciplined ones," who would be of great importance in the days of the future because no matter where I spoke, or when I spoke, they were to always be on duty holding the force-field of wrong identity at bay. It was said at that time that it was very dangerous for me and this had to be done. At one time, there seemed to be that group, but then the standard changed and options came in. However, instead of people realizing the importance of it, they *dropped* the importance of it.

Remember, it is stated that Jesus didn't send out one or two; He sent out seventy and then He sent out five hundred. I don't usually go into these things — but that's where you are, "in these things." How can you feed five hundred with a few fish if you haven't gained the scale of equilibrium? You never digest Truth; it is incapable of being regurgitated. Truth is its own originator of sound; in fact, it is one of the many jewels on the breastplate of the priest.[3] A stone may bear the symbolic pointing to Truth, but remember, a stone is always an inanimate object until its fire and meaning are perceived. Remember also, to-day the market is filled with *false* stones, and as I've always told you, watch for the star ruby, watch for the star sapphire, because *if the star never moves, it's fake!* When it's real it's only seen in a direct light and then it blazes forth in all its points of wonder. *That is the same with the attainment: it's only recognized by a similar one.*

Everyone in the sixties was preparing for the reappearance of the World Teacher, and some called it "the Reappearance of the Christ," but it was always so ridiculous because people would have crucified Him if He'd said He was the Christ! How can intellectualism discern the Christ when the Christ put an end to the solidity of thought-compresses? It is said, "Behold a wonder, a miracle, for I can do nothing of myself. 'Tis the Father, the Source, that doeth the work." And what is the work? *Extension, involuntarily happening by the radiance that becomes an unfettered state of Presence.*

Dialogue is always interesting. What's the other thing you engage in? Discourse, discussions, and these are usually aimless, worthless, for everyone's opinion is dropped into a pot that never boils, and if it does, it's usually one unpleasant mess! Dialogue makes you stick to a principal topic. Discussion allows you to describe how *you* see it dressed-up. Don't allow classes to be filled with discussion. **Dialogue has to be from the standpoint of the Self (Principle).** *If what you say can be contradicted, it isn't from the standpoint of the Self!*

"If thine eye be single, the whole body shall be filled with Light." What is *body* to you? This physical form? Is it physique? Body is *an idea,* and you make it up to be "you" with a body. But if it's an idea, why do you let it drop to materiality? Why don't you restore it to the realm of ideation? And what is that realm of ideation? *Where harmony, rhythm, and perfection abide.* Body is the natural rhythmic movement of conception unconfined and not at all interfered with by intellectual hypotheses.

Look at your scientists. They're always trying to discover something new for what ails you, and if nothing ails you, they're trying to discover how it might have an effect on a rat! [laughter] But how can one be an intellectual of such brilliance that one is termed a scientist, and have nothing of the science of Being as the foundation from which one views?! If thine eye/I be single, then you will perceive. No one ever questions the state of the *scientist!* How could a scientist offer anything new if the eyes were that of the old?

This is what the intellectual and the professional have succumbed to: the feeling that a specified study is the answer to living. It's the wrong study! How can you have a fine government when there is no one governing who is Enlightened? Where are the Priest-Kings? We don't want the robotized Atlanteans; all they could do was invent means for finding how to make others slaves by dwarfing, they said, by rays. But after all, why bother trying to dwarf the body when you can "ray-bombard" the computer, the mind, and still have slaves?

When you feel so tired and so lethargic, and you're not sure whether you've calculated this cost as this much or this cost as that much, be careful and say, "What state is my mind responding to? My personal methods? Or am I being bombarded by the ray of slavery to mediocrity?" Just look at your actions. Just look at your tardiness. Just look at how slow you are to bring about a change. Isn't it marvellous to prolong investigations about property, about jobs, about what you're going to do to the house — and never do any of it?!

Have you ever stopped? No. If you did, you would find the most unexpected Visitation. Remember, **the new always irritates the old.** The old can't stand the scintillating, energetic dynamism of newness. It reveals what? The aging process dressed-up as you! **Oldness wants agreement; newness doesn't.**

You're either there or you aren't. But be sure if you *are* there, you *are*, not *aren't*, because you can be present in body but absent — I can't say "in mind"; I could because you say that all the time, but you can't say "absent from the computer" — and still probe into the conundrum of this personification and the amorphous state of the Infinite. Remember, the diaphanous gown of the Ineffable always marks its trail by the confetti flowing from the *cornucopia* of the Unlimited and bearing fruitage to those who would say, "I have tended the garden and watched the miracle of the Unseen manifest in a gown becoming the ethereal wonder of Sun."

Remember, the sun doesn't rise or set. *Oh, you were taught that because somebody didn't know!* Isn't it amazing? They never told you that what you were on was turning. That's what you call putting the blame on something else. The sun doesn't mind; it just keeps on shining, and the cloud of unknowingness has to yield its dew, provided you don't look-up and just see a grey cloud, but some do say it bears a silver lining. I *think* not, I *know* that the **Light will never shine more brightly than it is at the moment, and it will never be dimmed by the suggestion of a time-space suggestion and a continuum of limitation. It is so *wonder*ful to live and transcend it by the voyages made on the ship of Soul into the harbour beyond all chance.**

Always be silent before the arrival of the Unexpected, and always be aware that you may want to chat; but unless you have the greetings from on High, it's better to contain your energy and die to the presence of Wonder.

"Wonder" is not known in Polish, neither is "miracle" or "marvel," and yet what they worship is nothing but a miracle and a wonder because it has allowed people to be found at that point in their incarnation where they find a way to worship what is known and named as God, just waiting to beam His Light upon this faithful follower and reveal that through your faithfulness you have found the key to open the door to the Presence of what you have prayed for: the Coincidence.

In some churches when a miracle happens at least once and others can testify to it, the one is called a Saint. But you have to have proof it happened at least once. Isn't life itself the evidence of the graciousness of the Light because you live as the antithesis and yet you are allowed to engage the possibility of not being "this" but being *That*.

> What is the point of saying "I AM" unless you add "That"?
> Then, what is the expectation?
> The *I* walks and the AM-ing evidences the creativity.
> That's why I AM *That* I AM, because creativeness is your life, is the fullness of it, framed so others may see a picture bearing scrutiny and an interpretation beyond the seeing of the eyes and the movement of the force-field that is termed "miracle," for then you may see a great Light.

It is said to "speak oft with thy Lord." Get to know your own inner perfection; get to know what state your will is in. (And the one that you've written out!) Get to know the state of your feeling. Get to know your emotions. They're astral; they belong to you, but, since they go with so many others that are not visible, you enjoy them too; you have that much more company. The ego loves company in the astral. It loves emotionalism because it's a substitute for the eternal movement of creativity appearing. **Emotion is the wasteful use of *energy* that could be used in the vocabulary that is becoming to the Source of creativity.** That vocabulary can't be used with emotionalism.

The vocabulary that surrounds and gowns our mystery of Source is dressed in the vocabulary of words bearing the train of a unity, Male-Female-One, and the wonder of a marriage made in a harmonic state and bearing the train filled with abundance, for All that I have is thine. That is the gift that we know we have. Why don't you make room for it by emptying your mind of the desert sands and allowing the Zephyr from the West to re-awaken the conscience so that intuition joins it hand in hand and you walk out of no man's land and onto the plane of Glory upon this stage, waiting to see a new Light.

I hope that satisfies your expectations.

Students: Thank you, Dr. Mills!

Terry was typing a transcript of 1978 and he discovered this:

> This is the morning of July 24, 1978, Monday morning, in the reception room at Ontanaka with Jaan K, Marc F, Gerry M, Peter C, and my mother is sitting in her chair knitting. It's a lovely sunny morning.

Perhaps before I read the next part, you should say what Jaan had said. Do you remember it? Just put it in your own words, about the DNA.

> *Terry S:* He did speak about the DNA and the RNA. The first part of the morning was primarily Jaan speaking; Peter said a few things. This was Dr. Mills' response after this whole morning ensued.

I said:

> Jaan mentioned the characteristics of the DNA and the RNA molecules, and as the result of a preliminary chat, the following has unfolded. Jaan wrote it down and I am now reading from the notes he has taken. We jump to the idea of language, and the following is the statement that was given.
>
> Language, in essence, is the gown that the primal electrical discharge comes to wear after the initial carrying wave of its origin has been utilized in a constricted dimension, the third. But its genesis came out of the wave of raw Power, unformed to this dimension but known to this dimension in its formed fashion as an urge. The urge finds expression as act and speech. Life has on a garment of recognition and pre-cognition, for the genetic stream carries within itself the power to meet any need so as to be always fulfilling the origin which is only known, but ever available, when life is seen in the raw (in other words, freed from the language of limits) and innocence is found gracing the brow of revelation.
>
> I AM That I AM is a garment: "I AM" is the charge; "That" the discharge; and the act, I AM, the origin of language. This evidences in a practical way of recognition and pre-cognition, all wrapped-up in the Urge.

And Jaan said, "Doesn't that point to the value of having the manifest Master?" I said:

> Attunement, consciously, as you become attuned to That termed "the Higher Teaching": "Do ye this in remembrance of Me until *I* come." In other words, by constantly remembering, by constantly practising, you are constantly imprinting upon the whole stream of generation unto generation the imprint of what can be, when language is free to alter, in the name of Love, and in its altering, free the finite from its limits, and the Infinite becomes the Sound given unto man, capable of wearing a Sound expression in Sound agreement and a Sound investment unto all those who would say, "In the name of God we praise."

Have you ever stopped to consider what power you have and you indicate it by your life? Consider it and then put it beside your name and see if it can change anything. Does one power by name (say, "imagination" or "strength" or "elimination" or "faith") by itself do anything? It can help and move, but it is not capable of the restoration of the divine Monarchy, because where "it" *happens* is when these are restored in the sense of an activity of each and every one evidencing these powers. That's what enhances a community, a city, a country, a nation. You think in such small terms!

Yes, Paul.

> *Paul S:* Sir, how important is our awareness of world events from the correct Standpoint?

If you watch world events, you perceive the error that is parading, and you know the Verity of Being, and therefore, it alters, it wipes out the suggestion that such error could have any tenacity in your thought-pattern. Yes, you stand, reducing the suggestion to its nothingness.

Yes, Barry.

> *Dr. Barry B:* Sir, what is the authentic power behind the ability to vote?

Wisdom. Every man should bear the wisdom to a vote. He shouldn't vote just because the majority are voting for somebody.

You should vote according to what you feel are the qualities that you'd want to live by. The nation is nothing but *"you"* magnified.

Remember, some of you agreed to come not only to rectify your own life experiences but also to resuscitate those dying in delusion. This Work was to re-awaken within the cache of your Inheritance the various gifts you have, to bestow involuntarily upon another when you have once gained the solution to the suggested problems of materiality. That solution is Love. "Love" is the name you give to a verity that you know is eternal because it's omnipotent in its power and in the force-field of its Life-force; and that Life-force, together with the omnipotence and the verity and the eternality of that, gives us this incredible *conglomerate* of Force termed "Love." Love isn't just a feeling; it's a unification of these force-fields of Power that *come together* . . . and the world is different! That is how Love sets the captive free. See?

Students: Yes, Sir.

Just love — it doesn't matter whether it's man, woman, dog, child, worm! You might as well love because you couldn't create any of them. It's a wonder! Even Freddie the fly! But don't love your*self* more than *That*. And it's obvious you do because the first thing that comes in your line of choices and preference is *"you."*

What if somebody said to you, "You've got to appear in Detroit and give a lecture to-morrow night"? Can't you imagine you running to the president of whatever your company is and saying, "Listen, boss, I've got a lecture to give to-morrow"? He'd say, "You do it and you'll lose your job." Would you do it?

I have people who stay away because they've got a headache or they don't feel just quite right. There used to be a time when people would come with migraines and they would walk free. Or filled with cancer and be going in two days later for an operation, and it wasn't there. You don't have to know the individual. I didn't know the woman; she was sitting close to me when I lectured. I was sitting like this, and she was right here, where the plant is.

Jackolyn E: Yes, Sir.

The doctor was an Egyptian. The incident is in my memoirs; she's had three major healings. And her daughter is with us. It's accurate, isn't it?

Lindy T: Absolutely, Sir.

She wrote it, thank goodness, in a letter in which she stated that the Egyptian doctor said, "How is this possible?" She said, "I heard a man speak the other night, and this is the result of it," and he said, "I agree with that."

Lindy T: Yes, Sir. He said, "I agree with that. I could understand that. I would know that that would be true —" from his background.

Then another time (she didn't like me or the Work at all), Lindy called me in Tucson. It was around one o'clock in the morning in Toronto; it was very late. She said, "Mr. Mills, Mother wanted me to call you." I said, "For heaven's sake, what for?" because I hadn't seen her in three or four years. "She said, 'Well, I don't believe Mr. Mills knows I'm in the hospital for another operation.'" I didn't know it, but Lindy told me she wanted me called to know it. And she went to the operating room, and there was nothing to operate on!

Lindy T: You gave her one statement to hold to, Sir, and that was the healing, as a result of holding to that statement. You told me: "You just tell her, dear, that if you can watch it, then you're not in it." It was a miracle.

Oh, wasn't it?!

Lindy T: It was incredible. I'll always testify to the accuracy of that, Sir, because it was just such a miracle.

Yes. And the most amazing one was my bird! One morning I put on my dressing gown and went out around five o'clock to sit in the Walled Garden and watch the sun come over the mountain, which was right in my view. We were only one road from the last road in the foothills of the mountain. I was meditating and then I started to walk around the garden. It was quite large and there was about a twelve-foot brick wall surrounding the whole area. The bedrooms on the northwest side of the house were all opening onto this walled garden and the pool in that garden. I was walking and I came to the Lemon Room. It had huge panes of glass: one window was ten feet by ten feet — just *one* piece of glass — and then on the other side there were two windows like that and some wall. In front of one of these windows, lying on the ground, was this Thrasher; it was a large bird and it was dead as could be, cold as a rock and as stiff.

I felt so sad for it, to think that it mistook the window as an opening. You see, it was so clear. So, I picked it up and put it up on the high brick wall so that nothing would touch it. I went over and sat down under the Palo Verde tree and just thought about the bird and the continuity of Life. Then I opened my eyes and I looked-up at it. Just as I looked, it went [Dr. Mills imitates a bird beginning to flap its wings]. One wing went . . . and it flipped over and flew away!

It just shows you how the dead shall be raised *incorruptible* provided you never give up your purpose and your intention. The intention of the bird is to fly, *and it did!*

Yes, Patricia.

> *Patricia J:* I would like to commend you, too, on your Web site[4] because that's where I found you. I looked at every aspect of it and loved every, every word. I just thank you for having that there, or else I would not be here.

[Dr. Mills responds by giving a poem.]

> I'm some glad that the Star never stops shining
>   and that you recognize it as your Self
> Because in that wondrous moment of cognition
>   there is only the I that dwells.
> The symbols are translated with the I unseen
>   in time,
> And then they are moved beyond the incoherent
>   mind.
>
> Then the coherency of expression, appearing as
>   gratitude, appears
> Because the I, that is hidden from the two eyes that
>   only reveal,
> Says, "I am the revelation and I am that Light
>   divine,
> And when I see your face, I see my own sunshine."

Good-night.

Students: Thank you, Sir. Good-night.

⌘

1. Don Watson, *Death Sentence: The Decay of Public Language* (Australia: Random House, 2003), quoted by James Button, "Fighting the Death Sentence," *The Age,* Melbourne, November 1, 2003.
2. Quoted by Don Watson, *Death Sentence.*
3. Exodus 25:7.
4. www.kennethgmills.com.

The I-thought

Chapter XX

The I that IS allows your search to be fulfilled in the realization that the I-thought is there without the I, thought.

The I-thought

Themes: I AM That ~ Reality ~ Identity ~ reason from a fixed Standpoint ~ mind/thoughts ~ false sense of substance ~ duality ~ ego

---

This is the evening of March 13, 2004, and with the possibilities of a new spring, it's always rather exciting to see what you have bred in the winter months of regeneration. The spring is always the time in which the fruit of your considerations starts to burst forth and to bloom for the sake of those who can still recognize beauty undefiled.

One of our great considerations in the experience of this plane termed "the Earth" is that we are seeing more and more the necessity of the enhancement of the spiritual considerations of the time, for the time seems to be devoid of all that is considered substantial. We are seeing people give-up their lives to chase a false sense of substance, give-up their lives to fulfill a hallucination.

One of the most serious defects in our whole pattern of awareness is that we are always succumbing to the subtle foe, and that subtle foe wears so many disguises that many do not dare to rip them off because they don't know what to do with what is left! This is why we never lose, in to-day's world, the arguments based on the supposition of duality as Reality, because there is a hidden fear that what lies at the root of our lives is being totally ignored. We have mistaken a false god and head towards the place of confinement within the comfortability of our friends and seek some sort of consolation in having company in our disillusionment.

You are of great importance because you bear within you the knowingness that your experience is just waiting to be tested. You have had a long time to prepare for the great day of what is termed "the dawning of the Light," which will mean that great masses will come to perceive the shallowness of their concepts and the foundationless structure upon which they have built their lives — because there is nothing in the realm of duality that isn't disposing of itself! Duality always leaves something to dispose of; Reality never does because Reality reduces the suppositional picture to what it is: a projection of your own inner creative Self.

What is the thorn in the flesh of everyone, or the thorn in the *side* of everyone, if it isn't that darned thing termed the "I". That darned thing termed the "I". Do you know that it arises at the same time as the ego? It arises at the same time as the ego. In fact, your false identity is, foundationally, the ego, and the ego is that which is obviously always up for reclassification — but it can never get the work permit of the Divine! [laughter] The ego cannot partake of the refinement of the Divine. It is abhorrent to it if it is preached unto it that the Divine is what it will become, because somewhere within the concept rests this very startling consideration: that it (the ego) only arises when "you" *need*.

Do you realize that you cannot find the I with the very situation that has produced it? The "I" is that state of false identity that *you* give it; you give it the privilege of inhabiting the netherworld and the Reality world, and truly, it's absurd! What do we say? The I — what? — thought. What is the purpose of meditation, what is the purpose of contemplation, if it isn't to do what?

Robert M: To still the thought.

It's to still the thought . . . to what degree? That is only the first step! To still the thought is to what? To see what is left if there isn't any. If you can't still the thought to see what is left, you'll never realize the accuracy that surrounds the **I**. You only say "realize the **I**" when the I-thought is present. (Listen carefully.) When the I-thought or the I, *thought,* is present . . . but the **I** is *not* thought! The first thought that arises is the "I," but it is only a thought! The **I** that IS allows your search to be fulfilled by the realization that the *I*-thought is there without the *I, thought*. That Presence is nameless but it is known, for there could not be the I-thought without the Super-consciousness, or the Consciousness that IS, being the Source of your comfort. That is how "I will never leave you comfortless."

If the I-thought — you see how I said *that* one. It won't look right on paper; *it has to be heard*. If the I-thought is held . . . to be your identity because you say "I thought" — all that verifies is that ego is now clad! The ego is now clad; it has a clothing in which "you" can be deceived.

> **If the I-thought is original, how do you happen to have this experience?**
>
> **Because the I-thought is without body;** *the I-thought is idea.*

Look at the comfort!

> **The I is your keynote; It is the very source of your solace in the Divine. It creates that which is necessary in your service role to fulfill your specific purpose for incarnating, and that is to restore to those lost in the mesmerism of mentality the way of escape from that land of bondage into the free land of unbounded and unconditional Love and its inherent ecstasy.**

When do you have your world? When do you have your friends? When do you have your bedroom? When do you have your drawing room? When do you have your car? When what happens?

Terry S: When you place your attention on them.

Yes, you can place your attention on them, but you're assuming that that's your gift, and it isn't. That's why they're a burden. You only have them under what condition? *You have to conceive them as idea and name them,* because the I is the source of ideation — but it isn't *in* the idea or the manifestation. It can never be in a limited *form,* but it can allow you to perceive the wonder and what must be that incredible condition that exists when I have realized the Allness of the entire creation and its acts!

How do you know you see, how do you know you feel, how do you know you sense, if they aren't the qualities sponsored by the mind — which is what? The name given when more than one thought arises. Your mind becomes contaminated with what? The abundance of unselected thoughts! Your desires and your propensities are thereby enhanced according to the control you have over the condition of the fructification in the realm of the lower mind. Why is the mind *lower?* Because it deals with everything that's passing, but it doesn't say it *isn't!* This is what you mustn't do. So many teachings in the High Way go to the point of annihilation; this doesn't. (This has been etched upon my awareness to give this always.) It doesn't eliminate your wonderful (I hope it is) experience, but what it does is call you to remembrance that it's all a result of imagination and it is passing, transitory, and bears no mark of eternity save in its uninhibited origin, its primal state of Source-dom termed "God."

What is our common tendency as being humans, or as human beings, is that we have used words and misunderstood them. We have understood being as humans instead of understanding Being *dressed-up* as humans. Why? Because we have to alert everyone: we are here to change our garments all due to the unique quality of choice. If you have chosen to be one with the Light, then your program is endowed with originality and uniqueness, and the only thing that would keep you from expressing it is if you have been contaminated by the wrong understanding of Identity. And every one of you has been!

There's not one who hasn't been contaminated by thinking you were "this" or "that." If they thought you were That, they wouldn't have known what That was because "this" is all-important; it would have been very difficult dancing with That from the standpoint of "this." So, this is why "this" and "that" are sort of a tit for tat! It never gives you anything but the possibility just to rap! [laughter] But who ever heard of rapping without knocking on something? It is said, "Behold, I stand at the door and *knock!*"[1] Everyone raps, but they don't realize *the obligation is to reveal the door to the wonder of rhythmic flow!* They don't understand the need of rhythm in their lives, and what begins to happen with the magnification of syncopation in so many areas — not only of rhythm, but of procrastination instead of instantaneity, of emotions instead of feeling — is that you start to create a veil. And you term that veil what? The veil of psychism, and this emotional veil is where you become open to invasion.

It's one consideration that you should think your own thoughts, *but how do you know if you're thinking your own thoughts?* How do you judge if you're thinking your own thought? There's one rule; it's a practice. What is it, Margaret?

> Margaret M: It has to be a thought that is in line with the Christ, with my highest Ideal.

Since your Standard is the Christ or the undefiled or the Source, then the thought has to be in keeping with That. What do we do to-day? We see limitations, we see fear, we see jealousy, we see resentment, we see what? A lack of awe, a lack of wonder, and a lack of brilliance. Why? It isn't in keeping with the mob psychology. Why does the mob want you and criticize your exclusivity and call you a cult or whatever? Why? Because a Standard always is threatening to those who have lost theirs. How can a Standard be raised if your mound is made-up of false predictions, false information, and false reasoning? You have nothing but a mound of dust and usually ending in the conflict.

One of the basic considerations is that you, as Light-bearers — "Light-bearers" doesn't mean you *carry* It! You *bear* It! A Light-bearer isn't one who carries *anything!* You can't carry *Light!* You can't carry Light. You don't "utilize Principle." (You all talk that way.) You don't utilize Principle; it's Principle *accepted* as the Love of your life that utilizes talent so that it glows in the adumbrations of time, and people say, "I *see* the Light!" Do you consider that the shadow can't stand the Light because as soon as the shadow faces the Light, it is no longer the shadow! It's one thing to see it on the back of the cave; it's another thing to face it. There is no one looking at a limitation in the Light of the orb of God shining as this golden symbol.

This veil is what clouds the clarity of your decision-making. How often do you make a decision, if it has to do with others, that isn't considering from your standpoint? How often is it ever done from the Standpoint "It is done"? We know, and it is said, that Jesus was such an Exemplar, and it's one thing to name it, and that's fine and dandy; but every word of Truth that He uttered has been echoing down through the centuries of your prolongation by desire and intent to hold the door so that it is available for knocking upon. You have got to perceive that all your desires, generally, are for "this," but I think the inspired Word is supposed to say, "One thing do I desire, and that is the Presence of the Lord. And one thing do I seek after . . ." Wow, is that *yours?* Or is it just after the topic so that you have a brilliant intellectual discussion with your, perhaps, somewhat dense or somewhat *tinsel-ized* intellectual friends? This is why you like the intellectual stimulation of having a language that can intrigue them? But what you should not do is *intrigue* them, you should *entangle* them in the Light Web of consistency!

How can you be what you call "friends" with those who know not what a friend is? Everyone should question: *What do you consider "friend" to be?* **To be a friend, be One. It doesn't mean "one to another"; it means be O-n-e, One! It's the only way you can be a friend, because it's Love undefiled and it's unconditional. You can't be a friend if there are two.** You *try* to be a friend and that's why you have a *trying time*. Don't try to be friends; *be* that Force and that Presence that causes each and every one to re-evaluate the circumstances surrounding their purpose of incarnation.

Have you ever stopped to consider that you were only meant to come here because you chose it, and because you knew somewhere in the deep recesses of your heart that you had not gained the purpose for all of this. Do you think you were ever made just to work as a secretary in an office, as a chauffeur or a cook or a painter, or as an architect or as a doctor? Never! Not when you're in this Light. Maybe the others have to fulfill it, but you're *here*, and that is not your state. You're not some petulant, little, frustrated urchin in the Light of the I. *You are a manifestation that is to bear witness to the Ineffable.*

Your work is to be what? Honest, faithful, responsible; fidelity present, commitment present, trust present; adjudication *absent!* That's hard (That's where it comes as an undercut! [laughter]) because, frequently, adjudication stands high. *Adjudication*, remember, is a marvellous sound, but it means to judge (in *my* consideration) righteously, which means to judge in such a way that what is revealed sets a captive free! I adjudicated so many people all my life in the realm of music and I never left an adjudicating state without everyone knowing their potential! You should never leave the contestant for first place feeling they have arrived. They may have been given first place only until a greater degree of performance is obvious.

If you are finding fault with someone, remember, it is to free them; it is not to limit them in that fault. That's the right kind of judgment. How can you really *judge*, anyway, unless you know their standpoint is as yours, and that's why each one of you knows the Standpoint from which you should live and move and have your being. It is not one of having opinions. **There is no opinion to Being! There's no option, no matter how many times you return.**

> **As long as your motivation is as a result of a remembrance of the past, you have karma in your to-morrows.**

I don't speak much of karma because it doesn't really enter much into This; it only enters into it when it becomes an unfulfilled effect after the Cause for activity is known.

What seems so necessary to-day is not the magnification of the Self but such a personal need for self-aggrandizement, and that is the wrong self. What do you spend your days doing? Lolling around, trying to be spiritual? Not at all. "The Spirit quickeneth." [laughter] What? What does the Spirit quicken?

Jennifer M: The spirit of adventure.

Yes, Nora.

Nora B: Creative action.

Yes.

Robert M: The Spirit quickeneth the realization of one's true Identity.

Yes, it should because it is your spirit of uneasiness that tells you that you're off home base. That's it. Watch for the signs.

Do you know, when you think you have arrived, you have hardly started. I always remember the high school principal. One of the boys said to him, "I'm all finished, Mr. Mowat," and he said, "Sorry, you've hardly begun." [laughter] That was the day when the principals wore a butterfly collar and a cravat and a black vest and long cutaway coat every day for school, either in brown or black or grey, and a pince-nez; every woman wore the most beautiful dress or suit; every teacher wore a suit or a sport coat, always with white shirt and tie; and the professors at the university wore their cap and gown, teaching the classes. I went to revisit it a few years ago. I was shocked at what walked on the campus! I couldn't believe my eyes.

Aren't you concerned about education? What is the most fundamental flaw is that you're not taught how to reason from a fixed Standpoint. I don't know whether people are taught "one and one is two" or not. I think maybe a computer does it. How can you start to work with the mentality, which is what you will have to work with, and *alter* it?

What is the mind? I've told you; somebody tell *me*. I haven't forgotten, but you tell *me*. I'm not so sure about *you!*

Dr. Barry B: A conglomerate of thoughts.

Yes. What's the point of the intellect? It chooses which thoughts go together at random. You have a great choice. That's your intellect. And your mind, where is it? Where is it? *Where* is the mind?! Where is it, Marshall?

Marshall O: In thought.

That's all it is. Then, why do you pay any attention to it if it isn't *I*-thought? The mind is just a thought. And what are you doing? Thinking. There's nothing wrong with it, but "choose you this day which thoughts you will serve." Because why? Each thought is a force-field ready for exhibition; it's bound to show.

If the mind is a thought, why do you go on making it up to be more than it is? Why don't you have the mind-thought as *I*-thought, as God-thought? It's your choice.

To be What-IS is the shortest distance that man ever has to walk. To be what-isn't is the most circuitous route that you can encounter because it's fraught with the temptations of finding yourself in the realm of duality on the turnpike of supposition and having to penetrate the veil of illusion.

What will happen when you realize? Will you still be here? Yes, you'd better be. It takes One to know One. That's the living Friend. It takes One to know One: Self, face to face.

The incredible wisdom and intelligence we seem to have is all the evidence of the magnificence that really is attributable to the One and only. But how can you release an impression (your friends) from thinking they're an expression if it isn't with the joy that reduces the suggestion to nothingness. The false can never stand happiness or joy, because salt, water, chalk, protoplasm, or slime, all strung together in a bag in time, can't be reduced to such a state — and yet it is, in the face of joy, because you can laugh at it and say:

"But for my God I would believe I am 'this,'
But for the Love that IS, I know I AM That
Which enables 'this' to personify for those who
      doubt

There is but one Person, and that is the eternal God,
    forever in action and constantly about.

"My days are not numbered, my years are not spent,
My time is eternal and the theatre of time is rent.
And mankind will see in the dawning light
That the Globe of glory fills the dome in sight,
And that insight reduces to time this incredible
    Fact —
It's wiped out, and the eternity is this:
    Thou art always eternally That."

So, in this knowing, rest assured you will find
The Glory becoming one so inclined
To see without doubt in the face of the Light
That what I see is all glorious and I AM that Light.

I thought, and I ran. Where?

What we are dealing with is this incredible objectification that we have produced, and we have forgotten that we produced it. *We have produced this entire experience.* **Every bit of this is a thought-projection manifested.**

Why is the tendency to always fill your life with attractions that sponsor not the Source? Music and art, singing, these are all wonderful. Salt, water, chalk, protoplasm or slime couldn't do it.

Students: No, Sir.

A beautiful tone, a beautiful sound,
Is the evidence at hand that God is around.

Every dimension has its characteristics, and there are only a very few that you, seemingly, can have any imaginative association with. Of course, it's never correct, because the time sequence doesn't exist other than on this one. Remember, it's only on this one that you have engaged that you are dealing with objectification as a *need*. You seem to be a solitary confinement. Have you ever noticed how different it is here [Toronto] compared to Quebec? In Quebec you are kissed on both cheeks, and sometimes *three* times. And do you notice here . . . ? That's about all you notice! [laughter]

It's so interesting to see how men embrace one another: shoulder to shoulder, creating an arch through which a car could pass! Do you know what I mean?

Students: Yes.

Why are you so afraid of being touched if you're embracing your Self? But you'd better be knowing that when you do it; somebody might think you're getting fresh, and that isn't good for you anyway!

What did you do this week that was exciting? Go to work every day?

> *David N:* I wanted to speak with you about the lecture that I attended that you were so interested in. It was quite fascinating. There were quite a number of speakers, and the future of democracy, particularly in Canada, was on the floor. It was quite interesting. The main speaker highlighted the significance of the parallels between the two democracies. In the ensuing discussion, education (which you spoke about to-night) came-up as one of the main factors in the future of the country, and just how important it is to be educated, and that civic interest be instilled. There were many, many aspects to it, but that was one of the most important ones.
>
> The area of the media (which I know is a concern for you) was a concern for everyone there, and what happens with the media, how it distorts and controls the information. One of the people with whom I spoke said he had all American channels removed from his television; he just did not want to even have that coming into his home, that type of bombardment, particularly the idea of sound bites where people are forced into making a fifteen-second statement on an issue of great significance. It's really impossible to define that way, but the way that society has construed things, it's forced people to do that. Donna was there, as well.
>
> *Donna C:* The main speaker spoke about imagination and how important that was in the forming of any society and how what we create as a society comes from imagination.

The society itself is an imagination of one person multiplied by several others. That's all. This Group, I'm imagining it, but I've opened my imagination to the fact that, although I know I am creating it, each in that creation is a reason for it being there. I have not selected what I should create; that's why my doors were always open. They were never locked, because I was open to allowing to see what others would create in their so-called Quest. So, I accepted it as part of my creation, when it's totally not mine at all, but by accepting it, it's hopefully graced.

> *Donna C:* Most definitely, Sir.

That is how imagination is such an important factor. The whole idea of democracy is "for the people and by the people," but we never have underlined *what type* of people. It can't be a people that is not attuned to the Source, God. You can't have a society that is afraid of prayer. No society has ever lived that didn't worship an unknown god or a thought-known god, such as Ra (why not?) or the wind, the rain, or the earth, or the water.

> *Donna C:* It's so important because, otherwise, you cut yourself off from that creative Source.

You cut it right off: just by one slip of the tongue, and you can do it. I've always felt that you were so important in this Work, and I always have found it so questionable why this whole thing hasn't moved beyond this stagnation, but I think that what happens here is you get so *in*volved with what *can't* evolve. You can't evolve intellectually; you evolve when you deny its supremacy and accept, because you knocked and the *I* heard you! The *I*, in that case, is fulfilling the grace of being someone who cognizes less than Allness, knowing that what's knocking is *All,* but only in ignorance thinking otherwise. That is the value of the *Unfoldment*™; It restores you to your own fullness. But it's very difficult to restore you to your own fullness if you don't allow yourself an empty cup. What you will do is, you'll use something or other to stir the thoughts until what I have said has not even been heard.

The reason what I say may be important is because the *sound* of what is said is *all-important.* The sound is the carrying wave of an Energy that is Earth-received but not transmitted from here. It's not transmitted from here. If it were on all the time I could never just talk with you.

Robert M: Dr. Mills, there's something you said in an *Unfoldment*™ recently that touched me very deeply, about our identity, and the word you used was "thought-probe." You've just spoken now about the sound being received on Earth; it doesn't come from Earth. Is that why I found that so comforting, that the thought-probe comes closer to that Origin of the sound?

That is actually closer to your Origin. The thought-probe — you can't name where it came from, but you want to because you think *you* have a source of *your* beginning. You don't. The only source you have of your beginning is by what you have been told and led to believe sensorially. It appealed to your vehicle as soon as it was freed from the sea of preparation, the ocean of preparation, within the uterus. As soon as it was freed of that, you were here, and you have to be reminded that you are not primarily "this." **You are primarily Consciousness supreme with a garment for this dimension of awareness that is a vibrating web of consistency.** In other words, it will allow whatever you are aware of to bear witness to whatever you need. It doesn't say it's right or wrong; it just allows you to have whatever you need.

Your awareness has vibrated to the point where I'm on it tonight, but just think, what you are hearing is a vibration. What is your web made of? Vibration! Where is the separation if it isn't in the thought that doesn't vibrate in keeping with the fundamental Pitch — which I spoke about earlier — the C. That's 440, which is an 8. It's the symbol of the Holy Breath, but it's movable. It's termed "a movable C": it can either be lowered to sound in the densities below or it can be raised to sound in the higher octaves of Tonality; and when they all mingle, you have a tonal framework that is so important.

The whole demand is to remember that if thought is immaterial, what is materialized is the attention you give unto it. That's why the attention you give unto a thought manifests. That's why you have a car if you want it, or that's why you have a home; you can have it manifested into this limitation if you are ready to sacrifice what is needed to sustain it. You can have anything if you're willing to sustain it. You can even have the Kingdom. "All that I have is thine," but *how many want it* (because then you are no longer concerned)? Your little ego has got to be *e*ternally on the *go*.

You don't try to tell anyone what you know until they ask you, "Why are you so *strange?*" [laughter] And you can say, "Well, my range is so very great."

Don't be satisfied with partials. See which string is not vibrating as it should be.

Yes, Susan.

Susan A: Earlier this evening, Sir, you said, "As long as your motivation is as a result of a remembrance of the past, you have karma in your to-morrows." Could you say more on that?

Yes. When you feel that you want to do something, you can't have the past as your motivation; it can't influence what you're going to do. You've got to do it with all the newness that surrounds originality. When the past colours it, then it conditions it so that it is not totally new. That's what I mean.

Yes, Barry.

Dr. Barry B: When you were giving the Unfoldment™ this evening, I remembered a very potent statement that you gave in the Summer of 1988 when you said: "*I* is not a thought; thought follows. If thought follows I, then how dare you think thoughts that are not following *I?!* That is the rigidity that is essential for the restoration of the monarchy of the Light."[2]

That's *exactly* what it is to-night! I'm concerned because there is such a destruction of the "monarchy," and it's *deliberate!* Do you know why it's deliberate? Have you ever thought, "Why am I disconsolate, why am I disquieted, why am I so restless, why am I so bowed-down, why am I so harried, why am I not successful?" *Where* are you looking, and where do those feelings come from?! They're not coming from Love, and if you feel inundated with them, go to somebody you know. Go to Rose or go to Hermine or go to Wendy, go to anyone you can get near who will say, "Get thee behind me, Satan!" That is terrible. You're fortunate to have someone, and you should really, truly beware of those times when this happens to you, because it is just exactly the influence of a mental voodoo or a mental Satanic force that is not yours and has nothing to do with you.

Yes, Nancy.

> *Nancy M:* Good evening, Sir. You asked earlier, What's the good news this week? What did you do besides going to work? I so appreciate the *Unfoldment*™ this evening and, particularly, when you mentioned that the important thing for the children is to be taught to reason from Principle, from a constant. I can see it's so important. What comes into their life — they don't know how to handle these forces that are present, but I can stay in a position where I can offer something. This is just what happened.
>
> It appeared on Thursday that there were all kinds of squabbles and difficulties happening with the girls, and it got to be almost too much. I know you can't solve a problem from within the problem. I thought, "What am I going to do here? Well, we'll sing." I said, "Let's sing the song that we haven't sung in months." It was "Let there be peace on Earth, and let it begin with me."[3] And, of course, that beautiful song — it's one that's sung frequently in churches — changed the tone of the whole class. It says, "As God is my Father, brothers all are we. Let us walk with each other in perfect harmony." That whole situation was quelled by music, and you'd mentioned the importance of the arts.

It's terribly important.

> *Nancy M:* It's essential. I'm just thrilled that I can do what I'm doing because of what you're offering.

The children are very fortunate to have you as their teacher.

> *Nancy M:* It's a testament in my life to Truth because I can see changes that happen when I utilize what you have given. Alterations happen, and it's remarkable. And the children would it easily.

[Dr. Mills responds by giving a poem.]

> They would love it because it becomes
>   something

That eventually they can think is a power that
    enables them to stand
Erect and bear what is becoming to a boy, a girl, or
    a man.

It's what becomes, at a tender age, the very fibre of
    an exciting pattern of thought
That allows them to weave their garment, to see
    what time in its time will bring to their slot
Of action proposed on this plane of Earth
To give unto everyone a chance of second birth.

And from the time the child perceived what is true,
His birth has happened, and it depends upon you,
Because it depends upon the teacher who can witness
    the fact
That the child has moved beyond what he thought
    was his mental trap.

He now sees without doubt this exciting fact:
That what he thinks he will exude, and will he act
Or will he consider, "Is it becoming to my Light?
For I am a child of Wonder and my action should
    be Light."

An exciting time. Why is time exciting? Because it's the moment that is fecund with unlimited possibilities. That's the way you can release time of a co-ordinate of space which defines our limits.

So, go on being middle-aged and worried about what's going to happen to your old age and what's going to happen to you when you haven't got a penny in the bank. Why don't you go to the Teller and find out what your account really is?

Why do you think you have to earn a living? I never thought I ever had to earn a living. I taught piano, and the money was there. That's what they said thank-you with. I didn't earn it; I just did what I loved. You only earn a living when you're doing what you don't love. When you're doing what you love, it's its own substance fulfilment.

Yes, Gayle.

Gayle K: Would it be wise for us as a group to image the full and complete experience of our divine nature so that we can really be the great Presence and allow It to master us as opposed to us mastering It?

You can't master It. You see, you never can master It. The great Presence is all that's present here now.

The great Presence is so great that you are nothing but a sparkle in its crown of recognition.

For in that recognition of the faceted Light,
You appear to be wearing a gem which others may
    call very brilliant and bright.
But remember, those who perceive your brilliance,
It's this wondrous thing at hand,
That they are awakening to recognizing a quality
    appearing as "you"
Which, of course, they think is dormant in their act.

But in the cognition of each and every one
By another who comes in from the shadow into the
    Sun,
You should find this glowing Fact
That they say, "Brother, what makes you glimmer? I
    want to know that/That!"

Gayle K: Thank you, Sir.

Glimmer and glow and don't deny the little glow-worm, either! [laughter]

⌘

1. Revelation 3:20.
2. Kenneth G. Mills, unpublished *Unfoldment*™, July 19, 1988.
3. "Let There Be Peace on Earth," words and music by Sy Miller and Jill Jackson.

The Resolution of Chromaticism

Chapter XXI

Unless leaders acknowledge the uniqueness of each and every being bearing sound as a viable part of the resonating keyboard of Life, there cannot be a harmonic or unified universal symphony of the Light.

The Resolution of Chromaticism

Themes: That ~ fundamental Pitch ~ unique individuality ~ overview ~ the world ~ acceptance ~ humanoids

This is the evening of March 20, 2004, and as we look over the world picture we must do so with the simplicity of watching a movie being portrayed and we the audience looking unto it. You must realize the verbiage that surrounds this phenomenon of living on this planet and the dire consequences of the suggested loss of power within the realm of liberated man.

We are a chosen race of people because we have been graced with the ineffable joy and beauty and peace, either we wouldn't be here. This is one of our significant purposes of being incarnates on this planet at this time.

> You are here because of your great privilege of
>   allowing others to perceive the wonder of the
>   undefiled
> Walking in the simplicity even of what appears as a
>   grown-up child.
> Bear the fruitage that you have been given when you
>   cease thinking through the limits of a mind,
>   and allow thought to come at rest,
> And see if you can see how that moment is
>   blessedness.
>
> Rest in the assurance that you would not be here
> If that God of Light was not revered
> Within your Soul and within your heart.
> And this is why you feel the impelling to start
> To rescind the suggestions of an errant mind,
> All conditioned by the propaganda of time.
>
> You stand supreme in this knowing Fact
> That you can discern what is Truth so that fiction
>   fades as a fact.
> You understand, either you would not have found
> That your state of thought is all Earth-bound

Until you meet a consequence of Power,
When it's reduced to smithereens by the Love of a
    bridal hour!

You are engrossed in the gross suggestion of time
But you know you're so brilliant that it can dash
    the mind
To the rocks of despair and you stand supreme
Because you know your life is not in this land of
    dreams.

You are the power to this glorious realm
And you come to service it with a free spirit and
    dwell
Giving unto mankind this Force divine
That comes from being simple when not lost in mind.

Take this fact and let it be known
That you appear to be one walking this Earthen
    shore,
But it's only a visit to this plane in time;
You are really a gadabout in the terrestrial vibration
    that exists, we know, within and without
    mind.

    The mind that we say is there for you and me is really all thought, you know. When you ask someone, "Where does the thought come from?" they say, "Well, of course, my mind." But, of course, the mind is a thought! So, you have what you call Edgar Bergen and Charlie.[1] [laughter] It depends on whose knee you are sitting. Unfortunately so many of us seem to be Charlie. Of course, we shun with dismay: "Egad! How under the sun could we possibly be manipulated? Don't we have our own mind?"

    You have the ability of the apparatus that is termed "mind" to engage this planet and allow you and your space-suit to be geared in such a way that it navigates easily. It's usually beautifully dressed, beautifully groomed, because, aside from the fact you want everyone to look at you and to see what a figure you can cut, remember, you are really a cut-out for time because what you seem to be is not what you really are at all.

    Of course, you're so bright, you know this, so it's like having oatmeal all heated-up again and gooey. But what is Fact is forever fresh and new and is always buoyed-up by the consideration of cream. But, I tell you, it's not quite powerful enough; you need some steak! It's the red meat that gives the blood what it needs, so they say: iron. What does iron do? It's that very, very hard metallic substance that is used in fortifications of your mind. You are geared to think a certain way because you've been taught a certain way, but it isn't certain that that is the way! [laughter] Unfortunately, not being certain that that is the way, do you suppose that you could be uncertain and *That* is the way?

Now, what is That? That is the only thing you can say or sound "That." It sounds like somebody hit you in the diaphragm: "That! That!" But we say, "Find That"; in other words, find that which is without thought. Only after it's heard do you give it thought. So, when you are searching for the needle in the haystack, don't waste time. Go to some store (I guess the popular one is, let's say, the "K-Supreme Market") and there, find one that your thought could not bear going through (the needle, the eye of the needle).

What man slit into time is so narrow and so fine that he is strung here on a thread of consistency and constancy, either he could not be vibrating to the supposition of a humanoid. Unfortunately, too many people are complacent and aren't annoyed enough! What happens? They are asleep in the cradle . . . of what? They're asleep, and you might call them "the walking dead." How do you know they're *walking?* They seem to be keeping in step with "you," unless you have caught the rhythm that goes with tapping feet and the knowing that your feet are here to tread upon this plane to spread *your experience* in a form termed "understanding," so that others may be caught in attention and given to pondering "Why is he or she so gorgeous, so gracious, so rhythmical, so slim, so lithe, and the spirit is blithe? How come I can describe it and not *be* it?" Silly! **If you can describe it, it's waiting for you to *claim* it.**

How can you possibly claim what you don't know exists? This is why you need to meet somebody who can tell you that you should claim something, because it is obvious there is a uniqueness about That which is unknown, and since you are so known — because "you" are just a what? A track of thoughts until somebody puts the light on and says, "*Stop* before it's too late; you're running on the wrong tracks!"

Non-duality is where the whole situation can be resolved. "This" is allowing you to appear dual, but in your depth of experience you know that that is for those who are on this plane waiting to see the practicality of the manifestation of That which is termed "the primal Pitch" that is uncontaminated by the hypotheses that you are "this."

In a world of such wonder, which seems so impeded in its beguiling beauty, our attention is always taken on the bonfires that are set in order to get you to run to see what's burning. But *you* should be burning . . . with the impelling force to rescind the restrictions of the errant mind and *move* into copulation with the divine Principle or Pitch that can rescind the disharmony which is trying to be claimed atonal and acceptable to the discrimination of the Light. *It isn't.* **Tonality is all based on the understanding that your instrument has got to be founded on an established vibratory frequency.**

This past week I have had a very interesting experience, another interview of several, *several* hours with the anchorman from New York. It was intense. Many, many questions were posed, and one of the questions that always arises is, "What can happen to resolve the dichotomy which is existing among people and thus manifested as the world situation?" Then, for the first time, I heard how something I've given in teaching piano years ago is applicable to the *entire* world! *We have the answer.* It's really world news. We have the answer!

For everyone who wants to play the piano, or who wants to play in a symphony orchestra, or anyone who wants to be the *art* (instead of the "-tist" and reducing it to personalization), we establish a pitch. That pitch is 440. Every instrument is tuned at 440. Knowing this, we can take any of the keys on the piano — and you have many choices: there are only eighty-eight! That should, in a way, satisfy you since your path is here for the fun of making choices — and the dire effect of not making the right ones.

So, what are we going to do? I said to my interviewer, "The most important thing is to have *the overview* of the entire keyboard of expression." What is the salient feature? That the notes are all white — it's a sea of white notes — *but* there's order to the black: twos, threes; twos, threes; twos, threes, right over the keyboard. What if "Johnny" is in the dark about how he is going to navigate this soundboard of expression when there is nothing there to give him any form of guidance? Ah, but there is if the teacher has caught it! It's the note between the two black ones.

We know that we must be founded on a fundamental Pitch; we can say 440 and call it "Principle." Did you realize that C had a name, D had a name, E had a name, A had a name, all because you agreed that 440 was the basic pitch. We never even mentioned it in giving the identity, because as soon as you are given a name you forget how it was possible for you to bear your unique individuality in the composition of life. You need somebody to remind you it's all based on an inner knowing that **fundamentally 440 is your accepted pitch of every possibility of expression in the realm of art, the art of being a harmonic pattern of resonating** *puissance.*

Why can't the *world* live like this? We don't have to be the *first* letter. Who cares what is the first letter?! A for America, B for Brazil, C for Canada. What does it matter? **We all have our individuality but we can't help but be related because we spring from the acceptance of a fundamental Pitch.**

There's your answer of simplicity to the whole world problem; but when you have *aggressive power* trying to solve the solution, there is *none,* because "aggressive power" is nothing but the name given to an imbalanced state. This is why it is said, in all the markings of the Way, that balance is so important. This balance is of encyclopaedic importance because it rests right back on the fundamental Pitch. You can't divide the Holy Name of the Creator just because you have a mind to/two. You can't divide the Holy Name by conjuring that you have any acquaintance with It. You say the Holy Name because the intellect lives on this ability to ascribe something unto It for *food.* You know you live, without ascribing any name to It other than *awe* and *wonder.* You worship It until you realize how close It is and how far your worship keeps you from It.

Who told you that if you could conceive of an apple, it was far from you? It was within your range of *acceptance.* An apple in your range of acceptance means you must have seen it, but how can you see an apple if you aren't willing to look for one? How can you find a living "That" if you aren't willing to look beyond the fodder of the mind?! You can meditate, you can pray, you can whistle, you can dance, but you will come to find that you still are not satisfied. You may, as Ramana Maharshi said, see a king or a monarch on your way, but just because you have seen the king or the monarch doesn't mean that you *are* the king or the monarch — even though you'd go home and tell everyone now you know what it is to see a king or a monarch!

The monarch isn't there, because it can't fly. The butterfly of Wisdom is not there to be found *in supposition*. Supposition is the greatest hook to the dilemma that confronts each and every one between what is termed "Conscious-awareness" and the magnitude of the objective confrontation. You cannot have the objective without the what?

Students: Subjective.

Exactly. But is the subjective *seen?*

Students: No.

What is the subjective then? What if the subject requires no object and the verb is "be"? If you think it's just "be," you're going to be stung for sure, because "be" is static! **"*Being*" is dynamic resolution.** Being brings a *bout* with the conflicts based on suggestion.

The grave mistake is that we become complacent and dream success, in reducing infinite possibilities to a circumscribed area of action. Now, mind you, pray intelligence is guiding you in your service role, but also pray that you realize the role is only for the appearance, for **your purpose is to reveal** *the scintillating, dynamic expression of what is termed "that elusive force-field of Soul."* And I tell you, don't go to sleep, but stay awake to what you are here for, either you will go on perpetuating exactly what you abhor, because *you are creating it*. If your attention isn't where it should be, you are allowing the spurious suggestions of war and pestilence to continue because your thoughts, you and your thoughts, are harnessed to projecting the propaganda that is aimed for those who are not fully awake to the manipulation of the parasites of the mind.

If you feel good after a Lecture — I'm not just sure what that means — but if you feel at ease after a Lecture, you shouldn't. It's been an unsuccessful Lecture.

What are the possibilities of world peace when the very people who are screaming for it and praying for it are really doing what? Aligning themselves to *fragments,* to quarter-tones! (A music that we are not used to.) Now, it's music to some ears. Just think, a quarter-tone has to have a fundamental one in order to be recognized as a quarter-tone. So, those who love quarter-tones, fine and dandy, but realize, if there weren't a fundamental Pitch, they would not be cognized. You don't kill it and you don't say, "That is a nation that needs to grow-up and hear it in a diatonic concept." What you do is sit in wonder that someone has developed that mode of sound that moves them — and *you* if you listen to it. You may be irritated, but that doesn't mean it's anything but *you;* it's not the sound.

Peace is not afar off. What is afar off is the willingness of leaders all over the world to realize how arrogance and ignorance can parade in high places. **Unless leaders acknowledge the uniqueness of each and every being bearing sound as a viable part of the resonating keyboard of Life, there cannot be a harmonic or unified universal symphony of the Light.** Impossible.

I do not understand how people can say, "I have a right to think what I wish!" Of course you do! It's obvious what's happened as a result of it: selfishness, arrogance, aloofness, wealth and poverty all come into it instead of the essential sound-ness, going to the very bottom of the key and letting it sing. You all have the key because you wonder, a bit, a little, how you came. If you don't want to wonder *much,* you forget about it and say, "Well, my mother and father married and I was the fourth or fifth child," or the first one, and that was enough [laughter] (Good!), or you may not have had any. That is of no consequence if the mother-father balance within you is ringing with the sincerity of knowing that there is a fundamental Pitch for which you will search in spite of the hypothetical origin of your presence.

Thus is the elucidation that surrounds the wonder of the Light Brigade that should blazon upon your living presence that you have found that which causes you to reduce the power of the mind to a place where it can become of service of the Sublime. You are all born to serve not yourself, particularly, but your Self, as you look upon the creation which you cognize only when you look upon it and focus upon it; *it doesn't exist otherwise*. That should shock you, because you say, "What's going on in the world?"

Well, what's going on within *you?!* And why do you like to look at the turbulence? To reduce it to its nothingness? Or to find it stimulating your fear?

What does fear rest upon?

The reduction of your awareness of the need of Fundamentality in living life.

How are you going to resolve the chromatic situations of the world to-day? Simply by *being authentic.* This doesn't mean you have to be staid, dull, afraid of embracing the wonders of others, or afraid of reducing that embrace to the evidence that the Divine *lives* in the embrace of All-inclusiveness. There is no such thing as love that amounts to a hill of beans if it's conditioned! Conditional love, oh boy, watch out! How can the very Source of Being be reduced to corporeality? You are so vain in thinking that it's possible. How can you conceive that that which is termed "the mind" is just nothing but the seat we give to the arisal of thought because you don't know where in hell it comes from. But that's where it comes from! Hell exists as a result of division.

What is Heaven?

It's a harmonic state of Being, and it's a harmonic state because the fundamental is accepted.

How could sixty, eighty, fifty, hundred, hundred and nine, hundred and ten people in an orchestra perform so beautifully if they all thought they had their own individual pitch?! What do they do? They surrender to the wonder of a sound baptism because when they agree to follow the conductor, each plays the notes becoming his choir. Then look what happens: an experience that is so forceful it can change everyone in the audience if they don't have what is termed "a tin ear." **What is the tin ear? One that doesn't know how to vibrate spontaneously to the experience of Unity!**

It's so fascinating, when the Star-Scape Singers used to sing on the stage here in Toronto (which they did many times), one of our "enlightened" critics said, "The conductor, Mr. Mills, seemed to mesmerize them." The jackass! How under the sun . . . ?! They don't say that about other conductors. Of course not! But they could see the Singers focussed because **what they were doing was so individual that without One Feature present they could not** find their individual parts and keep them in alignment with what was essential for a scintillating performance!

It was only in Canada that we heard the sarcasm cast. In Europe it was said to be "the choir of the twenty-third century." That is the difference of a nation based with music ringing in their hearts and sound emanating from their voice. They weren't afraid to embrace the Source of it, the Invisible or the visible. Never forget the Israeli paratroopers whenever you doubt the power of Sound! The hardiest of men and the handsomest of men, they were just wonderful, and what did they do? They had no sense of anything but a Sound experience. They cried and hugged me until my shirt was wet, and they said, "If you will come to our land, you will bring peace." Not personally would I bring peace, but the Sound could change. Remember, everywhere we sang when we were there behind the Iron Curtain, what happened? The walls came tumbling down!

Erika Z: They certainly did!

Star-Scape Singers: Yes, Sir.

Every story needs to be symbolically interpreted; it's much more than just our touring. *Every experience you have, if you look in depth, is an experience that carries a viability if you look at it more in depth.*

The answer to the chromatic situations of Earth is so simple! The child can see it. What do you suppose happens when it grows-up to be fifty and sixty, seventy and eighty? You can't string and attune each string just because you want it to sound differently. You would not have an audience! [laughter]

> This is why, if you are comfortable the way you are, consider, "Am I asleep?"
>
> If you are at peace where you are, ask how many you have awakened!
>
> If you are in Truth where you are, ask how many are irritated! If they're not, love, love, love until the irritation becomes the very force-field to the rapture of a moment of realizing where the King, the Origin, really dwells. It is not within your reach of materiality, but it is well within your

reach of conception unconfined and unfettered by objective confinement.

Remember, the equilibrium of thought-force is pertinent unto Origin, which is termed what? "Father-God." But God, the Holy Name — "God" really can't be holy! We use it because you can't name the Unnamable; we use "God" as a stand-in. But you can't imagine an imbalanced God-Force. Male-Female, One!

One of the startling new considerations, so I'm told recently, is that the intelligentsia have now declared in secret conclaves that they are worried about the reduction of masculinity in the country. I thought, "For heaven's sake, what has happened to *femininity?*" I said that and I was told, "It's sort of passé." I would hope it is, just from the standpoint that too many women have wanted too many delicate males. When the malehood, the manhood, of a nation is left considering what **its purpose is in being,** aside from procreating — **it's to stabilize and be that undeviating force-field for Good and allow the women to carry the expression and find a male-female situation bearing fecundity in its wake instead of selfishness and isolation.**

How many families ever do anything but include their own relatives? I was brought-up in a very simple home but *everyone* was included; no difference was made because of race or religion. **Do you make your meal prepared in such a way that all can partake of it? Is your menu so enticing that others are lining-up to partake of it?** Even if you give it away, people are very concerned about taking the Menu that is fulfilment, because *when you are satiated with the transitory, you are depleted.* **When you are satiated with the constant C of Being, others appear satiated; but there is neither satiation nor dissatisfaction, for you have offered the complete menu of Wholeness.** *It rests solely on the foundation of an accepted vibratory frequency which accompanies this three-dimensional experience.* Don't forget, you are not found in "this," neither is I AM. But it does point to that unknown thought-probe from another dimension that gave you confidence to assume this transitory figure in order to fulfill your heart's desire.

> **Don't be reluctant to face the dragon of your nature, for it was meant to give you the exercise necessary to develop the dexterity that is essential in coping with the suggested force of the objective resentment.**

Join in the rhapsody of Being and rhapsodize and create a tapestry of Wonder as your life and allow it to be, not a message printed on a wall of unknowingness but to hang on the wall of suggested blockage, the very tapestry that allows you to walk through it and enter into that state where you can appear to be in this world and yet not of it. The tapestry of your life is woven with a web of consistency, and the efficacy of your Work is in the benediction: "Well done, for you have traced, to those unbelievers, the great level of awareness that transcends belief and allows you to recognize the invisible Throne, as you carry, as your realization, the butterfly of wisdom on your shoulder."

Embrace your situation with Love and its expediency for all Good. Thus is the purpose of our coming together and sharing this Menu that has been deposited onto the invisible table of time, these ingredients offered by the Saints and the Sages of the Ages, for the enhancement of each and every one within the hearing of these Sounds and their relationship to the accepted Source of fundamental meaning.

Students: Thank you, Sir.

⌘

---

1. A popular vaudeville and radio act of a ventriloquist (Edgar Bergen) and his dummy (Charlie McCarthy).

The Precipice of Possibilities

Chapter XXII

Living in the Now is not seeing yourself doing something in the Now; living in the Now is doing without seeing "you."

The Precipice of Possibilities

Themes: God-Mind ~ unconditional Love ~ demands of Sonship ~ fundamental Pitch ~ the Higher Way ~ mind ~ humankind ~ emotionalism

This is the evening of March 27, 2004. As always, I never know what we're going to talk about. Let us consider.

One of the features of the to-day world is how we are all grasped by the news of the day and how we are all taken to scrutinizing the conditions that are offered unto us. We bear a responsibility, as you all know, to the denial of the opposite of harmony and peace. We are forced to reduce aggression to nothingness. Aggression is the evidence that somewhere within our perceptive patterns we are being challenged by that which does not conform to our way of "thinking."

In pursuing the Higher Way it is naturally expected that we will not behave in the manner of the lower way, and it behooves each and every one to consider just how we are moving in this zone of our lives. The tendency is to revert to the old way because the new way, under the aegis of Philosophy, gives us an ability to reduce what isn't conforming to the Higher Way. **Error unfed by attention dies, for it lives on your attention.** Now, this does not mean "I will not look at the television and see anything aggressive," but it does mean that you become the very force-field for peace. *Don't respond emotionally to what you see, but bless the humankind.*

Now that you have approached the Higher Way, do you consider yourselves to be a humankind or a kind of human? Or do you consider the human the gown your unbridled Spirit has utilized to experience the suggested confines of this three-dimensional space and the time experience that allows movements to be measured? After all, any movement that can be measured is a movement that is limited by the very concept of time and the concept of space.

We know that even adamantine matter is nothing but a level of vibration. We say it is hard and dead and lifeless but, in actuality, it isn't; it's just a reduction in vibratory frequency. The stone appears to be so hard and unyielding. Isn't it interesting how it resembles the state of many people to-day? *The vibratory frequency is so reduced by our reluctance to adopt the new energy-field that comes with the realization of our Essence.* We renege on the possibilities of that which surrounds a new way *of not only thinking but of being and doing* that comes naturally with the Higher Way. And when we consider that we are constantly forfeiting our right to *experience* newness, by emotionalizing the moments of pictorial events on the boob tube, we reduce our very power to open new ways for others to conceive, for we have been given a way of moving from the momentary impasses of suggestion into the realm of new possibilities.

This is why the Higher Way is so appealing. Anyone on the Quest should never be behaving in the way of others who are *not* on it. I feel so frequently that people behave and act as if they were not on the Quest and, by doing so, reduce the splendour of their own radiance. Another way of saying this is, you deliberately reduce your custodianship of a vibratory frequency that enhances your radiance and its level of radius.

Your radiant radius is so important because the circumference is outlined by your radiance. Do you extend for a mile from the area around you, or do you extend for twenty-five miles or fifty miles? It's the radiance that allows the wonder to be rekindled in those who have eyes to see. When one sees that there is a radiance that is unexplainable from the standpoint of being human, then there is the opportunity to question, "Well, why would you expect to understand it from the standpoint of being human?" Try to look at it from the standpoint of Being and the human the gown that the spiritual Force-field is wearing so as to set the captive free who has the perception and the ability to transmute the impossible state of affairs into the state that is becoming emancipation.

How much freedom do you really have? Certainly looking outside of yourself, with the suggestion that you don't realize that *you put it there,* you find yourself trapped in it. If you are believing that you are captured in this frail gown of flesh and bones, you are taking into consideration a false premise. **There is nothing that can confine the Mind that IS.**

As you know, in worship we pray to a God unknown. And how do we do this? In mind. It's the mind that allows, we say, a God to be considered. But if the mind is accepting a God unknown, then you are in that realm where you consider the mind to be the most important thing, next to your appetite, in your experience. However, when you question the mind — why *would* you, if you feel it is the one that can worship God? If your mind has to worship God, God is certainly afar off, and you would say, "In my mind I see God." That should be a warning sign, because if it is in *your* mind that you see God, you are imagining that your mind is capable of containing the radiance of the Ineffable. So, you might say that your mind is put into question because it could not *possibly* contain the radiance of the Ineffable. Therefore, the Mind that IS is that which allows the mind that isn't to have a sense of peace, because when you have once realized that God can't be contained in mind, then God *as* Mind is a bridge to that State. That God as Mind allows the mind that is worshipping God to be moved to the precipice where unlimited possibilities are now present. **The Mind of God, or the God-Mind, is what allows the dammed mind of the human to be blasted away in the blaze of the realization of the undivided State, in a State of Conscious-awareness.**

Awareness of God in a belief-system is meant for many people, but if you are on the Higher Way, the Mind of God is all that can bestow the Grace that allows those incarcerated in belief to once again spring forth and know the force that comes under the power of the Almighty in the adapting to the demands of Sonship. How can you say "I am the Son of God as divine Idea" and go on behaving as if you're the idea of someone else? There is one divine Idea; it's either zero or one. Your computer works on it. Either there's nothing and you call it something, or it's one that reduces the nothing to something: the evidence that *I* live and move and have my Being and reduce the suggestion of doubt to the dismal state of belief.

Can you imagine a God divided in stature?

Students: No.

Can you imagine a Son inheriting a divided state?

Students: No.

Why do you behave as if you were errant brothers and sisters and denied the legacy of those who have given their life-force to the wonder of Life living itself abundantly?!

You see, you are dealing with *ideas* on the Higher Way; you are not dealing with the thought-patterns of becoming something or other on the Higher Way. **The Higher Way demands that you reduce the crisis of identity immediately.** And we enhance this disturbance because we keep saying, "You say, 'I am,' but that has nothing to do with God." Ahhh! You thought *too much!*

The words are important because we know they bear much meaning when looked at in depth; but the sound itself bears such power if you are listening without putting thoughts to the sounds.

> **Let the sound be garmented in thought as you are in matter in order for your Essence to experience this plane.**
>
> **Let the idea be dressed in sound so that you can experience a sound that emanates from the vibration of a string that is set into your scheme of cognition as a heartstring responds to a situation.**

They say, "Seven strings, all strung to the tune of 'I love wondrous Light!'" It causes crystal to melt, and yet the adamantine nature doesn't feel secure in this nebulous world of vibration. Why do you always start your premise for reasoning from *matter* to mind, where it should be from *mind* to matter — and *does* it?! [laughter] As soon as you have matter, you have the solidification happening; and as long as you have mind, you have the sea of ideas that are either going to be garmented in sound, or if sound, then it may come forth as action; and then it can come forth as a materialization. Then when we say we have a materialization, we say, "Boy, this is just great. It works!"

That was the *Piscean* Age, and everyone wanted, guess what? Demonstration. That's why Jesus had to prove to people He was a divine Messenger by healing. But in this Age it's very different; it's appealing directly to the Conscious-awareness pattern of *experience!* This is why experience is a salient feature *for you* because, someway or other, you have got to reduce the suggestion of being part of a memory pattern that is totally capable of distorting because of its garment of emotionalism. You only *remember* when you have an emotion attached to it. When you are active in the moment, there is no memory of a moment ago. This is why it is said, "Live in the Now."

> **Living in the Now is not seeing yourself *doing something* in the Now; living in the Now is doing without seeing "you."**

As long as you personalize what you do, your person is moved into that place of feeling responsible. If you are capable of appearing to be personally doing something and know that "I of myself can do nothing; 'tis the Father that doeth the Work," then you can appear to be the knower, allowing those who only *think* they know to come to the point of saying, "If it were not for that realization that I just heard, I would believe I was coming to know. But what I have just heard allows me the wonder of *knowing* without thinking." **Knowing without thinking is the force-field to the moments that are so necessary to reduce the rubble of chaotic thought to the new super-structure of Conscious-Being and wearing the tonal garment in** *awareness.*

This is why I'm always checking, with people in the house, the awareness. "Did that envelope make the trash or did it not?" He said, "It did." I said, "I'm not sure; you better look." So David looked, and it didn't. However, this goes on all of the time because we get so taken-up with considering what we have to do that we hardly do *anything* that we *want* to do.

It's interesting to see everyone interested in something that is beyond their present possibilities. It's like the carrot: "If only I had this, I could do that." But have you ever put that statement into question: "If only I were *not* 'this,' could that be?" If that is put into question as a question, then you are in a position to start to see what you have done to make your life seem impossible to unravel. As long as you consider yourself to be one of a series, you're in a mass — and not even one that's *praying* for deliverance. You're in a *mess* and you don't know it because you may think you're alone until you see *me,* and then you have company. "You" and "me" keep each other company.

How can you expect to take the Kingdom by praying that you will be delivered? It says that "the Kingdom must be taken by *storm."* And what does that mean? You have to have the energy to confront the ensuing force-fields that arise to keep you from being liberated and a soundingness in time that reduces its tenacious grip on you and allows you to offer *a timeless tonality* that reduces a suggestion to the point where it can see, beyond the fog of the intellect, the landscape of infinite possibilities.

Have you ever considered a rather thorny subject: that if God is All, how does the *Son* fit in? Who said so? Isn't it a consolation given to those who, within, really want to find? And God is supposed to have said, "This is my beloved Son." How could it possibly be if God is a tonality of the Male-Female-One? How can it exist, if it isn't offered as a prize for anyone who sees the concept of God in the *real* sense of the divine Creator. Your perception of the Allness blazes forth as the Sun because you carry the radiance of knowing the immaterial nature of Actuality in the garment of the fractured picture of the humankind and the wonders of a belief-system that fades, for the lack of support, in the knowingness of the *higher* Way of the Light.

In the Light there is not a duality framework. That only appears to be your experience of your nature and the gowns you choose to wear. It doesn't mean that you are *confined* to them; you have just put yourself in them in order to experience how to extricate yourself from them so that the essence of your presence is the stimulating fact of a possible transmission and translation from the ordinary into the extra-ordinary Wonder of that which is termed "a celestial Visitor."

What makes your presence so formidable as a mass when *actually your presence can't be measured?* It has no weight! You cannot weigh Light, because you don't know what It is. What you term "the light" is fictitious; what you term "light" is just that which is keeping the door open for you to realize. You know it's possible to know what It is without limitations, because It exposes what-isn't, even its own false concept.

Love — oh, how we love that word. I don't know why, particularly. People seem to have so much trouble with it. They *fall* in love. Yes, they fall in love. Can't we think-up a different phrase? [laughter] What do you say? "We fell in love because we were so attracted to each other." What do they say about attraction? It's always where? It's always between opposites. Can that be *attraction?* That's what *you* have said to explain a faulty reasoning. **Love is the unifying factor of the *suggestion* of opposites!** That is why it is said that unconditional Love is the divine "attraction"? It should never have been used. Unconditional Love is the garment that is worn for those who would look for the experience of a God-Light in our midst.

Attraction is usually filled with emotionalism.

Unconditional Love is usually garmented in feeling, which is a continuous baptism of Wonder.

Emotionalism is a momentary absence of control.
You have lost the bridle from the horse's mouth and your mind runs amok in the emotional realm. Whenever you are emotionally bound,
listen carefully to some statement that allows you to move from the emotion to the feeling.

It is due, really, to emotion that you have memory.

It doesn't take time to think right;
it takes the willingness to do so.

You are all very special because you have continued to exist within this Enfolding Pattern and have met many emotional crises; you are also in a position where you have grown in the *feeling*. The feeling is your natural state, and the emotional is what makes you gloomy, moody, and you say you have the "gloomy, moody blues." [laughter] Don't enjoy such company; change the thought-structure immediately! *That is your job!* Just because you say "God is All" and you claim that State, it doesn't mean that what-isn't rolls over and dies! But it does mean you can't empower what-isn't with the emotion of "Oh, why didn't they do that! I can't stand that!" You'll have to stand it because you are supporting it by your energy and giving what you can't stand an opportunity to stand instead of *fall in Love!* What you can't stand *falls* in Love.

Utilize the power that is in translating the Transmission from words into the power of concepts unconfined and freed from the chaos of an unordered intellectualism. All we are ever dealing with are mental constructs. "Sick" or "well," it's the way we describe situations. When we came into the garment of this form, we came willing to be what it demands and living beyond its seeming demands. You can say, colloquially, "I don't feel like doing that," but you must know within yourself you are testifying to a condition that is describing the material state. It doesn't mean that it should be ignored, but it shouldn't be termed and believed to be "feeling." You could say, "My senses say I can't do that." Then you have something to deal very simply with.

What are the senses? They're the wonders of the world! Would you have any world without them? There's not a thing wrong with the senses, but where the problem arises is when you leave it with the senses instead of the awareness that allows you to stand at an experiential distance and see how they are operating under the panel of Light ministrations. You may sleep; that doesn't mean *I AM* asleep.

> **Fructify the statements that can offer unto you a whole stream of considerations that are blessed because they arise from the acceptance of your fundamental Pitch.**

The whole problem in the world to-day arises from the reluctance of people to accept or find the fundamental Pitch. "Principle," "God," "Creator," "Source," "Self" all sound so differently than the ordinary language. When you use the astringent language of that which accompanies the Higher Way, naturally there's a different tonality, there's a different impulse to the sound! If there isn't, you're not there. It's not some whispering hope on the branches of your thought. The Truth is not quiet. The Truth bears a shock. That's why it is said that to experience Truth, there's usually irritation.

So, if you are comfortable in your company (your own or with others), then know you have the first indication of the sleeping or the walking dead. You do! Knowing what you know reduces the possibilities of your *ever* being like you were . . . two (I'll let *you* say it! [laughter]) You can't go on, knowing what you know, and speaking as if you didn't know it. What you know springs from the Heart. What is Love springs from the Heart. And when you condition your response, you are nullifying the great gift of emancipation which is termed, by some, "the Christ." **How often your heart rings out and you reduce its impulse so that it doesn't show what it really wants to express!** "If only I hadn't!" But would you ever say it? Why would it come if it wasn't the heart feeling the bombardment of restriction? Yes, it's provocative. I can hear the change in the room.

Students: Yes, Sir.

It's wonderful to know that the Holy Breath knows nothing of time, but yet It allows you, seemingly, to be in a condition where you time it.

You should all sing because it's the evidence that you *have* breath. *How* you sing will be the evidence that you are being taught. *When the singing is the song and the song is the singing, then you'll know the Invisible is made visible.* This can happen in the magic of alignment to One, for in the song it happens. This is why you should never inhibit your gift of song. Don't make excuses: "I haven't got the time." It's purely an emotional response. *The breath knows nothing of time.*

Do you realize, even the people in the original Singers who were rebelling at something they could dream-up — remember, for years it was a joy, but there was always something to challenge what? The "dress" of your emotions: your ego. And yet, in performance, when the song was the singing and the singing was the song, all of the different strata of grievances faded out, because when you are concentrated on One, what other exists than the involuntary blessing of a voice set free? *That* gives a baptism and *gave* a baptism of sound to the audience. They were so moved out of their senses that they could not stop applauding, for they experienced a moment of blessedness. You can see why, viewing from this Standpoint, it was such a great moment of despair when people dropped out. They never did transcend their egotism. They'd "never want to do it again." Oh, dear boy and girl, you *will* do it again! Everything you don't *want* to do, eventually you *have* to do.

I once told you I always found it repellent to thought, the thought of kissing a dirty foot. Then, one time at my house on Hollywood Avenue, I said to this man, "Stand still. Don't be surprised by what I'm going to do, but I *have to face* what I don't want to do." He was startled. He was in sandalled feet, which had been walking the streets of Toronto, and I kissed his foot and made myself feel it; it wasn't just a rub, a brushing. From that moment on I was free!

Always remember, when you can sing the words of Truth (in other words, voice them!) and you don't, you are withholding the Holy Visitor from ever having an opportunity of being received by a state of awareness that would ask for "Food, Sahib!" What greater food can you offer them than the Invisible made visible, the impossible possible, and the wonder of attempting to describe what appears to be the precipitated from the zone of unknown splendour into the ever-changing grasslands of mentality.

What is set in the deep foundational Pitch of actuality forever bears the fertile seeds, and a garden will grow. Remember, the grass is always the passing, but you never forget a rose when you have once enjoyed its fragrance. A rose never dies when you ring it, first, in fragrance. The rose has a radiance and a radius according to your wonder as it unfolds its beautiful skirt and reveals the very centre that is invisibly gowned in that intoxicating fragrance of the Invisible.

Perhaps that is such as life, for life defined by form is a poor example of Life that is one with the very source of Being and, therefore, like Mind, It can't be contained in your concept. Ah, but It allows you to appear to live, so we say, "He has life. He moved. He started to feel."

> Thus were re-established the possibilities in the fluctuating picture of time,
> And the buoyancy of the newness appearing brought a bridle to the horse of the mind
> And in the verdant pastures where we may ride and play,
> Always with the tender knowingness that the bridle on the horse's mind gives it a horse-less way.
>
> For we ride the mind o'er the plains of doubt and climb to the mountain beyond despair,
> But the mind that knows it's usable is the one that evidences the Mind that is rare.
> For the Mind likened unto God is evidenced when the mind of time can declare
> In the wonder of being a tonal fragrance, "My mind was struck by the finger beyond, and that was the one of Light and Love, and so rare."
>
> So, listen for the Pitch clothed as wonder.
> Be accurate in your acceptance of such,
> For "this" can only shout the glad tidings which are beyond your thrust.
> That is the power to your knowing, that I came and I stood and I stand,
> Not equating the seeming passing with the "you" or "me" who tries to care.

I stand erect and offer you, under the panoply of the
 Love divine,
The grace to bestow what appears as "your"
 knowingness which will brace all the
 human . . . kind?
What kind of a human are you? Are you one that
 testifies to your limited garment of flesh?
 Or do you bear
The kindness that is one with victory and allows the
 human to bear a radiance rare?

Do you wonder at your apparel? Do you wonder at
 the opportunities at hand?
Oh, do! For there stands on the Summit that you
 have gained the High Point rare.
You have moved, from the fundamental Pitch of
 power that allows each man, each woman,
 each nation in your conceptual plan
To be at peace if they would find cessation from the
 turbulence of thought, which tries to solve
 problems that are its natural fare.

Stand supreme in the knowing Might that you
 caught the fragrance as it passed,
And give unto all nations the hope, when D in the
 middle was clasped.
But the Divine remained concealed in a code of
 expression; It was only revealed from the
 Standpoint of a Fundamental at hand.
But when you knew how to transcend the suggestion
 of limits, you moved from the ordinary man
To the octaves where man moves into a Frequency
 rare and vibrating and heard.
The Essence of All is nothing but a line of Wonder,
 and from this you attempt to solve.

Stay with the line that is perpendicular to your
 suggested horizontal in time
And reduce the suggestion of limits when I come to
 your horizontal in time.
There is a moment of lightning explosion, for your
 way is now perceived in a different way,

> For you now move from the valley of chaos and
>   despair onto the High Way of the Temple
>   Beautiful and rare.
> Move to this Temple and stand in wonder, for you
>   will be amazed as the portals open wide, for
>   you held aloft
> The banner of Principle and, lo and behold, you saw
>   how it was praised aloft.
>
> You may not get much praise on this plane, but
>   remember, it's no memory at all,
> For what you are can never be forgotten when the
>   Essence is revealed and the foot is shod
> To walk with a leather sole onto the plane of time
>   so that the feeling doesn't touch the mundane
>   of the mind
> But allows the splendour of victory to be the ecstatic
>   state of a God-filled Mind!
>
> This is the way you attempt to describe the
>   undescribable,
> This is the way we attempt to transcribe the
>   Transmitted,
> But you can never capture what the Tone is telling
> Unless you are moved beyond the auditor that is
>   thinking and then telling.

Don't be patient with error; just be kind to the one who's allowing it to pass. **Love is a vibration of liberation.** What It is in fullness can only be conceived, as there is no mind capable of limiting the conception.

> So, I don't know how practical this is, but it has
>   been offered, and may you find as the weeks
>   unfold
> That the numbering of days is nothing but a way to
>   continue the rhapsody as the Wonder unfolds!

Students: Thank you, Sir!

⌘

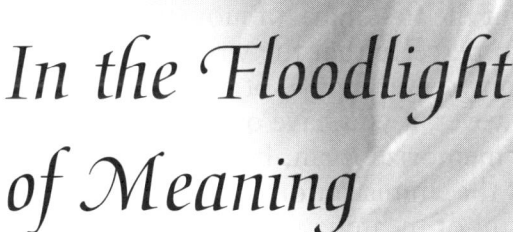

In the Floodlight of Meaning

Chapter XXIII

The reason you hear words of Lecturers is to alter your mentality and to rescind its hold upon you in this vestibule of time.

In the Floodlight of Meaning

Themes: Magic of the Invisible ~ vibrational scheme ~ free spirit ~ resurrection ~ drama ~ unanswered question

This the evening of April 9, 2004. We have all kinds of drama, all kinds of plays, all kinds of daily communion. We are dealing constantly with words, words, and more words, and I hope that you haven't met what I have so frequently met: the speaking to people, and after they recognize you've said words they know, they have assumed they've heard the rest of your sentence. This comes to that very subtle point of hearing the words (and we'll just say you're all marvellous) and everyone *hears* the words. However, one missing feature is that as long as you hear the words and *just* hear the words, you are just in the same spot when you leave! You are *taught* to hear words, but the first mark of moving beyond the entanglement of beliefs is to perceive that the word has *meaning*. The word you hear falling on your ear may not be dissimilar from others you have heard. However, if you have only *heard* them, all you can do is recite them, memorize them, but you cannot bear witness to change or to the ministrations that involuntarily happen when the word is full of meaning.

We have spoken of this, we have sung of this, and I continue the song of this, that "a word full of meaning is a life filled with love," but it seems to be a scarce commodity, this thing called "love." It seems to be as fluctuating as interest, commitment, sincerity, even fidelity, because I wonder how many people have realized that to take on any of these conditions, any of the meaning of these words of a higher vocabulary, means that you can no longer be referring to what's accompanying you as a mentality. A body is in the same place.

The reason you hear words of Lecturers is to alter your mentality and to rescind its hold upon you in this vestibule of time, and allow you to move into that auditorium of persuasive might where man comes face to face with the great Fiat "Create!", as Saint Germain once said. Why would anyone say "Create"? After all, you're here because somebody created! Well, you're perpetuating words. You're the result of words: "I love you," "Do you love me?" "Will you marry me?" et cetera. I'll let you all go through it. (Once is enough!) [laughter] What happens is that we come — *to?* My aunt used to shake me when I was a little boy. She'd say, "Come to, Ken! Wake-up!" I didn't know what she meant, because I was very aware of her shaking me! [laughter] *But* I always remembered the *words* because they carried meaning later in my life, and perhaps at that time but what child is perceiving what has been dropped from a chalice of wisdom into a receptive state of virginity?

You are enclosed, encamped within a fortress of beliefs, and as long as you are there, the only thing that can happen is you are besieged with a force of unanswered questions. There's nothing more challenging than to have questions and never receive an answer to them. Try to find an answer to some of the most simple questions, and you're just the simple answer instead of being a glorified presence to emulate. You should immediately see the victory as a result of the meaning of a word and how, upon its incorporation in your life, you are changed from the ordinary to a little above the ordinary. One word won't do it unless it's the *one Word,* but why not emulate That?

We are ensconced in a frail system of mortality and its multitudinous blends, but how many people are really looking to see how the crucifying effects of a belief-system (good and bad, light and darkness, victor and conquered) are really satisfying the framework of the great Fiat "*Now* are we the Sons of Light!"[1] No one to-day is really considering in depth the very delicate framework in which we are living these days. Have you ever stopped to consider what you are living them for? For *yourself?* Perhaps you *are,* but you shouldn't be *here* if you are! Or maybe you *should be!* Maybe that's why you're here! But you should be realizing — what? that to stay with the identification of a believer is never to put into question the belief that you are "this." As soon as you cannot answer this question, surely it should spike your interest and you should start quizzing everyone and seeing just how much company you have, and of course, you feel perfectly at home in it because you're all in the same boat! But you have the experience of mentality and physicality and you certainly have a spirit, which you say you have because you put-up with such partial experiences, leaving it mental and physical. "The spiritual, I'll take care of at a later time, but we *should be,* so we should go to church and show that we really are —" *That's* a question mark: *what?*

When we come to considering how we are going to rebirth — which spring is all about — if the tulip thought it had to come out of the old bulb it was twisted-up to be, I don't think you would ever see it unfold its turban! [laughter] And yet, it says, "I'm not going to go in the belief-system that I am dried-up and buried for the season. I have a rhythm to my beingness, and that rhythm is in keeping with the cycle that fulfills expectancy." Expectancy is always based on the result of actions which are in motion with the expectancy of a result as long as you are on the horizontal plane. This is where we seem to be and we wouldn't be here if it wasn't for a purpose. That purpose, perhaps, is to bring to all our friends, neighbours, and those with insecurity as to who and what they are — in other words, individuality is a big question mark — we are there to, perhaps, show them that there *is* an answer to all of these questions, because we have seen, through the exploration of suggestions, that there is a Light at the end of the tunnel of belief, and "that Light dispelleth all darkness."

The great magical feats of the alchemists were to turn the base metals into gold, but perhaps it also meant that we were to turn our attention from the obvious to the magic of the Invisible having the promise of bearing a corresponding identity. Unfortunately, people only believe and are only impressed with the objective verification; but there *is* an idea, where *the fruit* is relishing the meaning of the *idea* before it is *allowed* to be precipitated as part of your experience. If you don't *love* the idea, it is not *allowed time*. What do I mean by *allowing it time*? An idea is timeless, but as soon as you attempt to use your accomplishment to precipitate it, *are you ready for it*? Because as soon as you precipitate it into your experience you are responsible for it, and what are the most abhorrent words to-day? *Commitment, responsibility,* and the most fearsome of all is *obedience*.

No one wants to be obedient because everyone must express him or herself. But which one!? There are so many! Old Mother Hubbard may have had an empty cupboard, but "the old woman in the shoe had so many children she didn't know what to do"! Have you ever stopped to consider how many I's go under so many different headings? Just try — *don't!* You haven't the *time!* [laughter] There are so many I's inhabiting your fecund state of dreaming that it is very difficult to perceive how to bring them under control by donning one simple feature: the power of making an agreement, as a novice, with your invisible promise that there is a Source, either you would not be able to cognize your incompleteness, a Source of completeness!

Now, this Source of completeness has been called many things. It's been called "the Christ Consciousness"; it's been called "the Buddhic" — name them! It doesn't matter what it is called. Perhaps "Principle" is a wonderful word because when you really wrestle with that word, it starts to reveal its invulnerability, its constancy, and the very point from which springs the greatest gift that man can give to another: the ability to receive *Unfoldment* because *Unfoldment is **your** experience.* Whatever *my* experience is, is neither here nor there. What is important for you is in the nowness of Being to perceive that your awareness state is revealing the audacity of mentality to shackle you to a realm of inferior accomplishment.

No one here is born with an inferior accomplishment unless he wishes to use it as an excuse to evade being called a star capable of guiding another into the wonders of the kingdom of the celestial ideation that is beyond comprehension and yet viable because we have corresponding identities revealing: "Go beyond the confines of touchability and move into the embrace of a Conscious-awareness of universal significance." This comes under the heading of unification. This does not mean that everyone becomes One. "Everyone becoming One" is your experience of your mesmeric state. Everyone becoming one world, one government, one people is a mesmeric state. The only form of unification is in a framework of tonality when there is the evidence that Oneness is being perceived on the periphery of your enhanced awareness.

Oneness is perceived when you start to *realize* that without your attention supporting the vision of objectification and your experience sensorially of thinking, you may find there is no world other than within the confines of your imagination. What happens? What you imagine is *always* verified. Why imagine a paltry situation of a dark world in chaos rather than a pocket of people sitting in the grandeur of a promise and experiencing the fecundating of a seed kingdom bearing the fruit according to the condition of your contrite heart.

Your garden has been planted, and some of the movements are beginning to show through the encrustations of your systems of culture because you are bringing forth a different type of flowering. You are not out to convert anyone, you are not out to create a following, you are not *out!* Other people will say you're out, and you say, "Well, that is just great! It just shows you what I have attained. I can appear to be out when I am within, and when I am within, you can say I'm without." *But the difference is in the power to alter or create a new experience for each and every one you encounter.* This bears with it the stamp of the approval of everything that man has conjured: the Ascended Masters, all the angelic kingdom. It bears the seal of approval beyond good housekeeping! It is the evidence that you have been marked as a keeper of the vision of the unifying factor of Oneness and the nuclear force-field that surrounds it that can demolish, in the twinkling of an eye, the structures of limitation and, right on that spot, build a new structure. It's not made with hands, because it is glowing in the eternal, *in*ternal splendour of moving beyond the grass.

This is what resurrection is about. It's not making the old new; it's making the old *seen as a presumption* upon your ageless, eternal nature. It is that moment when you can see the spurious nature of belief and how it rescinds your natural state of manumission. How can you say that the world is a free place when it's confined to the mental gesticulations of chronic disturbance? Your whole system is being revealed in such a glaring way if you have the sight to see what the markings are telling: the ineffectiveness of your attempt to achieve wealth, fame, and so-called "success" at the expense of your identity!

"Well, I'm an individual. I have my own right. I can do what I want and you can got to H!" You can take it, "heaven" or "hell," it doesn't matter. They're talking about something that only exists in thought! Quite frankly, they really need your love, because anyone who thinks he or she is an "individual" and has their own right is interpreting the word from the standpoint of a dictionary that was written by an individual who didn't know really what it meant *to be* individual. Therefore, we have a dictionary of many words that most people don't use, but it's nice to know that we *have* them. What's the point of having a dictionary of so many hundred thousand words and using so few? It's because the more words that you can use that are not common reduce the common acceptance of your parlance to the place where another has to consider, "Boy, is he putting on airs of an educational ass!" or "He's making me feel silly. I don't know half the words he's using!" Well, sister or brother, do you know the meaning of half of the words *you're* using?! [laughter]

It is so strange that this is the topic that has come to me to-day to try to offer something on. It is such a subtle one, because we are so clever with imposing upon ourselves the wherewithal to think "It doesn't apply to me." You've been around, as they say, and you know your way with the subtlety of words. You've seen this all on the news: the delay tactics, the ability to have to face whether or not it's a truth or a lie or it's light or darkness. As long as you believe you are in that realm, you may *think* that you are facing this; but as long as you are thinking it, you're *in* it! That is why nowness and silence are so elusive, because when you think there is silence and there is no sound, you'll say, "Oh, boy, now I know what it is to be enlightened, there's silence!" I wouldn't fall for it! *(That* is the carrot, not just for the horse but for other animals!) I wouldn't fall for that, because whatever "to be enlightened" means — I have no idea other than what it says in the dictionary, and it is obvious that it isn't right because if it were, the world would never be in the state it's in!

Don't worry about being enlightened. I'd consider, though, "Am I *being?"* Do you know if you're *being* . . a genius or an ass? Of course you do! You're a genius when somebody says, "How did you do it? (Oh, I don't mean being an ass!) How do you do it, achieving what you have achieved?" If they can't tell you — oh dear!

Creativity is a mark of the free spirit. It is only limited by "you," and if you can only arrive at that point where Principle is held just long enough to subdue the thought-field and allow it to go out with the tide of desire, then that next wave will be in vogue with the Fiat of your Soul's desire. The only limit you have is imposed by the identification with the wrong self. The self you say you are is the self that everyone says you are, but the Self that IS allows the self that isn't to have a presence in order to be a Light unto the people. For the people are walking in darkness and they must "see a great Light."[2] Why would you keep yours hidden in the basket of mentality? Because you feel safe because everyone has dirty laundry in it? Why don't you wash it in the All! And if you need, have a little bit of Blue Cheer! But be sure if you use those things, use Oxi because it's supposed to give you something as white as the driven snow.[3] That is the way you were to be washed: you were to become as white as the driven snow. Why white? It was the Ancients' attempt to point to radiance!

The great difficulty that individuals face is remaining individuals. It's a lifetime's work! [laughter] That's why we have to do away with the "remains." *Be* the individual, one with the Source, by — what? Being the dynamic expression to the best of "your" (you would say) ability in emulating what you now know to be the fundamental factor of your life: the invincible Principle, the invincible Love, that is unconditional! Why do we say "unconditional"? Because, in emulating the Love of the Infinite, the finite can't help but experience the beams radiating from that pristine Source!

If you remember, "in the beginning was the Word and the Word was with God,"[4] it must mean that if "in the beginning the Word was with God and the Word *was* God," and there was a creation, they never stopped to consider the meaning. If they had, they would never have written the second chapter of Genesis, because the Exodus would have happened the moment the scribe who wrote those words put it to paper that "if the Word was with God and the Word *was* God, and that was *the beginning*," there must have been a *Foreword* to that! And that Foreword was that word that marked that moment with having the dispensation of Love's Light cast once again upon the pages of time to re-awaken in the unredeemed imagination the possibilities of a redeemed imagination giving us a world "without beginning or end." Thus is man perceived as glorified because he sees from the standpoint of the Infinite that the words so ascribed unto the Infinite in dynamic expression as "*I* will not leave you comfortless" do not mean person. He did not say, "I, as Jesus, will not leave you comfortless"; He said, "I will not leave you comfortless," in other words, *get to it and find what that I is!* It is only a symbol waiting to be what? Experienced in emulation.

Why do you behave as Earthlings with your spasmodic natures? Why don't you attempt to ride the Beam? Bear the radiance of emancipation and allow others to say, "I am so sorry you are a slave unto the humankind." And you can say, "Yes, but I have not an *underground* passage to freedom, **I have a vibrational scheme for attuning my receptors to the divine and clear intention of Being as I AM."**

You can appear to be a slave; it might even be better to be thought so than to be thought a master. What you must consider is the need of everyone to-day who attempts to rid themselves of a false identity and claim their creative genius, as never before, to realize that the whole attainment of intellectuality has to be baptized in the wonder becoming a clarified intention.

With this clarified intention, and with the knowing need of obedience to Principle, of fidelity to Principle and, therefore, to what appear as Principle's exponents, you are once again sanctified to walk this plane of delusion, bearing the power, as an alchemist, and transform the entire experience into a Light drama that allows everyone in the auditorium of expectation to see how, in the floodlight of meaning, Love, known and experienced, can only appear emulated as a Divine!

How many Divines walk among us? Have you ever considered you may be sitting next to one, but due to your insecure position you do not perceive?

We didn't come to this plane just to see someone coming through the rye. We may have come to dance through the tulips/two lips. But, remember, you have to be willing to let the leaves and the petals of your mentality appear to fall away in order for your crown of achievement to be recognized in the surrender of practically all that you had in time (your leaves) to get the attention. Those who waited to see them expand in glory found they were blessed by the corona hidden within their folds. This is what you are like! How many of you have this, and walk and talk as if you had nothing? What are you emulating? **This is the time that is marked for the escalation of Light.** Why do you let darkness seem to get a*head* of it?

Dare to be radical in what you accept as thought, because remember, if you accept a thought, it brings with it many others. The thought you accept, will it be bearing a train of splendour or the soil of an attempted movement in the morass of suggestion? The High Way of the Light is so simple. People say, "Oh, it's so elusive." No, it's the only thing that *isn't* elusive. It allows its presence to walk in the garment of ignorance while it's being searched for, and it is the very Light to even the darkness, and the darkness beholds it not.

So, the spring has sprung, and out of the box of suggestion has come something dressed-up as you, maybe tripping through the tulips/two lips in an attempt to find your words commensurate with the divine Fiat "Let there be Light. Create." There was Light. There was creating. Let others ask, "Who did it?" And you can say, "Who is asking the question?" 'Tis the Spirit that beareth witness to questions unanswered and gives you the strength and fortitude to say, "I bear the spirit of enquiry and I will not let you go, question of my life, until you have given unto me the nectar becoming the gods of Creation."

What a glorification comes in the form of a personification! The trick is, it's never *in* person. It's only evidenced *as* person but never found *in* it. Are you material? "You," of course! But what I AM is only known when you are not what you think. **So simple. Practise! Be obedient to Principle and see the wonder of Unfoldment**™. **As you unfold, you find yourself enfolded.**

What chased the clouds away?

> **Don't be so timid in putting what is important in your life first. It's amazing what you will put first. You haven't got much time.**

⌘

1. I John 3:2.
2. Isaiah 9:2.
3. All, Blue Cheer, and Oxi are brands of laundry detergent.
4. John 1:1.

Where Words Are Not

Chapter XXIV

The universal Plan is that men and women will reduce the language of limitation to a place in their life that satisfies the need of their appearance but inundates those who witness their state with a flood tide of possibilities!

Where Words Are Not

Themes: Principle ~ companion invisible ~ Fire of immolation ~ great Plan ~ creativity ~ jurisprudence

---

This is the morning of April 11, 2004. We find that synchronistic events happen all the time, and one that has proved very interesting, and I thought should be shared with you, is the one that Claude had just before coming. So, Claude, just tell them about it, please.

> *Claude C:* We've talked about magic in our lives since we've met Dr. Mills, and I certainly have done that on several occasions and on the occasion of writings, also. It's come to my experience, and I wanted to share that with you and really feel strongly, that when we come to a *Wordshop,* Dr. Mills prepares us in the Invisible also. We've talked a lot about being at one with a particular Pitch, and that's the way that I feel from this experience.
>
> What happened is that last week I was putting order in my study, as I am putting order in my personal life right now on many levels, and I came across a paper I had downloaded from the Internet seven years ago. It was under a pile of things, and I just took it out. It's a forty-page document, and I opened it up, completely by chance, and I fell on one page that was titled "The Degradation of Language." I had an intuitive prompting to bring it to the *Wordshop,* not really knowing if it was going to be something worth talking about. I kept it a secret until luncheon yesterday. It was so baffling to me that in the last two *Unfoldments* what Dr. Mills has been speaking to us about is almost word for word what's on this paper here!
>
> It's written by Rudolph Steiner. He was born in 1861 and died in 1925, so this was written at the beginning of the twentieth century. He started a spiritual science called anthroposophy and in his studies he came to realize the degradation of society. He was very unhappy about where society was going, and he outlined the dark forces that are

behind that. Among the characteristics of this degradation he outlined the degradation of language. [Claude reads:]

According to Steiner, it is characteristic of the present culture of [Dark Forces behind] scientists and Anglo-American economic imperialism that language has lost its instinctive spiritual meaning; that is, the connection is lost between the literal word and the spiritual impulse that constitutes meaning.

Without real spiritual content, language consists only of "empty phrases" such as "rule by the will of the people" or "the free world," "individual freedom," and so on. These phrases are largely devoid of reality in our socio-political structure; here the fundamental fact is the power of money over human beings and life. And where the empty phrase rules in language, mere conventions – rather than living human contact – rule in social life, and mere routine – rather than living human interest – rules in economic life. And: "It is only a short step from the empty phrase to the lie." Again, this is especially true in politics and economics, for the prevalence of empty words makes possible the falsification of realities – a potent weapon in the hands of those with occult, conscious intentions to manipulate people for devious ends. In our time, people en masse act as if they are possessed by evil forces, because, in a way, they are. The demons of materialism speak through empty words. A language in which the demons of materialism have taken the place of human spiritual impulses can lead only to destruction. . . .

If we do not put our wills into creating our original thoughts, then ready-made pseudo-thoughts, trite words and phrases, come automatically to mind and carry us along with them, resulting in "thinking almost entirely without thoughts."

Claude C: As Dr. Mills said yesterday, the thinker thinking thoughts should at least make sure he's thinking his own thoughts. [Claude continues to read:]

We can at least make the effort to resist these ready-made phrases and generalizations that effortlessly come to mind, and to form mental pictures of particular people, things, and events – and further, to make original word-formations describing these things and pictures from varying points of view. The essential point is that we not let our speaking and writing be determined by unconscious influences, but that we call forth *through our own efforts* new, original thought-creations and convey them with original, fluid, artistic word-formations. We will not always fully succeed; we are not all poets all of the time.

Claude C: Aren't we lucky to be with a Poet!

Students: Oh, yes!

[Claude reads:]

But if we consciously make this effort, then we will go far toward recovering the lost human-spirituality of language, and consequently, towards the humanization of culture – And, not incidentally, we will thus progress toward living consciously in the thinking-free-of-literal-words that is the "language" of the spirit-soul world in which we will live after death.[1]

[applause] I thought you would enjoy that.

Students: Thank you! It's amazing.

It's Easter; I should ring it in. [Dr. Mills rings the Tibetan bells.]

The spring season, with its decoration of Easter, brings to our attention that newness is never carried forth in oldness. The oldness is left buried, for it can only reveal what has been accomplished in another season. You are all new from the standpoint that you have taken on the journey from sense to Non-sense and from emotionalism to feeling and to What-IS so that It may embrace what appears to be and *isn't*.

The jurisprudence of the world rests upon the Law which must be fulfilled. They say "*Love* is the fulfilling of the Law," and this has rung into your attention so many times, but a very important part is the consideration of *will*. Frequently it is fortified by emotionalism, and if you have *that* present, you have it decked-up in egotism and you have yourself in obvious positions of dilemmas of all kinds. The will is such a subtle force, as I've often told you. Personalized, it's totally destructive and, therefore, it is not the will that is to be manifested for those who know it not, in the form of determination of personal sense.

The will is that part of our structure of conceptualization that is brought forth in the Light of devotion. Then it is that act of devotion that enhances the unspeakable and *unlimited* Will because devotion evidences the obvious tendency of reduction in the realm of interference. This is where there comes into this play of will the releasement from personally willing. You are then no longer the object of destruction, but you are in a position of the subjective power that is not only perhaps magnetic, as is Love — Love is very magnetic, as you know. However, as one Teacher pointed out years ago, and I wonder how many have ever considered it, just having Love as the only Force-field present in your life is only part of the picture, and that was part of the picture that we have said was yesterday. The part of the picture to-day is when *Will* enters into it, you have a *dynamic*. You can tell when the Will is present because of dynamics. The dynamics are fortified from the Invisible because there is no obstruction to the effervescence that comes when joy bestows upon the struggling a sense of happiness.

The joy that is profound is not subject to the whims of the people in the culture in which you find yourself. The whim of the people is fluctuating due to the propaganda that entices one to degrade attention to the lower level where the common man and woman have not yet been moved to enter into that state where they consider "What am I achieving?"

The Will is manifested in so many ways, but it is the *enhancer of vision*. **What is your vision?** It is a question that I am sure very few can answer properly. Oh, you'll say, "My vision is to find what I really am. And, of course, in finding that, I hope that I will have enough money to be able to do all I wish to do. But, of course, I have to go to work every day in order to make money so that I at least have a moment or two before going to work and when I come home tired from work to consider 'Who and what am I?'" Have you ever wondered why there is lack in your experience if there is? It's only there to awaken you. You never question "Why can't I get the right job?" There are all kinds of jobs, but you outline the limitations of a job according to your non-creative spirit; your non-creative spirit is only a supposition that Spirit could not be creative. So, obviously there is a lack of vision surrounding your penchant in your life.

The tendency is to complain about having to work or not getting enough pay for your work, but look at it the other way around, perhaps: Which should come first? "Oh," you say, "my spiritual way of life. And then, of course, I have to sustain myself." If you look, you will find that you may spend every evening studying (there's nothing better to do) and you may spend your whole day in business, but have you ever stopped to consider that the imbalance may be due to the fact that you have put what should not be first, first, and you have *really* spent your time on *the second phase*. Guess what? That's what you have: a second phase of suggested, superior intellectualism. You intellectually assume your studies and you read the words (having heard them, you read them now), but unless you're on that level where you are now demanding meaning, what hope is there? The intellectual pursuit of study, in itself, especially in the so-called spiritual realm, can be an evasion of facing inherent lethargy, indolence, and confusion.

When you study and *think* and don't *do,* you have minus income. **What is "minus income"? The abundance that could be yours is now unable to reach you because you have the wrong address.** It should be "The Devoted Mr." or "The Devoted Miss" or "The Devoted Mrs." And what is it? The business: "Madam Business" or "Mr. Business" — but there is no evidence of it being *God's* business or *the Self* in creative activity. It is in the quagmire of not understanding, when you are so spiritually sincere, why you haven't abundance; and anyone who does have it, there is the inclination to quietly, or very vigorously, resent it. This has often been the case that has been experienced in my home when people have seen the brilliance of the light in the Music Room and they have to look at it. They'll say, "This opulence, this grandeur, I can't stand it! He's supposed to be stricken in poverty; he's given-up all for the Search." Who told you you had to? The only thing you can give-up is that which you have. Can you give-up being entirely "this"?

Students: Yes.

I would hope so! Why can you give it up if it's the only objective in your life that holds your attention? You can't *possibly* give it up! *It doesn't know it is anything to give-up!* A thought has made it so, and it can't be found in this component you are utilizing, this space-suit that you expect is programmed to deliver you into the lap of your Infinitehood! It's rather ridiculous when we know scientifically that this is nothing but mostly empty space, and the residue can be placed upon the head of your pin, which could be used for your boutonniere of a nice red rose. However, it is wonderful not to pin your destiny upon the intellect of academic persuasion, because if you do you will have missed the point which is necessary to pierce the veil of materiality. If you can cognize a pin, it is obvious it is the name given to an object that is in the realm of the objective but whose value is in its ability to alter. A pin can alter your response. [laughter] You know then when you get the point!

Do you know, when you get the point, that the intellect is your dictator (and you allow it to do so) and the resultant poverty because you don't do what? You don't do what is realized when the intellect comes to a halt in the realm of "metanoia" or approaches its very perimeter. You wouldn't be wondering if you were at that point of metanoia. You're just at the edge, perhaps.

When you perceive that your mind is capable of being reprogrammed, it's nothing but the name given to all the "windows" of your utilization. Don't forget, if you have them you can open them and defenestrate! [laughter] And why wouldn't you when meaning has crossed the threshold and is wiping clean the hard disc of belief? You could lose it and then what will you do without your programming that "I am 'this'" and "How dare you tell *me* what to do! I'm not going to follow *anyone!* I don't want to be cajoled into a teaching or into a group!" Have pitiful patience with such a low level of attainment. By their language shall you know them. It tells you in the Bible, "By their gifts shall ye know them," and what is the greatest gift that you can receive? That another acknowledges the dynamics of your state, evidenced in body, in language, and in sound.

The dynamics evidence the crossing of the Great Divide. That is achieved, as I told you yesterday, as you move to the summit of the mountain, and then when you see it, you feel you have attained it. It is just the very beginning of the inverted picture you must enter now, because that inverted mountain is saying, "Take this one point of entrance, this very sharp point of perspective, and enter now into the ever-widening arms of the ascension!" No mountain would appear on Earth if there wasn't one unseen supporting it; it is so fragile. It's all part of your imaging, and you can't account for it other than to say the Creator laughed, and what was a hard crust of belief becomes a rippling rhythm for you to perceive.

That is a very important consideration because until you can break through the crust of belief, you cannot ever enter into the inner delight; there's a crust either way you go. If it's upside down or right side up, most people don't care as long as they find the

Centre. But how can you find it if Love isn't the handmaiden of your exploration and vision isn't clothing it with the limitless view and the dynamics that are the evidence of having found!

A word full of meaning is a life full of love, and a life full of love is gowned in words of meaning — but most people find they're more comfortable in slacks. Why? It shows you that the lower extremities of life are slack to appearance and the all-engendering force of the human. You know that below the diaphragm rests your power to utilize and to create and to enable one to move, in the dynamics of living freed from the rigidity of convention, into that high place where the Light shines and the Voice is like the one heard that cries in the wilderness.

What is going to happen in the world is entirely up to the density of the interest and the attention that people give unto the Good News. And one of the carrots of the New Age offerings is "one world, one government, and one people." The only thing that perhaps is *right* about any of it is "one." **You have to bring a halt to the flood tide of words that don't really have any meaning.** One world is the belief that there are others outside of your conception; so, it shows you immediately that your conception is confined. *There is only one creative Act,* and the worlds are as multiple and many as you create in the vision unhampered by mentality of limitation.

One government is possible if you look upon the One and Only that is the authority. A government should only appear to be the outer evidence of a lawful intention, manifested as the inhabitants of those who have found a great Light and *are* the great Light. It wouldn't be and couldn't be your experience if it weren't for you to be new! Don't put the new possibilities into the old bag woven on the looms of limitation. Don't keep counting your stitches . . . but don't lose any! [laughter]

How can you have a one-world government and a one-world people without those who view it having the vision of the fulfilment of the divine Plan? Have you ever considered it? I have mentioned it over the years in the Transmissions and in the *Unfoldments*™, but no one ever considers the great Plan; the Masters, they say, who have ascended, do. **The universal Plan is that men and women will** *reduce* **the language of limitation to a place in their life that satisfies the need of their appearance but inundates those who witness their state with a flood tide of possibilities!**

The only way that there can be one world and one government is by having the governed *realize*. What must be realized? How can the government be on His shoulders if you think you are the custodian of His vision and wisdom? It's impossible! That is what has happened so frequently, because when you think the vision is yours, there is no wisdom and the people perish. It is so obvious in the chaos of to-day how much people are really intrigued with its horror that they can even consider that it can be eliminated by the very forces that brought it about.

Look at the children in the world who are the result of an uncontrolled utilization of creativity and appearing now destitute. But stop and consider: *where are those who are seeking to find?* Most are just *looking*, and the mind is so capable of saying they are looking to find. Find what? They don't want to find anything like themselves, for heaven's sake! This is what they are looking, supposedly, beyond! But how many expect to find and be just like the lethargic and indolent and apathetic misery manifested of a world bent in mesmerism?!

The only way to "exodus" this limit is to build your barge of Soul and reduce the impinging force of limitation wrapped-up in emotionalism, and find, as your barge becomes worthy of your confidence, you can set sail not in the sunset but in the illuminating rays of the dawning Light of Realization.

Try to reduce what you have been taught: the sun rises and sets. You haven't been able to do *that;* you base your life on it rising and setting. What a strange basis for doing and not doing! When the Sun is our Ra, a divine Rama, it doesn't set! That is why the sun has always been and always will be the evidence of the constancy of the Invisible. Although we can say we see it, we are only seeing the *results* of it. Now they're trying to view its body, but look at the cost of attempting to view its body when it reveals nothing but "I'll burn you up if I'm not filtered by distance."

How far do you stand in distance from the Fire of immolation? Why wouldn't you expect what-isn't to become ashes and from it the proverbial phoenix rise again, not from the dead issues of a body but from the living embers of a realized State *embracing* the body so that others may see the invisible wings bearing the fruitage of the invisible octaves that enhance the vibratory frequency to the point where words are not.

Words are important but with the meaning are more so. That is why in the original text it says "*Meaning* (not *The Word)* was with God." "*Meaning* was with God." Why is meaning so important? Of course, it had to be changed because **when you have meaning you don't fall for supposition!** How can you build a belief-system if words have meaning?! *A belief is a system that is based on recurring word-patterns that seduce you into habit.* **What is habit? The mental state in which you can retire and not have to face the consequences of a dammed spirit until later!**

Habit has you repeating every day's activities and thinking you're attaining something. *That's* the drug! *It makes you think you are attaining something.* That's what habit does. But where is the attainment? Getting up at five o'clock to get to the office by seven-thirty so your employees won't think you're a nincompoop, and going home at night and filled with the day's dull activities and supposedly aroused by a husband or wife who is bored and children who are not sure they know you very well (male or female) and not really sure that you can read or write because you never hear their lessons to make sure that *they* can!

Have you ever wondered if your children think you may be somewhat illiterate because they never hear you question them upon the authenticity of their schooling? How often do your children recite the next day's lessons so that the teacher doesn't have to keep them in for two or three hours after school for not preparing their lesson? "Oh, Mr. Mills, we don't have a school like that to-day!" *That's why you have so many unprepared walking the streets of time. There's no discipline to-day.* What happens? "We just don't understand why so many thugs walk the streets and everything is so uncertain." Who are the dumb of this society? Those who don't want to hear, see, or have to correct!

Of course, the children should be disciplined! My father was not wrong. When the corporeal punishment went out of the schools, a few years after I had left them, he said to me one time when I was visiting at home: "The School Board has made the biggest mistake. Watch and see what happens when discipline has gone out of the schools." It didn't take many years for the area to become one that is filled with many police, and provincial police, because it has been said to be a great centre for crossing from the United States and for the drug business. When there was discipline in the schools, the generations that followed would walk a woman home if she was alone on the street at night. To-day, no woman would dare to walk the streets alone.

> Do you dare to walk the street alone in the darkness
> of the night?
> Or do you have a companion invisible that gives you
> second sight?
> Do you dare to walk those dismal miles where the
> light seems dull
> And the good have strayed somehow?
>
> Have you considered within the scheme of time
> How some of the streets are straight and yet others
> are blind?
> Have you ever considered you would take such a way
> And then find it a cul-de-sac with such dismay?
>
> But, you see, the habit of going 'round and 'round
> Is never considered a habit so bound.
> Without the vision that glows in the night,
> How can you walk with security without some
> fright?
>
> But knowing the vision that *I am not alone*
> Gives you the knowing you have not strayed far
> from home,
> For in that moment that you feel secure, you know
> That which IS is what is adored and on the throne.
>
> Take peace and see that it's bestowed upon all
> Who can stop the thought for a moment and find
> Wonder the All.
> Take the moment and what do you find?
> As long as there wasn't a thought, it was simply
> divine.
>
> What is that divinity without such thought?
> It's the Silence which gowns the Now — no thought!
> So, in this moment may you see in the Light
> That all great Masters have a vision, a sight:

The Plan to see all come to this salient fact
From the Point of Principle or the timeless, timeless
 That . . .
Move, look, do, and find
How the government is on *His* shoulders and it's
 simply fine!

No effort but joy, and you will find the fact
That it fills your cup and you may offer happiness to
 the saucer as act.
But don't be fooled by the personality bound
To being happy or miserable; that's just a human
 round.
Look to the wonder of having found the fact
That the vision of One is a dynamic act.

Watch your language. I don't mean cursing and
 swearing!
You may think you're being very sociably acceptable,
 but it may be a curse that you're carrying.
Watch your language and see if it has *meaning*
Because then you will find no wall for leaning.

When the word bears meaning, power stands
 supreme
And it allows the limited dreams of men dreaming
 dreams
To fall and find this glowing fact
That when meaning stands present, Love is in
 dynamic, creative act —
The very source of language imbued with
 manumission.

The black people were emancipated; now the very white people are in a position of having to be. The black people know what it is to be bound and freed; now the white people, or other races, have to know what it is to be emancipated from the limitations of race ordinances. **You must perceive how you are adjusting, in the dawning Light of freedom, the various force-fields that are now at your disposal, because no field of creativity should ever remain dormant; it should be the very avenue that allows the wonder of a vision to be fulfilled.**

The newness leaves the oldness in the realm of belief,
And the newness beckons all to bow to the Ra,
>   whose Light gives constancy to all those
>   who seek.
And may you find, as you wonder and stare
At the growing visions of those who dare,
The ability to see the majesty and the might
Of those who walk on the planes of Light.

Imagine it! Emulate it! Don't leave it as words;
Start to live as you are, the giants of Light for Earth.
To Earth you came, and where did you come from?
"You" are the result of the productivity of belief;
I reside as the Light to relief!

Students: Thank you, Sir.

I hope you will find the meaning of what you have heard. Tell it to the nations. Where are they? They're all your conception. They're not a precept or a percept; they're a conception. *Why do you have your concepts confined to the limits of mentality?*

Nations are a concept.
Why do you have them confined to nations and
>   **nationality?**
They all are divisions that you have made-up
Of the one undivided garment that is termed
>   **"the I-Trust."**
And this is the Foundation upon which you will find
The possibility of the reduction of those who would
>   **degrade the Sublime.**

⌘

---

1. Robert Mason, "The Degradation of Language"; available at the Rudolph Steiner Archive <http://wn.elib.com/Steiner/RelArtic/MasonRS/Ahriman/>.

Index

A
Absolute, 138, 248, 249, 259
adjudication, 218, 265, 325
Afflatus, 58, 107, 109
androgyne, 32, 33
Authentic, 7, 44, 254

B
Being, 233, 254, 265, 272, 274, 276, 287, 292, 293, 294, 298, 305, 309, 313, 323, 325, 343, 345, 347, 348, 351, 354, 367, 370
birth, 31, 72, 137, 154, 156, 174, 192, 196, 214, 234, 248, 276, 297, 334, 366
blueberry, 51
body, 222, 233, 249, 250, 252, 254, 273, 284, 285, 287, 309, 381
bonfire, 234, 291, 292, 296, 341
Breath, 35, 82, 109, 138, 331, 357
Buddha, 63

C
cathect/cathexis, 87, 94, 97
centre, 4, 43, 61, 74, 79, 96, 110, 184, 206, 260, 261, 293, 380
change, 11, 12, 14, 44, 45, 52, 60, 104, 149, 161, 176, 201, 214, 215, 222, 236, 264, 276, 279, 310, 313, 323, 346, 356, 364, 365
cherry, 86, 87, 91, 97, 105, 133, 150, 159, 175, 190, 191, 205, 219, 220, 223, 224
choice, 61, 71, 100, 162, 196, 212, 259, 260, 263, 296, 314, 323, 327, 341
Christ, 18, 31, 33, 59, 63, 77, 162, 202, 216, 230, 306, 308, 323, 357, 367

clones, 295, 296
commitment, 255, 274, 294
community, 132, 161, 296, 297, 313
Conscious-awareness, 3, 9, 18, 20, 35, 64, 71, 75, 79, 85, 98, 109, 115, 149, 192, 194, 195, 286, 343, 352, 353, 367
creation, 99, 135, 136, 146, 149, 154, 156, 168, 195, 221, 248, 258, 260, 261, 262, 293, 304, 330, 344, 370, 372
critic, 36, 345

D
darkness, 29, 33, 158, 217, 238, 365, 366, 369, 371, 383
discipline, 73, 78, 103, 106, 156, 184, 200, 251, 266, 267, 268, 274, 278, 306, 308, 382
discrimination, 47, 86, 207
disharmony, 36, 42, 63, 341
Divine, 4, 7, 29, 31, 33, 44, 58, 60, 63, 79, 87, 99, 109, 138, 139, 140, 153, 161, 234
dream, 69, 78, 110, 178, 214, 296, 339, 366, 384

E
ego, 228, 230, 263, 272, 274, 278, 311, 321, 331, 358, 376
Einstein, 138, 231
elegance, 61, 234, 287
energy, 6, 20, 60, 63, 64, 71, 74, 91, 93, 103, 106, 108, 126, 147, 150, 153, 157, 158, 159, 160, 161, 162, 175, 177, 178, 261, 267, 296, 311, 330, 351, 354
Enlightenment, 29, 120, 229, 268

error, 22, 36, 247, 313, 350, 361
eternal, 7, 9, 34, 56, 57, 71, 78, 79, 82, 85, 92, 178, 230, 247, 259, 260, 274, 314
evil, 60, 62, 63, 64

F

fear, 5, 7, 60, 63, 64, 103, 172, 176, 215, 292, 320, 345
fidelity, 126, 136, 263, 325, 364
Fire Mass, The, 36
fragrance, 5, 34, 86, 359
freedom, 10, 29, 60, 69, 73, 78, 85, 102, 132, 162, 164, 172, 176, 212, 249, 262, 273, 286, 351, 370, 384

G

gender, 33
Gift, 33, 94, 134, 159, 177, 208, 212, 291, 311, 314, 367, 379
guardian, 5, 10, 17, 264, 292

H

High Teaching, 30
history, 62, 233, 270
human, 272, 275, 281, 287, 297, 305, 306, 323, 340, 350, 351, 352, 360
humility, 52, 237

I

Ideal, 64, 287
Identity, 12, 37, 46, 174, 232, 323, 326
illusion, 14, 114, 115, 126, 130, 137, 148, 214, 222, 234, 327
imagination, 14, 63, 87, 105, 132, 169, 322, 329, 330, 367, 370
impression, 166, 327
Individuality, 32, 232, 263, 342

Ineffable, 29, 31, 33, 38, 253, 295, 310, 325, 352
insight, 137, 151, 152, 154
intellect, 34, 46, 49, 63, 64, 79, 138, 194, 195, 230, 248, 272, 276, 308, 309, 324, 327, 330, 342, 354, 371, 378, 379
intention, 10, 56, 68, 77, 93, 100, 118, 158, 162, 187, 213, 235, 239, 240, 278, 286, 287, 305, 307, 316, 370, 371
intuition, 136, 137, 151, 152, 153, 154
Invisible, 10, 34, 35, 68, 73, 75, 79, 82, 91, 160, 162, 202, 205, 206, 231, 235, 240, 261, 358, 359, 366, 377

J

Jesus, 11, 18, 19, 27, 63, 64, 109, 123, 162, 202, 260, 306, 308, 324, 353, 370
judgment, 325

K

karma, 107, 177, 251, 325, 332

L

language, 6, 8, 30, 43, 58, 74, 82, 104, 106, 107, 118, 121, 123, 135, 190, 218, 230, 232, 237, 248, 252, 291, 304, 312, 313, 324, 357, 379, 380, 384
Life, 7, 16, 34, 52, 78, 79, 104, 175, 219, 248, 250, 312, 314, 316, 344, 359
lily, 34, 51
Love, 4, 7, 8, 11, 12, 22, 35, 46, 48, 75, 78, 79, 80, 104, 105,

126, 135, 139, 155, 159, 174, 186, 200, 215, 230, 233 255, 262, 274, 278, 280, 305, 314, 322, 324, 345, 346, 348, 355, 356, 357, 361, 364, 370, 376, 377

M

Madonna, 30, 41
matrix, 69, 70, 72, 76, 102, 105, 115, 199, 229
mediocrity, 59, 62, 297, 310
meditation, 35, 46, 78, 82, 161, 321
memory, 62, 79, 86, 89, 93, 353, 356, 361
mentality, 31, 33, 35, 38, 62, 64, 133, 150, 158, 212, 228, 262, 265, 322, 326, 364, 367, 369, 371
metaphysics, 11, 59
Mind, 5, 6, 7, 15, 33, 44, 72, 78, 125, 176, 202, 250, 254, 259, 351, 352, 359
monarch, 132, 134, 149, 150, 224, 313, 332, 343
money, 123, 124, 132, 232, 277, 278, 334, 377
music, 26, 31, 36, 62, 184, 240, 252, 325, 333, 344, 346

N

Nathanael, 63
news/newspaper, 7, 30, 60, 247, 258, 350
Now, 56, 58, 238, 270, 276, 354, 383

O

obedience, 224, 274, 278, 366, 371

One, 12, 28, 36, 43, 186, 197, 206, 214, 217, 230, 232, 249 255, 260, 296, 303, 311, 324, 327, 347, 358, 367, 368, 380
ordinary/ordinariness, 30, 56, 57, 58, 59, 61, 63, 82, 121, 190, 216, 248, 253, 355, 357, 365

P

passion, 207, 208
peace, 8, 34, 191, 234, 262, 304, 338, 344, 346, 350, 352, 360, 383
perfection, 290, 291, 293, 296
personality, 33, 63, 84, 172, 263, 272, 275, 384
philosophy, 59, 69, 70, 350
piano, 116, 117, 252, 341
Principle, 7, 9, 13, 29, 31, 33, 62, 78, 96, 103, 118, 134, 136, 180, 196, 199, 215, 228, 247, 248, 258, 260, 263, 284, 309, 324, 341, 342, 357, 367, 369, 371, 372
promise, 2, 58, 77, 123, 124, 131, 236, 250, 366
purpose, 4, 9, 28, 45, 56, 59, 85, 100, 185, 218, 229, 231, 234, 239, 242, 245, 274, 275, 292, 306, 316, 322, 325, 338, 343, 347, 366

R

ray, 6, 309
Real/Reality, 9, 12, 16, 27, 36, 37, 46, 59, 60, 75, 114, 125, 147, 175, 176, 185, 190, 192, 207, 208, 214, 229, 230, 231, 236, 247, 274, 305, 320

Realization, 21, 38, 75, 214, 229, 265, 268, 381
resolution, 31, 81, 247, 343
resurrection, 18, 28, 368
Rumi, 40, 42, 125, 214

S

Self, 16, 31, 33, 37, 52, 86, 109, 117, 118, 135, 172, 205, 212, 228, 230, 238, 246, 248, 255, 272, 276, 279, 309, 320, 326, 327, 329, 344, 369, 378
Selfhood, 31
serpent, 40, 127
service, 43, 56, 89, 99, 139, 141, 156, 215, 278, 322, 339, 343, 344
song, 220, 240, 358
Soul, 2, 3, 9, 11, 20, 23, 68, 72, 88, 93, 105, 108, 176, 187, 193, 194, 213, 253, 262, 294, 310, 343, 369, 381
sound, 4, 28, 35, 43, 68, 73, 75, 82, 106, 114, 117, 118, 120, 125, 153, 184, 214, 221, 222, 246, 252, 253, 263, 304, 305, 306, 313, 328, 330, 331, 342, 344, 345, 346, 353, 358, 369, 379
Source, 5, 7, 17, 30, 33, 59, 85, 114, 132, 133, 134, 195, 197, 202, 203, 222, 230, 234, 261, 278, 305, 311, 323, 330, 331, 345, 367, 370
space, 7, 31, 56, 71, 93, 107, 108, 109, 111, 112, 113, 114, 138, 153, 155, 159, 160, 260, 295, 306, 310, 350, 378
Spirit, 6, 7, 9, 78, 107, 176, 186, 196, 234, 248, 251, 254, 262, 276, 326, 350, 372, 377

Star-Scape Singers, 81, 122, 220, 239, 345, 346, 358
sun, 9, 20, 33, 47, 196, 219, 269, 306, 310, 381

T

talent, 32, 35, 117, 134, 324
temptation, 56, 57, 58, 59, 82, 327
Tonality, 31, 33, 53, 213, 214, 217, 221, 331, 341
Truth, 7, 30, 33, 34, 44, 47, 57, 68, 74, 75, 76, 78, 102, 103, 106, 107, 112, 167, 174, 176, 196, 231, 247, 249, 251, 255, 276, 292, 305, 306, 308, 324, 338, 346, 357, 358

U

understanding, 29, 46, 75, 102, 113, 248, 263
unity, 28, 43, 102, 230, 232, 297, 311, 345
Unseen, 43, 75, 310
utopia, 75

V

vampire, 60
vibration, 154, 219, 243, 247, 248, 252, 261, 263, 275, 331, 350, 353, 361, 370
virtual, 27, 29, 86, 104, 125, 176, 190, 208, 242, 247, 249, 279
vocabulary, 9, 38, 59, 82, 104, 107, 118, 224, 311, 364

W

weather, 181
Will, 139, 262, 280, 305, 376, 377
wonder, 4, 7, 15, 33, 34, 52, 57,

58, 80, 82, 104, 116, 130, 153, 214, 231, 237, 295, 307, 310, 323, 348, 351, 356, 383
Word, 19, 21, 33, 46, 48, 61, 106, 114, 135, 138, 221, 237, 279, 305, 370, 382
work, 31, 43, 82, 140, 175, 198, 199, 278, 291, 293, 308, 325, 354
world, 4, 5, 23, 31, 52, 62, 68, 69, 71, 75, 79, 85, 86, 91, 93, 102, 104, 106, 115, 116, 121, 131, 132, 134, 137, 140, 148, 157, 167, 178, 184, 213, 216, 219, 222, 223, 224, 261, 262, 264, 274, 313, 322, 338, 341, 342, 344, 345, 350, 357, 367, 368, 369, 370, 376, 380, 381

Notes

Books by Kenneth G. Mills

Change Your Standpoint ~ Change Your World
Tyranny of Love
The Key: Identity
The Golden Nail
A Word Fitly Spoken
The New Land!
Given to Praise!

Poetry
Words of Adjustment
Embellishments
Anticipations
Surprises

Aphorisms
Food for No Thought
Food for No Thought II

Audio Recordings by Kenneth G. Mills

Change Your Standpoint ~ Change Your World
The Golden Nail
The New Land!
The Tonal Garment of The Word (poetry and music)

Orchestral Compositions by Kenneth G. Mills

Majestic ToneScape
Promethean Fire
Arrival of the Unexpected
Let Robots Melt

Kenneth G. Mills and The Star-Scape Singers

The Fire Mass
Tonal Persuasions I & II
The Song — The Heart of Christmas
Greatest Hits, Vol. 1
Greatest Hits, Vol. 2

Please visit *www.sun-scape.com* for a complete list of publications.

Sun-Scape Enterprises
P.O. Box 793, Station F, Toronto, Ontario M4Y 2N7, Canada
Tel. 1-800-437-1454 or 905-951-3155